Art for Life's Sake

Essays on D. H. Lawrence

Keith Sagar

Art for Life's Sake

Essays on D. H. Lawrence

Keith Sagar

Critical, Cultural and Communications Press

In association with the D. H. Lawrence Research Centre,
University of Nottingham

Nottingham
2011

Nottingham Lawrence Studies
General editors: Macdonald Daly, Sean Matthews and Andrew Harrison

Art for Life's Sake: Essays on D. H. Lawrence
by Keith Sagar.

First published in Great Britain by Critical, Cultural and Communications Press in association with the D. H. Lawrence Research Centre, University of Nottingham, 2011.

Critical, Cultural and Communications Press is an imprint of *Jet*stone Publishers Ltd.

Cover design by Andrew Dawson.

Cover Photo 'D.H. Lawrence seated under an olive tree at the Villa Mirenda, Scandicci, Florence, Italy' by kind permission of the University of Nottingham, © University of Nottingham.

Contents

About the author

Keith Sagar was educated at Bradford Grammar School and King's College, Cambridge. Formerly Reader in English Literature at the University of Manchester, he was then Special Professor in the School of English Studies at the University of Nottingham. He was the author or editor of over twenty books, most of them on either D. H. Lawrence or Ted Hughes. His most important book, on which he worked for over thirty years, is *Literature and the Crime Against Nature* (2005), which covers sixteen major authors from Homer to Hughes. His website (www.keithsagar.co.uk) contains more than forty essays for free downloading, including discussions of Shakespeare, Blake, Tennyson, Lawrence, Eliot, Hughes, Larkin, Ibsen, Chekhov, Pirandello, Brecht, Beckett, Tennessee Williams, Pinter, Mishima, Friel and Fugard. Keith Sagar died in 2013.

About Nottingham Lawrence Studies

The D. H. Lawrence Research Centre at the University of Nottingham was founded in 1990 to provide a focus for research and teaching in Lawrence Studies, and to promote the Lawrence Collections. The Centre hosts conferences, symposia and lectures, as well as coordinating Lawrence-related classes and courses at undergraduate and postgraduate level. We also work closely with Lawrence Societies around the world, particularly the Eastwood D. H. Lawrence Society, and offer support for Visiting Scholars wishing to use the Lawrence Collections. Nottingham Lawrence Studies was established in 2008 to publish work in the field. We welcome submissions, and proposals, of work of interest to academics, students and general readers. These should be sent to:

The D. H. Lawrence Research Centre
School of English Studies
University of Nottingham
University Park
Nottingham
United Kingdom
NG7 2RD

Acknowledgments

As these essays span the work of half a century, I cannot acknowledge all the fellow Lawrenceans to whom I have been indebted in many ways. Suffice to say that, unlike many other academic specialisms, Lawrence studies has been very much a common pursuit, characterized by generosity and friendliness, inspired by love of Lawrence.

I must, however, acknowledge the tireless support I have received in recent years, and particularly in the production of this book, from Sean Matthews.

I have been fortunate for the whole of my career to have as my agents Laurence Pollinger Limited, first Laurence himself, then Gerald, and now Lesley Pollinger. I am grateful for her permission, on behalf of the D. H. Lawrence Estate, to publish the copyright material in this book.

Reference Abbreviations

The earliest essay in this book was written before the Cambridge University Press edition of Lawrence's complete works was even thought of; and some of the later ones before works in question appeared in that edition. Nevertheless, for consistency and the convenience of the reader, I have given all references to the CUP edition. References to works not by Lawrence are given in the footnotes.

Letters of Lawrence

1L	*The Letters of D. H. Lawrence Volume I: September 1901–May 1913*. Ed. James T. Boulton. Cambridge: Cambridge UP, 1979.
2L	*The Letters of D. H. Lawrence Volume II: June 1913–October 1916*. Ed. George J. Zytaruk and James T. Boulton. Cambridge: Cambridge UP, 1981.
3L	*The Letters of D. H. Lawrence Volume III: October 1916–June 1921*. Ed. James T. Boulton and Andrew Robertson. Cambridge: Cambridge UP, 1984.
4L	*The Letters of D. H. Lawrence Volume IV: June 1921–March 1924*. Ed. Warren Roberts, James T. Boulton and Elizabeth Mansfield. Cambridge: Cambridge UP, 1987.
5L	*The Letters of D. H. Lawrence Volume V: March 1924–March 1927*. Ed. James T. Boulton and Lindeth Vasey. Cambridge: Cambridge UP, 1989.
6L	*The Letters of D. H. Lawrence Volume VI: March 1927–November 1928*. Ed. James T. Boulton and Margaret H. Boulton with Gerald M. Lacy. Cambridge: Cambridge UP, 1991.
7L	*The Letters of D. H. Lawrence Volume VII: November 1928–February 1930*. Ed. Keith Sagar and James T. Boulton. Cambridge: Cambridge UP, 1993.

Reference Abbreviations

Works of Lawrence

A	*Apocalypse and the Writings on Revelation*. Ed. Mara Kalnins. Cambridge: Cambridge UP, 1980.
AR	*Aaron's Rod*. Ed. Mara Kalnins. Cambridge: Cambridge UP, 1988.
IR	*Introductions and Reviews*. Ed. N. H. Reeve and John Worthen. Cambridge: Cambridge UP, 2005.
K	*Kangaroo*. Ed. Bruce Steele. Cambridge: Cambridge UP, 1994.
LCL	*Lady Chatterley's Lover and A Propos of 'Lady Chatterley's Lover'*. Ed. Michael Squires. Cambridge: Cambridge UP, 1993.
LEA	*Late Essays and Articles*. Ed. James T. Boulton. Cambridge: Cambridge UP, 2004.
MM	*Mornings in Mexico and Other Essays*. Ed. Virginia Crosswhite Hyde. Cambridge: Cambridge UP, 2009.
MN	*Mr Noon*. Ed. Lindeth Vasey. Cambridge: Cambridge UP, 1984.
PO	*The Prussian Officer and Other Stories*. Ed. John Worthen. Cambridge: Cambridge UP, 1983.
Poems	*The Complete Poems of D. H. Lawrence*. Revised Edition. Ed. Vivian de Sola Pinto and Warren Roberts. Harmondsworth: Penguin Books, 1977.
PS	*The Plumed Serpent*. Ed. L. D. Clark. Cambridge: Cambridge UP, 1987.
PU	*Psychoanalysis and the Unconscious* and *Fantasia of the Unconscious*. Ed. Bruce Steele. Cambridge: Cambridge UP, 2004.
R	*The Rainbow*. Ed. Mark Kinkead-Weekes. Cambridge: Cambridge UP, 1989.
RDP	*Reflections on the Death of a Porcupine and Other Essays*. Ed. Michael Herbert. Cambridge: Cambridge UP, 1988.
SCAL	*Studies in Classic American Literature*. Ed. Ezra Greenspan, Lindeth Vasey and John Worthen.

Cambridge: Cambridge UP, 2003.

SEP *Sketches of Etruscan Places and Other Italian Essays*. Ed. Simonetta de Filippis. Cambridge: Cambridge UP, 1992.

SL *Sons and Lovers*. Ed. Helen Baron and Carl Baron. Cambridge: Cambridge UP, 1992.

SM *St Mawr and Other Stories*. Ed. Brian Finney. Cambridge: Cambridge UP, 1983.

STH *Study of Thomas Hardy and Other Essays*. Ed. Bruce Steele. Cambridge: Cambridge UP, 1985.

VG *The Virgin and the Gipsy and Other Stories*. Ed. Michael Herbert, Bethan Jones and Lindeth Vasey. Cambridge: Cambridge UP, 2006.

WL *Women in Love*. Ed. David Farmer, Lindeth Vasey and John Worthen. Cambridge: Cambridge UP, 1987.

Foreword

The studies of D. H. Lawrence published in the 1960s established the critical parameters for interpreting Lawrence's works. The 1960s were the years that produced such critical classics as Julian Moynahan's *The Deed of Life* (1963), H. M. Daleski's *The Forked Flame* (1965), George Ford's *Double Measure* (1965), Colin Clarke's *River of Dissolution* (1969), and David Cavitch's *D. H. Lawrence and the New World* (1969). The foundational study that is obviously missing from the above list is Keith Sagar's *The Art of D. H. Lawrence* (1966).

As Keith Sagar explains in his fascinating, instructive Introduction to this selection of his Lawrence essays, he attended F. R. Leavis's lectures in his second and third years at Cambridge, shortly before the publication of *D. H. Lawrence, Novelist* in 1955. That is to say, Keith was more or less present at the creation. Leavis helped him 'learn to read,' and he also taught him to perceive Lawrence as a great visionary artist whose writings seriously and passionately addressed the crisis of modern civilization. But Keith 'never became a hard-line Leavisite,' partly because of his independent habit of mind, partly because Leavis and his followers were disdainful of scholarship. From the beginning Keith Sagar has believed that art is the central human enterprise. Art is for 'life's sake.' But he has also always believed that the study of the arts must be grounded in sound scholarship.

I scrupulously underlined my own paperback copy of *The Art of D. H. Lawrence* while I was writing my dissertation at Princeton in the late 1960s. Needless to say, the book is still on my shelves—along with all of Keith Sagar's other Lawrence books. Keith was one of the first Lawrence scholars to recognize the need to ground the interpretation of Lawrence's writings in the complex particulars of their compositional history. One of the important features of *The Art of D. H. Lawrence* is the series of chronologies of Lawrence's writings that preface each of the chapters. Keith subsequently published *D. H. Lawrence: A Calendar of His Works* in 1979. He also became an original member of the editorial board of the Cambridge edition of Lawrence's letters after being instrumental in bringing together the Cambridge University Press and Laurence Pollinger, Ltd., the agent for the Lawrence Estate. Along with Jim Boulton, the general editor, Keith edited the seventh volume of the scholarly masterpiece for which all Lawrence scholars and serious readers of Lawrence are grateful.

In 1980 Keith Sagar published *The Life of D. H. Lawrence*. After having published studies of Lawrence's art and Lawrence's life, Keith completed his unofficial trilogy by publishing a study of the relationship between the two. That book, published in 1985, is *D. H. Lawrence: Life Into Art*. In 1982 Keith edited two notable books about Lawrence: *A D. H. Lawrence Handbook* and *D. H. Lawrence and New Mexico*. In 2004 Keith published *D. H. Lawrence's Paintings* with its splendid reproductions and expert commentary. As you might suspect, Lawrence also figures importantly in *Literature and the Crime Against Nature* (2005). Most recently, Keith published *D. H. Lawrence: Poet* (2008), a comprehensive study of Lawrence's poetry. His own selection of Lawrence's poetry, published by Penguin in 1972, stayed in print for thirty-five years.

In the summer of 1980 I made my single foray into Ted Hughes scholarship when I travelled to Manchester to participate in the First International Hughes Conference, organized by Keith Sagar, yes, the most prominent Ted Hughes scholar. I especially remember the lovely evening that several of us spent at Keith's cottage, during which he showed us his marvellous Lawrence collection (including the 'grubby, well-worn, once-white silk jacket' that belonged to Lawrence during the 1920s). Eight years later both of us travelled to Shanghai for the first truly international Lawrence conference. We discovered that our hosts had arranged for us to be roommates in the dorm where the international participants were housed. It was easy to discern the logic of the conference organizers in placing Keith Sagar and Keith Cushman in the same room. Perhaps the same logic is once again operative in my having been asked to write this brief Foreword to this selection of Keith Sagar's Lawrence essays.

In addition to being roommates, Keith Sagar and I have also been scholarly collaborators. Keith had figured out that the striking painting known inanely as 'Italian Landscape', which had always been attributed to Lawrence, was actually the work of Achsah Brewster. In the early 1990's two Keiths published a short essay in the *D. H. Lawrence Review* in which we were at last able to give Achsah credit for one of her best pictures.

My brief description of Keith Sagar's Lawrence books, along with a casual glance at the table of contents of this collection, makes it clear that he has done it all when it comes to Lawrence criticism and Lawrence scholarship. The collection begins with a biographical study, 'Lawrence and the Wilkinsons', Keith's first Lawrence publication. In the other thirteen essays Keith engages with the poetry, one of the plays, the short novels, and several of the novels. 'Lawrence and Frieda: The Alternative Story' and 'D. H. L. and R. L. S'. are biographical studies. In 'Beyond D. H. Lawrence', published in 1980, Keith looks back on what Lawrence meant to his generation in the 1950s and 1960s: 'He asked us the necessary questions, the questions St Mawr asks Lou: what is real? are you alive?' [89]. In an era of narrow academic specialization Keith Sagar has always been interested in Lawrence as the writer who boldly asks such ultimate questions. This Lawrence is also found in several other essays collected here: 'D. H. Lawrence: The Man and the Artist', 'How to Live? The End of Lawrence's Quest', and 'Lawrence's God'. The fourteen essays of *Art for Life's Sake* are but a sampling of all of Keith Sagar's essays on Lawrence.

In our post-modern, indeed post-literary world, Keith Sagar writes about literature with the sort of high seriousness that first drew many of us to the profession many years ago. He also writes with the scholarly precision and clarity that we can all aspire to. The passion in the prose is not always readily discernible because the style is so unassuming. His criticism is always direct, textually grounded, sensible, and useful. If this makes him rather old-fashioned in 2010, Keith would be the first to say 'so be it'. Indeed he reports on his website that in 1995 Manchester University 'threw [him] out seven years early for teaching the Western canon'.

Keith Sagar is also a poet, a photographer, and a gardener. He has bred endangered Australian finches. His two books that have enjoyed the most commercial success are about tropical fish. And let's not forget that he is the man who taught me how to pronounce Ursula: '*Ursyula*,' not the flat, American '*Ursuhla*.' As a quintessential Englishman and the father of a daughter named Ursula he should know.

What a pleasure it is to have these fourteen essays collected in one volume.

Keith Cushman
University of North Carolina at Greensboro

Introduction: Lawrence in my Life

The choice I made, unconsciously at school and consciously at university, to specialize on Lawrence, was the most important choice of my life. It determined not only my career, with thousands of hours spent reading, researching, teaching and writing on Lawrence, but also my thinking, my travel, my friendships, and even my marriage.

I have often been asked when my interest in Lawrence began. I can date it very precisely to the year 1949, when I was fifteen. My main interest at that time was in animals. My ambition was to be a zoo-keeper. I was saving up to buy a Royal Python I visited weekly at a pet shop in Leeds. But pythons were sold at so much per foot, and the snake grew faster than my savings. However, I did keep many other animals, including snakes and birds. One day I was browsing in the school library when a title caught my eye – *The Plumed Serpent.* How could a snake be feathered? To find out, I borrowed and read the book. Its author's name, D. H. Lawrence, meant nothing to me (not even *Lady Chatterley's Lover*). *The Plumed Serpent* was the most evocative, powerful piece of writing I had ever read. I wanted more. My second choice (for similar reasons) was *The White Peacock,* which was less interesting, but did not deter me from going on to *The Tales*: all Lawrence's short fiction in one volume, an inspired choice.

By the time I went to Cambridge in 1952 I had read everything of Lawrence that was in print, and that was a good deal, thanks to Allen Lane, who had published almost his complete works in 1950 to mark the twentieth anniversary of his death. In almost every student's room at that time, irrespective of his subject, and even if there were no other literature, you would find a few of these Lawrence Penguins. He was saying very much what we wanted to hear, especially on sexual matters.

Scrutiny was still being published in 1952, but I knew nothing of the Leavis controversy; and when my supervisor, F. L. Lucas, advised me not to bother with Leavis's lectures (without explaining why) I took his advice. In my second year

I did go to them, and in my third year went to little else. Leavis helped me to learn to read, to pay proper attention to the words on the page, but I never became a hard-line Leavisite. I was much more in tune with David Daiches, who was my supervisor in my second and third years.

I stayed in Cambridge for a fourth year to do a Teacher's Training Certificate. For my thesis I wrote on 'The Educational Implications of the Writings of Plato, John Stuart Mill and D. H. Lawrence'. That course, and especially the term of practical teaching of semi-delinquents in Bradford, made me realize that I did not really want to be a schoolteacher. I consulted the Senior Tutor at King's, Patrick Wilkinson, who told me about Adult Education, of which I knew nothing. When he had finished his long description of Extra-Mural Departments and the Workers' Educational Association, he asked me what I thought. I replied: 'That sounds made for me'. At the end of that year, through Patrick, I was offered the opportunity to teach at the Cambridge WEA Summer School. I taught, of course, Lawrence.

***

My first job, after nine inglorious weeks of National Service, was as an Administrative Assistant in the Extra-Mural Department of Leeds University. Our head of department suggested that I should take advantage of the fact that members of staff could take further degrees without fees to do a part-time Ph.D. Apart from Shakespeare, the only author in whom I felt I could guarantee to sustain interest for five years was Lawrence. The Cambridge English tripos had contained a paper on *The English Moralists*. The title of my thesis was to be *D. H. Lawrence as a Moralist*; but the new head of the English Department, Norman Jeffares, asked me what my qualifications were in the moral sciences, and hearing that they were nil, vetoed the idea. I then came up with *Vision and Form in the Works of D. H. Lawrence*.

The Leeds EMD at that time had a splendid team of literature tutors. I joined two of Walter Stein's weekly classes, one on Shakespeare and one on Twentieth Century Literature, in which *The Rainbow* was a primary text. I never missed a meeting of either class for two years, and learned more from Walter about literature and how to teach it than I had learned in four years full-time at Cambridge. (His book, *Criticism as Dialogue*, is a neglected classic.)

After two years I moved to Chesterfield, as WEA Tutor-Organizer for NE Derbyshire. Though my thesis was critical, not biographical, I naturally wanted to see Lawrence's birthplace and the country of his heart. I had never before set foot in Nottinghamshire. Hitherto I had lived with my parents in Bradford. We had no car at that time, and Nottingham seemed a very long way. But now I was only half-an-hour away, and within days of my arrival in Chesterfield I set off for Eastwood on my Lambretta scooter, with my trusty Kodak Colorsnap camera.

It is difficult now to imagine how little interest there was in Lawrence in those days. One even had to specify 'D. H. Lawrence, you know, the author of *Lady Chatterley's Lover*'. 'Oh, yes,' the response might come 'and didn't he also write *Sons and Lovers*?' If you simply said Lawrence you would be taken to be referring to Lawrence of Arabia. But I assumed that in Eastwood at least there would be some recognition. I went to the library for guidance, to be told that there was only one person in Eastwood who knew anything about Lawrence. 'Go down the other side of Nottingham Road until you come to a large shoe shop, and ask for Mrs Hopkin.' Of course I knew all about Willie Hopkin, Lawrence's close friend and mentor in Eastwood, who had died aged ninety in 1951. Olive Hopkin, Willie's second wife, whom he had married in 1925, not only gave me directions to the four Lawrence houses, Beauvale Primary School and Haggs Farm, Lawrence's rural bolt-hole, where he had met his first sweetheart Jessie Chambers, but invited me to tea at 165 Nottingham Road afterwards. There she showed me all

Lawrence's then unpublished letters to Willie and Sallie Hopkin, and many photographs. It never occurred to me to raise with her the possibility of publishing the letters, publishing of any kind being at that time something quite outside my experience. I was to visit Olive Hopkin on most of my many subsequent visits to Eastwood. She also put me in contact with her step-daughter Enid (who had helped Lawrence with the distribution of *Lady Chatterley's Lover*). I had a long correspondence with Enid, whom I was to accompany to the Lawrence festival in Santa Fe in 1980. She was then eighty-four.

Eastwood at that time was very different from Eastwood today. The mines were still in full production, and the whole area was much closer to the mining countryside Lawrence depicted. Those who have visited the area only recently might well feel that in stories such as 'Odour of Chrysanthemums', in *The Widowing of Mrs. Holroyd,* in the opening of *Sons and Lovers,* in the Wiggiston chapter of *The Rainbow,* and in *Lady Chatterley's Lover* (to name but a few examples), Lawrence exaggerated for fictional or ideological purposes the contrast between the 'old England of the forest and agricultural past' and the degradation of the mines and the villages built to serve them. That contrast was much more stark in 1959. The war and post-war austerity had ensured that, apart from the sprouting of a few television aerials, the area was much as it had been in Lawrence's day. It is easy to understand how, before he began to write or form any ideologies, the natural world must have presented itself to him as a source of the clean, the sane and the sacred by which the works of men were to be judged.

The Squares, for example, were exactly as Lawrence had described them thirty years previously in 'Nottingham and the Mining Countryside':

> On the down-slope of the north side the company erected what is still known as the New Buildings, or the Square. These new buildings consist of two great hollow squares

> of dwellings planked down on the rough slope of the hill, little four-room houses with the 'front' looking outward into the grim, blank street, and the 'back', with a tiny square brick yard, a low wall, and a w.c. and ash-pit, looking into the desert of the square, hard, uneven, jolting black earth tilting rather steeply down, with these little back yards all round, and openings at the corners. The squares were quite big, and absolutely desert, save for the posts for clothes lines, and people passing, children playing on the hard earth. And they were shut in like a barracks enclosure, very strange. (*LEA* 288)

To get to Lawrence's favourite countryside, at Underwood, Felley and Annesley, I had to walk, like Lawrence, through Moorgreen pit, but then, just across the road, alongside the beautiful Moorgreen reservoir. The northern horizon was still dominated by Brinsley pit, where Lawrence's father and grandfather had worked, and his Uncle James had been killed. So the colliery engines were still running just a few feet from the door of Vine Cottage, the cottage of 'Odour of Chrysanthemums' and *The Widowing of Mrs. Holroyd.* As a stranger to the area I had no idea as I came to the top of a hill whether the next valley would be totally unspoiled or sickeningly disfigured and polluted. A few miles further north there were the horrors of Selston, Jacksdale and Ironville.

My photographs were not up to much. Fortunately a proper photographer, George Roberts of the County Library, had taken a large portfolio. This was part of the excellent Lawrence collection assembled largely by Lucy Edwards in the building in Shakespeare Street which had been Nottingham University College when Lawrence attended it.

My next visit was to the University Library, where I expected to find a significant Lawrence collection, but there was very little. I learned later that this was largely due to the influence of Emeritus Professor Ernest Weekley (whose wife Frieda had run off with Lawrence in 1912). Even after Weekley's death in 1954, there was considerable hostility to

Lawrence among senior members of the university. It was not until the sixties that Professor Vivian de Sola Pinto, head of the English Department and himself a Lawrence enthusiast, was able to start to build the major collection which is there now.

My visit, however, was far from wasted. What I did find, which proved of immense importance to me, was an unpublished thesis by Gamini Salgado presented in 1955 on *The Poetry of D. H. Lawrence*. It was this work, the first full-length study of Lawrence's poetry (until then almost completely neglected) which alerted me to the importance of Lawrence's poetry and the greatness of the *Birds, Beasts and Flowers* collection in particular. It much improved the three chapters on the poems in my thesis. Without it I might never have proposed to Penguin Books my new selection of Lawrence's poetry.

At the start of the third year of my thesis it came to light that due to an administrative error in the English department my registration had been for an MA (which I already had) rather than a Ph.D. When I pointed this out to Professor Jeffares, he asked to see the work in progress. He found it insufficiently 'critical', and prevaricated about setting right the mistake.

This was about the time when Professor Vivian de Sola Pinto staged the first significant Lawrence exhibition at Nottingham University, 'Lawrence After 30 Years'. I attended almost all the events staged in connection with the exhibition, including an inaugural talk by F. R. Leavis. As the audience waited for that lecture to begin, I noticed two Lawrence specialists, disciples of Leavis, sitting immediately in front of me, Harry Coombes and Roy Littlewood. I had met Roy at Staff meetings of the Leeds Extra-Mural Department, where he had been employed in Services Education at Catterick. I remembered only one previous conversation with him. I had asked him if he had seen an interesting article by Ian Gregor in the current *Essays in Criticism* on Lawrence's story 'The Fox'. He seemed amazed than anyone should have presumed to write on 'The Fox' at all: 'Leavis has already dealt with it'.

We began a conversation in which I mentioned the three versions of *Lady Chatterley's Lover.* They interrupted me – there were only two versions of Lady C. 'But', I objected, 'all three versions have already been published in Italian edited by Professor Nardi – *Le Tre Lady Chatterley.*' This cut no ice at all – they insisted there were only two. This was typical of the disdain the Leavisites had for scholarship, for mere facts.

Leavis's talk was inspirational, especially his characteristic analysis of Lawrence's informal prose in a letter describing the death of Rupert Brooke:

> The death of Rupert Brooke fills me more and more with a sense of the fatuity of it all. He was slain by bright Phoebus' shaft – it was in keeping with his general sunniness – it was the real climax of his pose. I first heard of him as a Greek god under a Japanese sunshade, reading poetry in his pyjamas, at Grantchester upon the lawns where the river goes. Bright Phoebus smote him down. It is all in the saga. O God, O God, it is all too much of a piece: it is like madness (*2L* 330-1).

But the lecture was marred by Leavis's equally characteristic contempt for the work of American Lawrenceans, especially Harry T. Moore. Harry Moore was neither a particularly distinguished critic nor a meticulous scholar, but he made up for this by his utter dedication to Lawrence. No other criticism, English or American could at that time compare with Leavis's *D. H. Lawrence: Novelist,* published in 1955, but it was American critics and scholars such as Tedlock, Spilka and especially Harry Moore himself, who, at least as much as Leavis, had kept Lawrence's reputation alive through the forties and early fifties.

In the exhibition were several previously unknown photographs of Lawrence taken at the Villa Mirenda in 1926-7 by his neighbour Arthur Gair Wilkinson. I asked the university for copies, which they said they would be glad to provide given the permission of their owner, Frances Gair Wilkinson, Arthur's daughter. I wrote to her, and in her reply she told me that she had much more material than had been in the exhibition: over thirty letters and postcards from Lawrence to her family; more photographs; and the diaries kept by her parents detailing almost daily meetings with the Lawrences – walks, picnics, parties, trips into Florence, countless conversations… She said that she had offered to sell the collection to Nottingham, but that de Sola Pinto had replied that the university would be glad to accept them as a gift. I suppose no funds were available for such purchases at that time.

I asked if I could visit her, and subsequently spent two days at her delightful cottage at the foot of the Quantocks, transcribing the letters and diaries, which were a joy. I was working upstairs. When I came down after my final session, Frances had spread on the table a dozen lovely watercolours by her father of the Mirenda at the time the Lawrences were there. 'Take your pick,' she said. She had described picnicking with Lawrence by a stream above the Mirenda, and feeding the fresh-water crabs with their chicken bones. She drew me a map of the route from the tram terminus at Vingone, past the pagoda and the 'due cipressi'. The following year I went there with a group of WEA students I had taken to Florence. As the Mirenda came into view, there on the path in front of it was a red cart drawn by two white oxen, exactly as in the painting I had chosen.

I had no intention of intruding on the occupants of the Mirenda, but some children playing nearby ran to the Villa Poggi (where the Wilkinsons had lived) to report the presence of strangers. A couple came out, the wife from Manchester, and they insisted on taking me to meet Signor Mirenda, Lawrence's landlord, and his wife. It had never occurred to me they might still be alive. They showed me the rooms occupied by the Lawrences. Then we found the stream and fed the crabs. I have returned to the Mirenda several times, culminating in 1995, when I took a group of Lawrenceans on an Etruscan tour. It is still a splendid walk, but the crabs are there no longer.

Professor Norman Jeffares was head of the English Department at Leeds. He had looked at my work in progress on my thesis, and expressed disquiet that it was 'not sufficiently critical' (whatever he meant by that). He was also editor of the *Review of English Literature,* which had just published the important early letters from Lawrence to Blanche Jennings, which the Allotts had unearthed in Liverpool. I asked him if he would be interested in publishing some more new Lawrence letters. I had never before been a welcome visitor, but now it was a case of 'Come in, my dear boy. Pull up an armchair. Can I get you a sherry?' As I left he said: 'Oh, by the way, I don't think there will be any more problems about your Ph.D.' 'Lawrence and the Wilkinsons' became my first published piece on Lawrence.

Publishing these typically sparkling Lawrence letters was the beginning of an interest which led to the campaign by Harry Moore, Gerald Lacy and myself to get an edition published of all Lawrence's several thousand letters. We eventually succeeded in bringing together the Lawrence Estate and the Cambridge University Press, whose seven handsome volumes appeared over the next twenty years. With the General Editor, Jim Boulton, I edited the seventh.

Several years later, when the Cambridge edition of Lawrence's letters was launched, and I had acquired a portable photocopier, I thought I had better return to Somerset and get a more accurate record of the letters. Frances had, in the meantime, become Mrs Miller, and moved to a neighbouring village. Again I received the kindest hospitality. They seemed a perfectly contented couple. As I was about to leave, Frances asked if I had ever met her Uncle Walter. Walter had been a frequent visitor to the Villa Poggi, and had got to know Lawrence, who reviewed his book on puppeteering, *The Peep Show,* in the spring of 1927. It had never occurred to me that he could be still alive. I was told that he was very much alive, and that his wife Winifred, also in her eighties, had just published her first novel *God in Hell*. They lived not far away, at Selworthy. Frances telephoned them, and they invited me to tea. As I said goodbye she gave me a copy of *The Lost Girl* inscribed by Lawrence, and a napkin ring painted by him.

Walter and Winifred were equally charming and hospitable. At one point Walter disappeared upstairs and returned wearing a grubby, well-worn, once-white silk jacket. He told me that he had arrived at the Poggi from England one very hot day wearing his English worsted suit. 'For goodness sake, Walter, change into something more comfortable,' said Lawrence. 'I can't,' said Walter, 'my trunk is in Florence; I've only what I'm wearing.' 'Here,' said Lawrence, taking off his white jacket, 'keep it; it's time I had a new one.' It is probably the jacket Lawrence had worn throughout his years in America, and is wearing in most of the Arthur Wilkinson photographs. As I was leaving, Walter thrust it into my hands: 'Here, it's more use to you than to me.' Christopher Miles was later to borrow it to have a replica made which Ian McKellen wore in *The Priest of Love*.

Shortly after this visit I learned that Mr Miller had died. Frances did not long survive him, dying in 1976.

***

Soon after my arrival in Chesterfield I had met Lawrence's nieces, Peggy Needham and Joan King, daughters of his sister Emily. After my move to Manchester in 1963 I would usually stay with Peggy on my visits to the Lawrence country. At her house at Heanor, she had all Lawrence's letters and postcards to her mother and herself, many photographs, and many of his early paintings. Joan had yet more photographs and paintings. Emily had recently died, but on my first visit to Joan at South Muskham I met Emily's husband Sam King. Sam told me that while Lawrence was visiting them in 1926, Sam was leaving the house one morning, and Lawrence asked him where he was going. He replied that he was going to see his solicitor in order to make his will. Lawrence commented that he ought to do the same while he was in England, as he had never made a will; yet his widow Frieda and Middleton Murry had persuaded a court in 1930 that Lawrence *had* made a will in 1916 leaving everything to Frieda and nothing to his family. Peggy remained an active advocate of Lawrence into her nineties. Joan, happily, is still with us, probably the only person living who knew Lawrence.

At that time it was still possible to obtain Lawrence first editions at reasonable prices. I bought a lovely copy of *The Rainbow* from a Cornwall bookseller for fifteen pounds. When it arrived there was a note saying: 'You might as well have the enclosed Lawrence postcard, the only one which remained unsold from my previous catalogue.' My first Lawrence manuscript! It was Lawrence's first communication on his return to Florence in 1919: 'Italy is a good bit spoilt by the war.' I also obtained a copy of the Mandrake edition of the paintings, and my favourite first edition, the Black Sun Press *Escaped Cock*, with Lawrence's delightful watercolours, before they became unaffordable.

***

Enthusiasm for Lawrence as a 'priest of love' peaked in 1960 with the *Lady Chatterley Trial.* Not only did that trial vindicate Lawrence's views on sex, it marked the last gasp of Lawrence's England, the England of censorship, mealy-mouthed Puritanism, and class-distinction; the England in which it was still possible to say in all seriousness: 'Would you wish your wife and servants to read this book?' The sexual revolution which followed (though entirely lacking the religious element in Lawrence's view of sex) largely removed the appeal of that area of his work, especially for younger readers, who could not see what all the fuss had been about.

The early feminists chose Lawrence as an easy target, demonstrating his male chauvinism by means of highly selective quotation and by ignoring his major contribution to female emancipation, especially in *The Rainbow*.

My own interest did not decline, because I had already moved on to a more literary interest in Lawrence's mastery of a living prose and verse, and of so many diverse literary forms. My work on him moved gradually away from the novels towards the poems and novellas.

I finished my thesis in 1962, and began to rewrite it as a book. Boris Ford, Professor of Education at Sheffield University at the time, and editor of the influential Pelican Guide to English Literature, gave a lecture at Leeds, which I attended. He had a return train ticket to Sheffield, but when I offered him a lift (I was going to Chesterfield), he gratefully accepted. On the journey it came up that I was looking for a publisher. He suggested that I should approach Michael Black at the Cambridge University Press. After unstinting guidance from Michael, the book was published, as *The Art of D.H. Lawrence* in 1966, and remained in print for about twenty years, and the Press has recently reissued it. Michael later claimed that it was the chronologies of Lawrence's writings in this book which first engendered the huge and still continuing Cambridge University Press enterprise of the Complete Works of Lawrence, meticulously edited in about fifty volumes.

Harry Moore had also been a speaker at the 1960 Nottingham conference. After his lecture I had joined a queue of people waiting to question him. I asked him two questions: why there were no British contributors to his recently published critical anthology *A D. H. Lawrence Miscellany,* and whether he knew the whereabouts of any of Lawrence's paintings. Little did I imagine that this brief encounter would be the beginning of a relationship which would last until Harry's death twenty years later.

I had a friendly correspondence at this time with F. R. Leavis. He soon insisted on first name terms. He fulminated against Graham Hough for trying to get *The Dark Sun* published before his own *D. H. Lawrence: Novelist.* I sent Leavis two framed unpublished photographs of Lawrence.

He was delighted with them and gave them pride of place on his piano. I had eight letters from him in all. When my book was published I sent him a copy, which was unacknowledged. My next project was to have been to edit a collection of essays on *Wuthering Heights.* Michael Black told me that the Leavises had just returned from a lecture tour in the States during which Queenie had been lecturing on *Wuthering Heights,* and suggested I should invite her to contribute it to my anthology. I wrote to her, sending also my greetings to her husband. She replied in a single sentence: 'Neither my husband nor I remembers ever having met you. Q. D. Leavis'. This charming rebuff was just as well because her essay, subsequently published, was so bad that I would have had to reject it.

Later, in an article, Leavis berated me for revealing in my book that when Lawrence spoke of his work in progress as 'really a stratum deeper than I think anybody has ever gone, in a novel' he was referring to *The Insurrection of Miss Houghton* (an early version of *The Lost Girl*). Leavis insisted that anyone with a grain of critical sense should see that it was obviously about *The Rainbow.* It was a test case for Leavis. His critical sense told him that it *must* refer to *The Rainbow,* and this overruled the mere fact that the letter in question was written several months before Lawrence conceived of the novel which was to become *The Rainbow.*

Fortunately, my book was well received by the Lawrence establishment, one of the most generous reviews being by Professor de Sola Pinto, who described it as marking the beginning of serious Lawrence scholarship in England.

***

1966 was also the year in which I bought my first house. Now my interest in animals which had brought me to Lawrence in the first place began to rival my interest in him. The freedom to keep whatever livestock I pleased went to my head. I converted the garage into a menagerie in which I kept a large stud of exhibition Himalayan cavies, an aviary of Australian finches, and a bank of breeding cages of new-colour canaries. In the house I had two large aquaria of marine tropical fish and one of freshwater tropicals. Humming-birds were flying free in the hall. I travelled far and wide exhibiting my cavies and buying and selling creatures. My academic work inevitably suffered, and my eight years in that house yielded only *The Art of Ted Hughes* and some editing of Lawrence for Penguin Books. When I moved house I decided that I must curb this animal-keeping frenzy, and settled for just two marine aquaria. One reason for preferring fish to cavies or birds was that I could combine fishkeeping with my growing interest in photography. In the mid-seventies I published *The Love of Tropical Fish* and *The World Encyclopedia of Tropical Fish.* These two books earned more money than my twenty academic books put together, but they delayed my return to serious work on Lawrence by another couple of years.

***

One great benefit of following in Lawrence's footsteps is that one has the motivation (and even sometimes the funding) to visit some of the world's most beautiful spots. I had already seen most of Lawrence's Italian homes, culminating in the magical Fontana Vecchia in Sicily, surrounded by lemon groves, with Etna smoking behind and the Calabrian Sea sparkling in front. In 1967, having had no contact with him since the Leavis lecture, I received a postcard from Roy Littlewood postmarked Taos, New Mexico, saying that I must go there. I had never been outside Europe, and it had not occurred to me that New Mexico was a place one could actually go to. Air fares had recently plunged, so I started to plan my first trip to the States.

I wrote to Harry Moore. He not only remembered me from Nottingham, but remembered the exact questions I had asked him there. He also provided me with an invaluable list of contacts for teaching and lecturing engagements.

My best friend from Cambridge had emigrated to the Bay area, and had several times invited me to visit him. I now took up this invitation, and was able to arrange a five-week course on Lawrence with the Continuing Education Department at Berkeley. I wanted to take the opportunity to work on the *Sons and Lovers* manuscripts at Berkeley, particularly to see exactly what Edward Garnett had deleted from the novel, but I was denied access on the grounds that Mark Schorer was working on them. He had been sitting on them for about ten years. I did not get to see them until several years later, when Carl Baron obtained copies for his work on the Cambridge University Press edition. My initial response was to approve of Garnett's pruning; but over the next decade I gradually came to see the importance of much of the excised material, particularly about Paul's older brother William. The novel is, after all, not *Son and Lover*, and Lawrence called it 'the tragedy of thousands of young men in England' (*1L 477*).

After five weeks I boarded a Greyhound bus in Berkeley and set off for Taos, stopping for a night in Angel Creek lodge, overlooking the Grand Canyon.

I stayed at La Fonda de Taos, where the owner, Saki Karavas, had the world's largest collection of Lawrence paintings, most of those which had survived from the 1929 Warren Gallery exhibition, in his poky, smoky office, where they could be seen for a dollar. Saki had been a great friend of Frieda's third husband, Angelo Ravagli. Angie hated Lawrence's paintings, and after Frieda's death simply wanted them out of the house, so he sold them to Saki for a song. I knew the paintings from reproductions, but the originals were another matter. I could express what they meant to me only in little poems (as Lawrence himself wrote a few Pansies corresponding to some of his paintings). I had written a few poems at school, and published a couple in the school magazine, but reading English at Cambridge had soon cured me of that, and I had then written not a single poem for sixteen years. The five I wrote on my return from Taos kick-started me again as a poet.

Saki's paintings were always for sale, about to be bought by Greeks or Japanese. But the price kept rising, always just ahead of any possible sale. Saki did not really want to lose what he called his 'spiderweb'. He loved the daily flow of visitors, especially the glamorous young women. Saki was waiting to take me to breakfast every day, and would then offer to chauffeur me wherever I wanted to go, even several miles into the mountains to the Lawrence ranch, still kept (by the immortal Al Bierce) much as it was when Lawrence lived there in 1924-5. He would take me to the best restaurants for miles around for dinner. And he knew everybody, and was liked by everybody. One of the few good things Richard Nixon can be remembered for is having given back to the Taos Indians their sacred Blue Lake. Saki was the only non-Indian invited to the grand ceremony. As if that were not enough, there was a film crew at La Fonda making a film for the BBC on Lawrence in Taos, and they took me around with them, meeting everyone still in Taos who had known Lawrence.

Dorothy Brett, who was the main focus of the film, was 85 and still painting – beautiful paintings of the fish she had seen a boy catching in Mexico. Having just lost her driving licence because of her failing sight, she was talking of getting a motor-bike, apparently in the belief that she wouldn't need a licence. Brett, who was living with the Lawrences at the ranch in 1924, had typed out *St Mawr* day by day as Lawrence wrote it. She told me that he pronounced the name 'Seymour'. Since 'mawr' is Welsh for big or great, and Lewis, St Mawr's groom, pronounced it 'with a Welsh twist', this seemed highly unlikely, despite coming, as it were, from the horse's mouth. When I got home I looked up Seymour in a dictionary of surnames, to find that it derives from the Norman French 'de St. Maur'. St. Benedict, the founder of Western monasticism, had founded the great monastery at Monte Cassino. St. Maurus was his disciple and successor.

This information triggered my interpretation of *St Mawr* in 'The Monk and the Beast'.

Joe Foster befriended me, and took me to see the cave at Arroyo Seco which Lawrence used for the ending of 'The Woman Who Rode Away'; also to see the herds of buffalo which the Indians had reintroduced to the plains under Taos Mountain. 'Spud' Johnson was running the office for the Eugene McCarthy presidential campaign next door to La Fonda.

When the time came to leave La Fonda, I went to pay my bill, and was handed a note by the cashier saying 'No Charge'. I remonstrated with Saki that he couldn't run a hotel that way, but he insisted that whenever I wanted to stay there it would never cost me a cent. I stayed there as Saki's guest every year for the next thirteen years, and would gladly have paid the going rate. My love affair with New Mexico culminated in a book, *Lawrence and New Mexico,* in which I arranged in chronological order, with commentary, everything Lawrence had written about New Mexico.

When Saki died a few years ago he left both the hotel and the paintings to his friends the Sahds, who have had the paintings restored and now display them in a properly appointed room at La Fonda. But seeing them crammed together with many of Saki's other fascinating paintings, photographs and mementos, through a haze of cigar smoke, with Saki's twenty pairs of immaculately polished shoes lining the wall, had been a different experience altogether.

I met few natives in Taos. Most of the people I met had come as visitors and simply stayed. I asked how long it took for the magic to wear off, and they all gave the same answer, 'Never'.

From Taos I headed for Texas. The most important of the introductions Harry had given me was to Warren Roberts, the Director of the Humanities Research Centre at the University of Texas at Austin, where I was subsequently to spend a great deal of time working on the huge Lawrence collection. Warren in turn introduced me to one of his graduate students called Gerald Lacy, who was looking for a Lawrence topic for his Ph.D. I had dinner with him and suggested he should make a calendar of all Lawrence's extant letters. This calendar was later to form the basis of the seven-volume Cambridge edition of Lawrence's collected letters.

At the HRC there were yet more Lawrence paintings, including two of the finest, *Boccaccio Story* and *Resurrection.* The Lawrence collection was so vast that I spent my whole week in Austin working on the catalogue. Obviously many more visits would be needed. There was still at that time much unpublished and unstudied material. One thing which particularly interested me was the large number of unpublished photographs. I obtained copies of a great many of them. Together with the photographs I had obtained from Peggy and Joan, these formed the basis of the collection from which I was able to illustrate so fully my biography of Lawrence a decade later.

My 1970 visit to Taos was to attend a Lawrence conference at the ranch. I was not a speaker, but felt obliged to speak up in defence of *St Mawr* when David Garnett dismissed it as 'that story where a woman falls in love with a horse'.

On some of my later visits to the States, Harry Moore arranged lectures for me at Southern Illinois and put me up at his home.

***

By 1970 Gerald Lacy was well into the daunting task of locating and describing as many as possible of Lawrence's letters. I gave him what help I could on this side of the Atlantic. I knew that Lawrence and Frieda had visited Sir George and Lady Ida Sitwell at Montegufoni, near Florence, and that Sir George had suggested that Lawrence should make contact with his children and visit Renishaw Hall, the Sitwell family home in Derbyshire. He would almost certainly have told Lawrence of the battle his son Osbert was fighting to save Sutton Scarsdale Hall, which Lawrence knew well. At least one of the excursions of the Pagans had been there. Yet I noticed that no correspondence had come to light between Lawrence and any of the Sitwells. I wrote to Sir Reresby Sitwell, son of Sacheverell, and the then incumbent of Renishaw, to ask if he knew of any such correspondence among the family papers. He did not, but our subsequent correspondence led me to an exciting discovery about the origins of *Lady Chatterley's Lover.* It is obvious from the topography of the novel that Wragby, the Chatterley home, was to some extent based on Renishaw Hall, which Lawrence had visited on his last visit to England in 1926; but I did not suspect a much closer connection. Sir Reresby suggested that I should talk to Harold Taylor, 'self-instructed village historian', who knew more than anyone else about the history of Sutton Scarsdale Hall.

Harold Taylor told me the story of William Arkwright, grandson of the famous inventor, and last of the Arkwrights to live at Sutton Scarsdale, which he sold in 1920. Born in 1857, educated at Eton and Oxford, William had suffered terrible injuries when thrown from his horse at the age of twenty. He lay unconscious for six weeks, and had a silver plate inserted in his head. He recovered sufficiently to write three books and become an expert linguist, but the accident had left him impotent. Seven years after the accident, against the advice of his family, he married a beautiful young woman from an aristocratic family, Agnes Mary Summers-Cox. The marriage was unhappy, and they lived apart for most of their lives. Sir George must have told this story to Lawrence. Though no gamekeeper appears in it, it clearly contains the germ of *Lady Chatterley's Lover.*

***

1971 saw the first of a series of four summer schools on Lawrence held on the Nottingham campus. The initiative came from Michael Draper of Hull Extra-Mural Department and myself, and Michael directed the first, on *Lawrence and England*. The tutors included Bridget Pugh and Graham Martin. When I mentioned the school to Harry Moore he expressed great interest. I explained to him that the school would be nothing like an international conference. It was simply an Adult Education residential course run primarily for the students of the Extra-Mural Departments of three northern universities, Nottingham, Hull, and Manchester. Yet Harry insisted on coming at his own expense. He had no regrets, stating afterwards that he could not remember ever having experienced a more genuinely Lawrencean atmosphere. He was particularly struck by the depth of knowledge and interest in Lawrence for his own sake among both tutors and students. That this was no mere gesture was attested by the fact that Harry subsequently attended both the 1975 and 1980 summer schools. Harry had to be wherever Lawrence was being discussed or celebrated or performed. (Can we imagine Leavis attending a summer school?)

At the 1975 school Harry was upstaged by a lady from Chicago called Lois Ascherman. We were alerted to something out-of-the-ordinary in Mrs. Ascherman when her application arrived in a bright pink and highly scented envelope. The school was held at Derby Hall during a sweltering heat-wave. Arriving early, I went out into the courtyard for some air, and picked up from the ground the longest cigarette I had ever seen. It had been lit but not smoked. As I walked on I found another identical one. Then another. Eventually I caught up with a large lady and saw her take a cigarette from her bag, light it, and throw it away. I presented her with my handful, saying: 'I believe you dropped these.' 'Oh, I've finished with them,' she said. I pointed out that they did not improve the appearance of the courtyard, and she apologized profusely. Later, I found myself seated next to her at dinner. She was holding forth about how exited she was, and how she had promised all her friends Lawrencean souvenirs. I suggested that she should collect several of the paper napkins which we had had specially printed with the letters DH, and she began to do so until someone pointed out that DH stood for Derby Hall. She took this in very good part. After dinner everyone repaired to the bar. When I entered, Lois was sitting with her back to the door, complaining about the heat. I took an ice-cube with a pair of tongs and pretended that I was about to drop it down the back of her dress. Seeing from the faces in front of her that something was happening at her back, she turned and dared me to drop it. So I did. She went rigid. Then an expression of ecstasy crossed her face and she said: 'That is the most beautiful thing anyone ever did to me.' That was the beginning of a lasting friendship. Lois attended every subsequent Lawrence summer school and conference, and enlivened them all with her wit. She proved to be the best reader I have come across of Lawrence's satirical poems from *Pansies* and *Nettles.*

***

The most memorable of my visits to Taos was in 1977, when I had study leave and a Fulbright grant to work at the Humanities Research Centre at the University of Texas at Austin. Most of Lawrence's manuscripts are there. I was working simultaneously on my *Calendar* of Lawrence's works and on my biography of him. Acquiring so many excellent photographs from Peggy and Joan, many of them unpublished, had implanted in me the desire to produce an illustrated biography, and I had spent some fifteen years augmenting this nucleus with more photographs from all over the world, but especially from the HRC.

I could have gone at any time, but wanted to see Taos under snow. I had been at every other season, including the fall, for the aspens and the San Geronimo Indian festival. Taos, at seven thousand feet, is a ski valley in the foothills of the Rockies. So I went in January to be certain of snow. When I got to Albuquerque airport they told me there had been not a flake of snow all winter, and the ski resorts were desperate. As my Greyhound bus climbed out of

Albuquerque into the Sandia Mountains huge flakes began to fall. The bus could get no further than Santa Fe. I had to stay the night in the de Vargas Hotel, where Lawrence had stayed. By morning the snow-ploughs had cleared the way to Taos. The valley came into view under eighteen inches of virgin snow. Three days later there was a fresh heavy fall. Up in Ski Valley they were searching for their cars with long poles. By now photography had become a major interest for me, and this was a photographer's paradise, especially the ranch and the pueblo.

It was 3 December 1978 when I finished the first draft of my biography. I had decided that I did not want it to trail off into anticlimax with details of the survivors, the literary reputation, and so on. I wanted Lawrence's death to be the closing page. It was getting very late, but I was so close to the end that I did not want to leave it unfinished. Yet I dreaded the end. I had come to feel so close to Lawrence, and now I was about to kill him at the age of forty-four. 'Why,' I thought, 'I am almost that age myself, and my life has hardly begun. Perhaps I am already older than Lawrence was when he died.' I did the calculation. He was forty-four years, five months and nineteen days. Then I calculated my own age: forty-four years, five months and nineteen days.

The biography of Lawrence was published in February 1980. It was very well received, and I had every reason to expect it to have at least as long a life as its predecessor, Moore and Roberts's *D. H. Lawrence and his World*; but when the publisher, Methuen, was taken over a few months later by one of the faceless multinational publishing groups, the title was dropped.

From collecting my first copies from Methuen I went straight to the home of Christopher Miles, who was keen to use the photographs in my book for both locations and costumes in his film *The Priest of Love*. I spent the afternoon discussing these with his designers, then he took me out to dinner, and from there to Euston for the last train home. On the way to the station Christopher invited me to join the company on location in Oaxaca at his expense as an advisor. I had always wanted to go to Mexico, and had made two abortive attempts to get there (thwarted by the last minute unavailability of the American friend I had planned to go with). As we parted, Christopher thrust into my hand the first draft of the script by Alan Plater. I read it on the train. It appalled me. It created artificial situations nowhere near as dramatic as what had really happened. It bristled with unnecessary inaccuracies. Though it was three o'clock when I got home, I immediately typed a letter to Christopher saying that I could not possibly have anything to do with the film. He replied that shooting scripts never bore any resemblance to first drafts, and that if I came I would be able to influence its development. But I stayed on my high horse and did not go. Christopher was right; there was little wrong with the final script. I have never made it to Mexico.

***

In July 1980 there was a huge festival in Santa Fe and Taos to mark the fiftieth anniversary of Lawrence's death. All I can remember of it is the surfeit of celebrities, literary and otherwise. I thought Trevor Howard was the worst reader I had heard of Lawrence's poetry until Elizabeth Taylor began to read 'Snake'. I found myself sitting next to Margaret Drabble one morning. She asked me what I had thought of Derek Walcott's talk on Lawrence's poetry the previous day. I said I thought that his comments on Lawrence's free verse were not very intelligent. 'Oh, but he's a wonderful poet,' she replied in a huff (meaning Walcott, not Lawrence). In her subsequent report on the conference in *The Observer* she wrote that I had been a stand-in for Dr. Leavis, which surprised me.

That same year I directed a summer school on Lawrence and Italy at Nottingham University. When Michael Draper was forced to withdraw because of illness, we recruited a new tutor, Melissa Partridge, who was doing a Ph.D. on that very subject at Cambridge. I began to pursue her, in complete ignorance of the fact that one of the students in my group, who had deliberately registered in her maiden name, was in fact her mother.

On the final evening of that summer school we rashly decided to stage a re-enactment of the Red Indian playlet performed by the Natcha-Kee-Tawara circus troupe in *The Lost Girl.* Peter Preston, who played the bear, barely survived my overenthusiastic assault.

The British Lawrence Society had been founded in 1974, based on Eastwood. I was closely involved from the start, and have probably given more talks to the society than anyone else. One of the society's activities is to provide guided walks in the Lawrence country. I later heard that a certain tree above Felley Mill had acquired mythic status as 'the very tree under which Keith Sagar proposed to Melissa Partridge'. We had, indeed, sat under that tree during the summer school, but the proposal came some months later in the rather different setting of Paris.

During my long stay in Austin in 1977 I had met Harriet Gay, who was also working on Lawrence in the H.R.C. We subsequently kept in touch, and when I told her that I was soon to be married, and that we were planning a honeymoon in the States, she and her husband Larry invited us to spend a week (by ourselves) at their second home in Hawaii, with the use of their car — amazing hospitality to near-strangers . It was the highlight of the honeymoon, which we remember as dominated by the almost overpowering scent of flowers. I was able to snorkel with some of the same species of coral reef fish I had been keeping and photographing for many years.

In 1982 the British Council invited me to give a lecture tour on Lawrence in what was then Yugoslavia. Melissa accompanied me. I lectured in Ljubljana, Zagreb, Split, Belgrade and Novi Sad. The beauty of Split was balanced by the ugliness of Novi Sad. Our Yugoslav hosts were extremely hospitable. I lunched with the great Yugoslav poet Vasco Popa in Belgrade. Tito had died in 1980. Everything seemed perfectly normal. There was no sign (or nothing evident to visitors) of the horrors into which Yugoslavia was to descend within ten years.

Our first child was born in Lawrence's centenary year, 1985. We called her Ursula partly after the main character in *The Rainbow*. Ursula, though an avid reader, does not, I regret to say, read Lawrence. She began *The Rainbow*, but did not persist, even though I told her that without Lawrence she would not exist.

In 1980 I had staged a Ted Hughes exhibition in Manchester, and had borrowed some items from Colin Franklin. When I went to collect them we were having afternoon tea in his garden. He said: 'You're also a Lawrence man, aren't you? I've got something which might interest you'. He went into the house, and came back with a small watercolour. 'Good heavens', I gasped, 'it's *Dandelions*'. Lawrence's painting of one of the peasants on the Villa Mirenda estate pissing into a clump of dandelions had never been heard of since he sold it to Orioli for £20 in 1929. Colin offered me a sizeable commission if I could find a buyer for him. I told him I was about to go to a huge Lawrence festival in Santa Fe, where there were bound to be many potential buyers. I let it be known at the reception meeting that I had a major Lawrence painting for sale. Several men jostled round me, reaching for their chequebooks, but when I produced a colour photograph of the painting, they mysteriously melted back into the crowd. Apparently sex would have been o.k. for these Texas millionaires, but pissing was beyond the pale. Five years later Carl Baron and I were working on a proposal for a volume on the paintings in the Cambridge edition. It occurred to me that I must keep tabs on *Dandelions*, so that it did not disappear for another fifty years. Colin Franklin confirmed that he still had the painting, and it was still for sale at the same price. 1985, Lawrence's centenary year, seemed a likely time to find a buyer. It suddenly occurred to me that I could now just about afford to buy the painting myself. When Melissa returned home from hospital with the new baby it was to find *Dandelions* on the wall, her 'birthday' gift, the only mature Lawrence painting in England. Carl and I reluctantly dropped the project when the C.U.P. told us a few months later that the illustrations in it would all have to be in monochrome.

1985 saw the publication by Penguin/Viking of my most ambitious book on Lawrence — *D. H. Lawrence: Life into Art,* which attempted to show how Lawrence transformed the raw material of experience into novels, stories, plays and poems. It was also the year of my British Council lecture tour in India. The tour began with a Lawrence conference in Hyderabad. I did not realize until I got there that the name Sagar (meaning, apparently, any large body of water) was very common in India. It was almost certainly in the belief that I was Indian that I had been invited. In fact my name is Scandinavian, meaning 'sayer'. I was the only non-Indian at the conference. No timetable was available until after the conference had begun. I was taken to the first meeting by the conference director. On the way he said that they had hoped to have an inaugural address by the Vice-Chancellor, but that he had cried off at the last minute. When I asked who was now giving the inaugural address, he said, 'You are'. That gave me some five minutes to think of a theme. What I rashly said was that I felt it would be more useful and more 'Lawrencean' if Indian scholars were to approach him from the perspective of their own culture and religion rather than aping Western academics. I don't think that cut much ice. I subsequently lectured on both Lawrence and Hughes at Madras and Trivandrum.

Three years later there came another British Council tour, this time to China. It was a time of apparent liberalization. The Shanghai conference was memorable for the number of bright young Chinese academics greedy for Lawrence. A few months later came Tiananmen Square, and all that enthusiasm was nipped in the bud.

After that, apart from editing the seventh volume of his letters, I rather drifted away from Lawrence to work on Ted

Hughes, and on my *magnum opus*, *Literature and the Crime Against Nature* (which has a large chapter on 'Lawrence and the Resurrection of Pan'). I gave an early version of this chapter as my contribution to the inaugural day of the D. H. Lawrence Research Centre at Nottingham University in 1991. Being all too aware of the fact that, despite the widespread celebration of the centenary of his birth in 1985, Lawrence's stock among both academics and the reading public had dwindled sadly in the eighties, what I wanted to do was to draw attention to a neglected aspect of his contemporary relevance, his contribution to deep ecology.

I have spoken at the Centre several times. Perhaps the most important occasion was a day-school in 1994 to mark the completion of the great Cambridge Letters project with the publication of the seventh volume. But equally important was the unveiling of the delightful statue of Lawrence holding a gentian by Diana Thomson, which now stands outside the library.

***

Only once has my decision to specialize on Lawrence worked against me. There was a financial crisis at Manchester University in the early nineties. By that time I had the status of Reader. One of the measures the university adopted was to close down its Extra-Mural Department in 1995. This meant relocating over forty academic staff, most of them in the appropriate internal departments. I assumed that I, along with the other Literature tutor, would go into the English Department. When the rest received notification of their new positions, I did not. When I approached the chairman of the Arrangements Committee, he said that a decision had not yet been reached in my case. Months passed, with frequent assurances that I would have a decision not today but surely tomorrow. In June I did not know what my job would be in September, so I wrote to the Vice-Chancellor. He asked me to be in his office at eight on Monday morning. To my amazement with no preamble he outlined terms for Enhanced Early Retirement (I was sixty-one). When he asked if they were acceptable, I replied 'I can't answer that until we have discussed the alternative'. 'What alternative?' he said. 'Going into the English Department', I replied. V.C.: 'I wouldn't regard that as an alternative'. Me: 'Why not?' V.C.: 'The English Department does not regard your work as fitting what it sees as its changing profile'. Lawrence, in other words, was not flavour of the month. Neither was Ted Hughes, nor, for that matter, the whole of the Western Canon. The 'changing profile' referred to the desperate attempt of the department to climb belatedly onto the Post-Modern Critical Theory bandwagon. Shortly afterwards I was introduced in the refectory to a new member of the English Department. I asked him what his specialism was, and he replied 'soap opera'.

I lost any desire I had had to enter that department, and accepted the retirement terms. Since that decision probably saved me from several years of misery, I can hardly say, in retrospect, that my allegiance to Lawrence had worked against me.

***

In retirement my first intention was to wean myself from academic work altogether. When I had finished the Ted Hughes bibliography I was working on, I intended to cultivate our garden, and breed endangered Australian finches in the large octagonal aviary I had designed as a retirement present to myself. (Ted Hughes called it my 'stately pleasure dome'.) I had given up hope of ever doing a book on Lawrence's paintings, of ever getting my short-lived Lawrence biography back into print, of ever finding a publisher for *Literature and the Crime Against Nature*, of ever getting the Harry T. Moore award for services to Lawrence studies, and, of course, of ever getting a Professorship. I do not believe that all things come to him who waits. But I do believe that all things sometimes come to him who has abandoned hope altogether. In 2002, without my stir, out of the blue, came an invitation from Chaucer Books (prompted by John Worthen) to edit and introduce a volume on Lawrence's paintings. It was published in 2003. In 2004 Chaucer published a new edition of my Lawrence biography, and in 2005 *Literature and the Crime Against Nature*. In that same year I got the Harry T. Moore award (appropriately in Santa Fe), and in the following year a Special Professorship in the School of English at Nottingham.

When I chose Lawrence as the topic of my Ph.D. thesis in 1957 because I felt I could maintain my interest in him for five years, I little thought I should still be working as keenly on him in fifty.

Lawrence and the Wilkinsons

First published in Review of English Literature *3, October 1962. For the background to this piece, the first I ever published on Lawrence, see my Introduction, pp.22-3.*

The Wilkinsons, or the Wilkses as Lawrence came to call them, were a family of artists living at the Villa Poggi, San Paolo Mosciano, near Florence, at the same time that the Lawrences had a flat in the neighbouring Villa Mirenda. From April 1926 to March 1928 they were neighbours. The family consisted of Arthur Gair Wilkinson, a tall, rather gaunt, red-bearded man, three years older than Lawrence, who painted delicate, spacious, landscapes and made delightful puppets for his own puppet theatre; his wife Lilian (Diddy), a Scotswoman several years older than her husband, also an artist, though a shared interest in Marxism rather than art had brought them together; and their two children Frances (Bim) and William (Dino), adolescents at the time, with musical as well as artistic leanings. Arthur's younger brother Walter, also a puppet-player, stayed with them for long periods.

The Wilkinsons were great walkers and nature-lovers, concert and theatre-goers, strenuously pursuing health and culture simultaneously. Though priding themselves on their social, political and religious nonconformity, they were very conventional in their cultural interests and aesthetic standards. Bach, Mozart, Brahms, Chopin, are appreciated 'without reservation' – not so the moderns: 'then they whined away for hours at a noise by Béla Bartók and everybody was bored stiff. Then a lot of silly sentiment, all perverted, by Ravel.' They found Blake 'repulsive', and Lawrence's own paintings 'lewd', 'horrors'. Lilian even found *Etruscan Places* 'queer stuff': it made her 'fume a good deal'.

The Wilkinsons took each day and tried to make it a work of art, unsullied by care, by the 'unpleasant' doings of other people in the great world beyond the Tuscan hills: 'In such a mad world, how thankful we must be if we can live quietly and simply and more or less harmlessly.' A book which Lawrence lent them was indeed 'a bad indictment' but made 'unpleasant reading'. Lawrence was often too precise and critical for them – 'exasperated' with the mad world, but committed to it. This commitment the Wilkinsons rather patronised: 'Poor chap – what a nightmare he does suffer.'

Both the life and the art for which the Wilkinsons stood must have seemed to Lawrence frankly escapist. It is clear from Gair Wilkinson's less formal sketches that he would have made a fine illustrator of Kenneth Grahame or A. A. Milne. 'Village-arty people' Lawrence called them in an early letter.

Despite the basic differences, the Lawrences and the Wilkinsons formed a warm and lasting friendship. Lawrence soon learned not to ride his hobby-horses in their company and his lack of sympathy for their way of life found expression only in the lightest and most genial banter. Lawrence was a very sick man during these years, but usually managed to cheer up as an evening progressed so that by the end he would be leading the festivities and jumping about with infectious enthusiasm.

From the letters Lawrence wrote to the Wilkinsons and the diaries which Arthur and Lilian kept alternately one gets little impression of a man hard at work writing. He appears to spend his time in bed ill, travelling, doing housework, shopping, walking, talking, visiting and entertaining. During the twelve months or so that the two families were in residence together, they visited each other some eighty times, usually for tea or supper. On at least a score of occasions the gathering developed into a full-scale party, with games, sing-songs, charades, etc. There were also several walks and picnics and one visit to the theatre. The Lawrences frequently entertained other friends, particularly the Brewsters and the Huxleys. Yet during these two years Lawrence produced the three versions of *Lady Chatterley's Lover, The Man Who Loved Islands, The Man Who Died,* several short stories, *Etruscan Places*, translations from Verga, many essays, reviews and introductions, twenty or thirty paintings, and an incredible number of letters, including about forty to the Wilkinsons.

There follows a number of extracts from the Wilkinson diaries and from Lawrence's letters, all previously unpublished, with a minimum of explanatory comment.

Arthur Wilkinson was introduced to the Lawrences in Florence on 26 April, 1926, because they were interested in a flat at the Villa Mirenda. He undertook to show it to them the following Sunday, also inviting them to lunch.

29 April, 1926. Letter from the Pensione Lucchesi, Lungarno Zecca, Firenze.
We both liked the spot immediately: and the old house. I think surely we must take that apartment, and just keep it as a *pied-à-terre*. If we decide on it on Sunday – and I think we shall – I hope we can move in quickly. I do hate this sort of hotel-pension life. (*5L* 443)

On Tuesday, 11 May, the Wilkinsons went to the Villa Mirenda for tea 'and the party went as merry as a marriage bell'. Lawrence talked 'with whoever would talk with him' and told them about the strike 'from the miner's point of view'. The following Friday the Lawrences went to the Villa Poggi for coffee after supper, taking with them a book of French songs: 'We sang the chorus to Lawrence's lead – he chanting away as bold as brass in the solo parts'. On the Sunday they called again 'and the talk waxed fast and furious'. Notes like the following began to pass frequently between the Villas Mirenda and Poggi:
'Will you all come in this evening after supper, as there is a cake and the promised Kummel, and, let us hope, a tune or two going.' (*5L* 460)

Tuesday, 22 June, 1926.
The Lawrences give us tea by the stream. We set up the primus and made the most successful picnic possible. It was so indescribably lovely there – a fresh wind blowing – the air so translucent, the water limpid and the tea and cheese

sandwiches and cakes so good. We just sat and talked and talked and the Lawrences were very happy. We mostly discussed the stupidities of other people. He has an exasperation against English bourgeoisie and he thinks riches inevitably spoil any man – cut him off from all that's worth while in life as if a glass jar were clamped tight down over him.

Friday, 25 June, 1926.
Found the author embroidering a panel – a design adapted from an old Etruscan design – in the brightest of colour. Mrs. Author was ironing with vigour and great satisfaction – and both very happy.

Summing up for June, 1926.
Our new neighbours have added to the interest and enjoyment of life here, and we are already fond of them both, and have a natural and very pleasant relationship with them.

Friday, 2 July, 1926.
Lawrence poured out tea himself and made it too, while Mrs. Lorenzo waved a towel at the flies, which made it a rather disturbed tea-party. They had funny stories to tell of their town adventures and kept us amused and were very friendly.

21 July, 1926. Post-card from Baden-Baden.
I like it better here than Italy, it seems more peaceful, not such a nervous tension. The forest here is very dense. This year the foliage is so thick – and the little clearings are so bright green. It is country one can really walk in. (*5L* 500)

12 August, 1926. Post-card from Newtonmoore, Inverness.
I was never in the Highlands before – find it rather attractive, though a bit cold and showery. Today grouse-shooting begins, but of course I'm not one to go banging at the birds. – The heather is just out – bell-heather dying – and the harebells are very lovely. The motor-cars spoil it all, though –

they never cease passing on these narrow little roads. We motor to the various lakes and picnic, making fires with very damp wood. Which is my news. I am always glad to hear of you all. (*5L* 508)

15 August, 1926. Post-card from Newtonmore, Inverness.
I went to church this morning – the Church of Scotland. What do you think of that! We want to take a trip to the West, tomorrow – to the Isle of Skye; but of course, the weather is very Scottish and drizzly. Probably we shall go, in spite of it all. – I would not like to live all my life in Scotland, but it's nice to see it. I sort of expect to meet Mrs. Wilkinson coming striding off the moors with a walking stick. It is rather obviously her country – only a bit too damp for human habitation. (*5L* 511)

29 August, 1926. Letter from Sutton-on-Sea.
I like the Lincolnshire coast – knew it when I was a boy. It is so very bracing and tonicky – picks me up like a shot. There are not many people – and the sands are so big, such a great sweep, and a big sky over-head, and a low sea growling in the wind… I like England again, though, especially up here in the Midlands. There's life in it – in spite of the coal strike: which last is looking pretty serious. (*5L* 518)

12 September, 1926. Letter from Sutton-on-Sea.
We leave here tomorrow – and I'm rather sorry. I've got quite into touch with my native land again, here – and feel at home. It's a lovely September morning, with bright sun and a wind, and nearly high tide, and long thin waves uncurling down the long, long sands. I think perhaps next year we may come here for five or six months. The sea-side is such a good place for doing nothing in. One has a hut on the sands, and the sea does all the shuffling about that is necessary… The coal strike continues – and in the coal areas it's a serious business. For the first time, the iron seems to be entering the soul – or the consciousness – of the workers. This will be the beginning of

a slow revolution, here in England – but a serious one. It's a funny country – so safe, and so kindly. And yet, way down, a certain ruthlessness... I do hope, in the fresh autumn, we'll have some walks and picnics – and really discover the place a bit. I ought to do some work – I don't touch a pen all this time – but the Lord sends the wet with the fine. Tell Mrs. Wilkinson to tie a string to her ankle, when she goes off into the 4th dimension, so that she can be pulled safely back when she's got beyond recall. Four is a dangerous number, as you realise when you're forty. (*5L* 534-5)

Thursday, 21 October, 1926.
Mrs. Lawrence came in just as we finished tea and we made her a cup and had a cigarette for her of course. She was very talkative and happy and sent A. off to tell Lawrence to come too. So A. went and found Lawrence whistling so loud he could not hear the knocking at the door and busy peeling hardboiled chestnuts for their supper. So we finished the chestnuts and joined the others. Then we produced cherry brandy and all our toys and all got on very merrily together.

First quarrel between D. H. L. and Frieda in front of the Wilkinsons: Sunday, 24 October, 1926.
L.(of the upper classes) 'I've done with them: they're hard – cruel, cruel' (crescendo).
F. 'Why didn't you marry one of your own class then, you'd have been bored stiff.'
L. (Very sad and vinegary) 'I may have my regrets.'
F. 'Well you can be off. You can go now if you like.'

Sunday, 14 November, 1926.
In the afternoon we went to the Lorenzo villa to see the new room and have tea. The room is very bright and pleasant, except for a large picture painted by Lorenzo which seemed to us a revolting blot on the wall. Uncle Roger and an imbecile fat woman with most of her clothes missing, and a pert child, are bunched together in a most unpleasant group.

Lorenzo explains that it is a modern painting, all in rounds and curves and colour, and we let him have his say and offered no criticism. In spite of this picture we had a quite nice party, and lots of talk and fun. We had a concert at night and some solo whist.

The picture was 'Holy Family'. The resemblance of the father to Uncle Roger was coincidental.

Thursday, 18 November, 1926.
We treated Lorenzo to a concert; and he treated us to criticism as usual, telling Bim about her painting, and Pino about violin music in his superior way. We smiled.

The following week the Wilkinsons went to Florence for the children's studies.

25 November, 1926. Letter from the Villa Mirenda.
Dear W., Mrs. W. and P. and B.,
Ooray! You'll all come home as fat as porpoises with a fleshpot of Egypt under each arm.
I've stopped in bed two days with a cold, but am rising now to blink an astonished welcome to that great stranger the sun. More borrowings! Did you take your easel to Florence? If you didn't would you hate to lend it me, and I'll see if I can get that Scandicci carpenter to make me one like it. Cute idea! My new picture – feel I should say `Pic-chah!' – is going to be suggested by Boccaccio's scandalous story of the Nuns and the Gardener. Hope your virtuous easel won't swoon, and let my canvas fall from her arms. (*5L* 587)

Sunday, 19 December, 1926.
The Lawrences came before 3 and we had a nice tea ready. She was enthusiastic about our room and everything else – he as usual a bit dry, but nice too!

In the evening they all went to the theatre to see Stenterello, and L., insisting he would not be able to hear from the W's box, took Mrs. W. and Pino with him into the front stalls.

Sunday, 26 December, 1926.
Then we got a famous reception from the Lawrences. They had high tea ready and relit the tree. We had a very congenial party indeed – singing and feasting and all six of us as sympathetic and merry as could be.

Monday, 17 January, 1927.
In spite of the pouring rain the Lawrences and their visitor Brewster came to tea and a very noisy nice and comfortable party we had.

Thursday, 20 January, 1927.
Bim and Pino had tea with the Lawrences and it seems to have been a very merry party and they laughed all the time.

Thursday, 27 January, 1927.
Lawrence's latest hatred is for America and everything American. He says the Yanks have no taste. Nothing fine has come or will come from America. Their women are not really beautiful – they have no taste to them – they are like the asparagus very large and white – but tasteless. The Americans want their asparagus large and white – but they don't know whether it tastes or not. You soon lose all taste yourself there!!

Sunday, 30 January, 1927.
Lawrence was very unhappy when we went in for he had a potato cake in the oven and he was over anxious. However the cake came out a great success and was eaten hot - but he was still thinking how much better they used to be in Mexico. Mrs. Lawrence was in great form and just went for the piano in the most relentless way and sang as well as played the accompaniments.

Thursday, 3 February, 1927.
Lawrence came in very cross and doesn't look very well. He was pretty rude to Mrs. L. several times and said his aunt 'was a fool like most women', but we pulled him through! We had a grand singing – she being a most willing accompanist and now getting quite slick – though she has not played the piano for 12 years.

Sunday, 6 February, 1927.
We marched very gay and talkative to Romola… We counted it a very successful day indeed.

In the summer of 1927 Lawrence had several severe haemorrhages and was confined to bed much of the time. Mrs. Wilkinson baked a cake for him and sat playing cards at his bedside. But the Wilkinsons soon lost patience with the invalid and found his departure for Austria a 'real Relief'. On August 3 they watched the Lawrences packing. Frieda was also unwell.

3 August, 1927.
We came back pretty critical of their ways of doing and thinking – she's too vague and unconsidering for anything – and he's too precise in some ways and dreadfully scatter minded in others and has such a way of jumping to conclusions and just making things up.

7 August, 1927. Letter from Villach, Austria.
It's queer to be in a country with practically no government – a queer shabby kind of populace – quite nice – and no bosses or bossing at all – a queer empty sort of feeling, all the forza of Italy suddenly removed, and the sforza too. It is much more restful to the nerves. I am much better already – went out to the lake yesterday – then down to the end of the lake on a motor-boat – all the Viennese sunning their large and naked bodies like whitish seals on the shore – save for little bathing drawers – it is de rigueur (*sic*) to be naked all day long – and nobody making the slightest effort for anything – the

slackest world you ever knew. In the evening was a firework fiesta by the river – very funny – home-made fireworks, in this destitute country – pans of fire blazing and floating swiftly, very swiftly, away on the full icy river, one after another – squibby fountains of fire from damp powder, on moored rafts – and a few rockets that let out six red sparks – and crowds and crowds of queer amiable people in odd dress, and nobody to boss; dancing, beer-drinking, skittles, etc. A queer world. I feel a different creature here in this cool – and am eternally grateful to you for getting me out. There are such amusing men's jackets, that the people wear – all colours, in checks – am so tempted to buy you one – and myself – we'd look such shoots – I'd buy you a green and purple check, – myself, I think, yellow and pea-green – shall I? (*6L* 119)

3 September, 1927. Letter from Irschenhausen, München.
The little house sits - brown wood and red roof – in its corner of meadow on the shoulder in the Forest and looks wide away over the Isar Valley, and the big mountains shadowy. It is so still, so motionless, and nobody – as if there were nobody in the world. The woods are beech and fir – lovely, quite lovely really – the squirrels so tame they don't run away. In the spring and early summer the deer come round the fence – but now they are deep in the forest. It's surprising how little this country has changed – a big open landscape striped with forest and strips of field. I like it very much – there is no time, and no event – only the sun shines with that pleasant hotness of autumn, and in the shadow it is chill...

I feel it must be cool in San Paolo by now. Here the nights are really cold – and we shut the double doors – the doors and windows are all double. The autumn crocuses are out in the lush green meadows – in the stillness of autumn, only ducks quacking. I am just going to take my little afternoon doze on the balcony...

I hated Munich – such a big town, though beautiful in its way. But big towns worry me. (*6L* 139)

12 September, 1927. Letter from Irschenhausen.
Sunday poured a black and ceaseless rain all the hours God sent, and I began to feel like – plinosaur or an ichthyosaur or something sour. But today it's finished – and turning colder. – The peasants have decided that this is the hour to let their cows eat off our grass – so up they trail every afternoon, with such a ringing of bells all round the house till nightfall that you'd think you were going into a hundred village shops all the time – or that you kept a shop with a hundred doors and a roaring trade – they're just like village shop bells. We lead an uneventful life – the mountains come and go and lovely is the show – sort of thing – I play patience!! Oh Lilian Gair, I've come down a peg or two, lower than bezique, lower than piquet – patience on a stool instead of a monument! But you can teach me some other sorts when I'm back: you're bound to know my one and only sort. – The woods are simply uncanny with mushrooms, all sorts and sizes and shapes and smells, in camps and circles and odd ones – the brightest red, the blackest black and the sea-weediest green – and we pick the little orange-yellow ones and eat them fried in butter. – The dark blue Autumn gentian is out – and the deer are about – little roe-buck – they fly across the paths just like a Persian picture – and then they stop fascinated by my famous little white jacket. The jays are so cheeky they almost steal the tears out of your eyes. I really like it here – but when it's dark and rainy then you sing: 'A little ship was on the sea' – for the oceans of old Time seem to sweep over you.

I expect we shall go to Baden next week – Frieda wants to. We have a good cook – and she goes in to Munchen and brings out food: today for lunch, fine trout, for supper – partridges. Der mister muss futtern – she says. We spend more than we earn – and, as Richard Aldington says – you can't even have poor relief if you've been two years out of England!! So you see you'll get no poor relief either!! When you go back. Well, be warned, and don't eat your chickens before they're hatched. (*6L* 158, dated 26 September)

6 October, 1927. Post-card from Hotel Eden, Baden-Baden.
Here it is a frosty morning, yellow sun earlier, now rather clouded over – beech trees going yellow – that funny sort of stillness of a threatening winter. Now we shall be glad to see a bright day again. – really bright. We've got an invitation to Egypt – shall we go? I feel I don't care much what I do or where I go… I really feel like coming back now – wouldn't mind starting tomorrow. (*6L* 169-70)

12 October, 1927. Post-card from Hotel Eden, Baden-Baden.
I am doing an Inhalations cure – sit in a white shroud and hood in the steam or vapour rather, and look at the other dim shrouded figures sitting across the room! – but I think it does me good. (*6L* 186)

14 October, 1927. Letter from Hotel Eden, Baden-Baden.
I feel like painting a large picture of Adam and Eve driving the Lord God out of Paradise: Get out of here, you righteous old bird! But it's [on] the knees of the gods. The doctor says I'm really better than last year when he examined me. But with this catarrh of the bronchials and top of the lungs, you just have to go slow, and build up the general condition. I cough and puff uphill just the same – otherwise feel pretty well. (*6L* 190)

The picture was 'Throwing Back the Apple'.

19 October, 1927. The Lawrences returned to the Mirenda.
Lawrence 'still a very sick man'.

She was very happy to be back – as we came along in the car she enthused enormously – but he refused to be pleased or glad – said it was all like a dream and Italy had no life in it. Villa Mirenda looked lovely at first sight – but even that failed to rouse him.

20 October, 1927.
They came to tea in the afternoon – very happy and bringing

such a lot of pretty things from Germany... Of course we talked fast and furious... He was very irritable indeed with Frieda and she was dreadfully sharp with him – but on the whole it was a happy time. We could scarcely leave off discussing them after they'd gone and we feel he's a very sad case and glad as we are to have them back, at the same time, rather an embarrassing problem.

Friday, 28 October, 1927.
He says there's no life in Italy – you feel the want of something. The woods are thin – no depth to them – they are thin and scraggly – the olives are scraggly, the vines are scraggly – the PEOPLE are scraggly – that's it – everything is scraggly. Poor chap – what a nightmare he does suffer.

Friday, 27 January, 1928. Post-card from Chalet Beau Site.
Sunny weather, blinding snow, me in dark glasses. It seems quite difficult to believe that the Mirenda is still there. I trudge patiently up the hills, and pant – don't think of sports. Aldous goes mildly skiing – all stalk and claw – but doesn't get far before he slithers home again. No fun, struggling uphill with seven foot of ski on each foot... No sound, some sleigh-bells – and no motion, save a few people little as flies on the snow. (*6L* 276)

6 February, 1928. Post-card from Les Diablerets.
We drove in a sledge, tinkletinkle, to the top of the pass yesterday, F and I – the others came on skis – and we picnicked on the pass, very high, very sparkling and bright and sort of marvellous – and some men did some fine ski-running. I liked it very much – and it sort of puts life into one. – But today it snows again!! But I can go quite nice long walks. (*6L* 290)

7 March, 1928. Lawrences return. 'A very friendly meeting it was and they both look very well indeed!'

20 March, 1928.
L. got very animated and happy telling the funniest stories about Ezra Pound and Ford Maddox Hueffer and Violet Hunt… Ezra Pound was the first live literary lion he met and he found him in an attic with some pliers and a patty pan heating frankincense over a candle 'to recover some of the aroma of the East in your filthy London'.

28 March, 1928. Wilkinsons leave San Paolo Mosciano.
Lawrence sat amidst the wreckage and smiled sadly for half an hour and at last all was ready and we waved to Lawrence all down the Hill.

10 April, 1928. Letter from Villa Mirenda.
I am pretty well – going in to Florence tomorrow – We're having tea on our grass, under the ippocastagni, which are nearly in flower. – The grove of aspens above is a lovely feathery pinky colour. We'll leave here at the end of this month; then probably Switzerland till July – then England in August – then if I can afford it, we'll go round the world by those Messageries Marittimes (*sic*) in the autumn, and to the ranch that way. (*6L* 362)

13 May, 1928. Letter from Villa Mirenda.
Dear Wilkses All!
So glad Pino's measles are coming out all right. If they're a bit slow, make him drink camomile tea, hot, lots and lots of it. Some cure! – And Bim safe so far – and enjoying London and gadding round. – Here the wind has come so cold, I light a fire after supper – and snow on the mountains… It was queer to see the light in your end window at night as if you were there – and in the day the shutters open. I swear I hear the ghost of Pino's fiddle wailing… We are still here, probably till the end of the month. If we'd gone to Switzerland we'd have found ourselves sleighing again. Ugh! I don't want to see any more snow this spring. (*6L* 398-9)

20 December, 1928. Letter from Hotel Beau Rivage, Bandol. We are here in this quite pleasant little hotel by the sea – it's been sunny nearly all the time, and good for my health. Of course I still cough like a brute, but am much stronger... Frieda says she wants a house – but she doesn't know where, – and you can't have a house nowhere. – Where does one want to live? Tell me if you can! – How do you like London? I hear of you giving shows at Heals, and showing A's pictures, and selling them – *beato lui*! So that's all to the good. And I suppose Bim and Pino get more melodious every day! We shall have to see you before long, to see all the strides taken. What a game life is! (*7L* 80-1)

31 May, 1929. Hotel Principe Alfonso. Palma de Mallorca. Spain.
Dear Wilkses,
Your letter this morning – as I was sitting in my pyjamas on bedroom floor painting a little picture which you would all thoroughly dislike, I'm sure – so you'll see things are pretty much as usual. You seem to have a busy time – which I suppose is highly admirable – but here on this island it makes one wilt to think of so much doing. This is called la isla de la Calma, but it should be called worse names than that. It's a marvellous place for doing nothing in – one just doesn't want to do a thing – and even to write a letter costs great efforts. In seven weeks I have painted one small picture and written nothing at all. But I suppose it's good for me. I'm pretty well – so is F.

The place is curious – very attractive, and quite unattractive. Not beautiful like Italy – nor *vivace* nor *allegro* – people a bit dull, dreary, really. Yet it's all so easy, and so thoroughly indifferent to everything – except, perhaps riding along the coast in motor-cars. The people don't seem to care about a thing – and nobody bothers – not even I. One feels, in a sense, one has dodged the 'world of care' and settled down in the world of indifference. The climate is very good – today is a brilliant blue day, beautiful, with white surf running in to the little bay. We are in a rather big, fairly dear hotel on the sea's edge – very good food, and too much of it. We are only six guests and about ten servants – so very spoiled – and we have the run of the place – are waited on hand and foot, given everything we want, let to do as we like, and altogether ruined for life. Sounds about the reverse of your strenuousness – and I'm sure the young ones at least don't envy me.

When it gets too hot – the sun is wildly hot already, but the breeze fresh and cool – we shall get on the steamer to Marseilles, and go probably to Italy to collect a few things, then somewhere cool. Frieda says she wants a home in Italy. I am not sure. Anyhow we can look. We might come back here, to the isla de la Calma. *Quien sable* – which we say now instead of *chi lo sa*!

We hear from Giulia, they like their new podere and new padroni very much, for the present – and the *padroni* sends us an invitation to go and stay in their villa. Florence seems to be the same, very social. The Brewsters are in Capri, but again without a house – and the court in Boston sent them a notice that a long lost cousin of Achsah's, supposed dead in the San Francisco earthquake twenty years ago, has now turned up and claims the money that Achsah inherited from an uncle – about three-quarters of all they possess. – I'm not going to put my trust in Buddha. – The Huxleys have left Paris this week for Forte Dei Marmi – having come to hate that little Paris house of theirs.

I think that's all our news. Do you have letters from the Nencione still? What news of the Poggi?

I suppose you'll go and see my pictures when Dorothy Warren shows them, just to renew the acquaintance. Remember me to them.

Now I fizzle out!

Belle cose! D. H. Lawrence.

I'm pining to know the election results, though – and this island has nothing to divulge, so far. So I'll take my siesta, close the balcony doors and nod off, for it's nearly 3.0. (*7L* 313-4)

Lawrence never met the Wilkinsons again. Nine months later he died. There is no doubt that the middle years of his career had been vitiated by caring too much. His works had staggered and sometimes collapsed under that 'world of care'. His new-found world of indifference, or rather of insouciance, which he celebrates in the essay of that name, in many of the *Last Poems*, in *The Man Who Died*, and, particularly, in *Etruscan Places*, no doubt derives largely from his experiences in the living tombs of Tarquinia in 1927. But perhaps the mellowness, 'the deep calm at the heart' which pervades these works also draws some of its quality from gay golden mornings and hilarious evenings spent in the company of this unique family.

The Wilkinsons returned to San Paolo for a few more years, then settled in a cottage in Somerset where Arthur Gair Wilkinson died in 1957. His wife survived him by only a few months. Pino had been killed in the R.A.F. in the war. Frances Gair Wilkinson still lives there, painting and teaching art in adult classes, surrounded by her father's paintings of those sun-drenched Tuscan hills. My sincere thanks are due to her for allowing me to rummage freely through her collection of letters, diaries and photographs, and for permission to publish the extracts in this article.

Introduction to D. H. Lawrence: *Selected Poems*

First published by Penguin in 1972. Most of the influential Lawrence critics of the fifties and sixties had either ignored Lawrence's poetry completely, or taken for granted that it constituted a mere footnote to the fiction. For many readers the only access to the poems for those decades had been the Penguin selection, edited by W. E. Williams, which contained only 86 of Lawrence's thousand poems, and an introduction of less than three pages. The Complete Poems was not published in paperback until 1977. I offered Penguin a selection of 150 poems, with the following introduction. To my amazement they accepted. It remained in print for thirty-four years.

The very scope of Lawrence's achievement in so many other forms – fiction, travel-writing, essays, criticism, letters, and plays – has told against his standing as a poet. We have come to think of his poetry as something of a by-product of, or relaxation from, other more strenuous and important work. Though it certainly came more easily than his fiction, I am sure that, except perhaps in *Pansies*, Lawrence did not think of his poetry in this way. At the outset of his career he devoted much time and care to his poems and cherished them when written. And at three subsequent periods of his life his poetry became the primary channel of his experience and creative energy: the first year of his relationship with Frieda (*'Look! We Have Come Through!'*), the two years in Sicily (*Birds, Beasts and Flowers*), and the last year of his life (*More Pansies* and *Last Poems*).

Lawrence wrote nearly 1,000 poems, and we must concede that an unusually high proportion are unsuccessful. He needs to be read in selection. Reviewing Lawrence's *Complete Poems*, D. J. Enright wrote:

> It must be granted that this *Complete Poems* — however grateful many of us will be to have it — makes for oppressive, confusing and blunted reading. There is still room for a critical selection; none of those I have seen

> conveys a true sense of the fantastic variety and scope of Lawrence's verse.[1]

I have tried to fill this gap. Moreover, I have tried to bring together in one volume all Lawrence's really successful, achieved poems – the poems on which his claim to the status of a major poet must rest. I believe that on the strength of these one hundred and fifty poems we can support the claim that Lawrence is a great poet in every sense, including the technical. The technique for making something out of nothing he had not, nor the technique of highly finished formal craftsmanship. Such technique might have improved some of his early poems. It might equally have prevented him going on to write the great poems, where the form is the perfect incarnation of the content, the perfect vehicle for the liveliness of thought and feeling, the freshness and depth of perception, the wit and wisdom he has to offer.

Many of the early poems printed here are in versions different from those with which the reader may be familiar. Lawrence extensively revised, and in some cases rewrote, these poems when preparing his *Collected Poems* in 1928. In his introductory note to that edition Lawrence says that he has tried to establish a chronological order, 'because many of the poems are so personal that, in their fragmentary fashion, they make up a biography of an emotional and inner life'. Yet he goes on to say that some are:

> a good deal rewritten. They were struggling to say something which it takes a man twenty years to be able to say… A young man is afraid of his demon and puts his hand over the demon's mouth sometimes and speaks for him. And the things the young man says are very rarely poetry. So I have tried to let the demon say his say, and to remove the passages where the young man intruded. (*Poems* 28)

[1] H. Coombes (ed.), *D. H. Lawrence: A critical anthology* (Harmondsworth: Penguin, 1973), 444.

The result, even when the poems are improved, which is not always, is a kind of ventriloquism, with the voice of the mature Lawrence speaking, sometimes grotesquely, through the mouth of the dumb young man. How ridiculous, for example, to suppose that the young man of twenty-two, out of his actual virginity, could have written the version of 'Virgin Youth' which appears in the *Collected Poems*. It is a poem by the author of *Lady Chatterley's Lover*. It seems to me much more important that we should have what the young man actually wrote at twenty-two than what Lawrence at forty-two (a much better poet, but a different man with a different demon) thought he should have written. I have therefore taken the texts from *Love Poems, Amores, New Poems* and *Bay* where they first appeared in book form.

The earliest poems date from the period 1906-8 when Lawrence was a student at Nottingham University College. The girl who figures in many of them is his first sweetheart, Jessie Chambers, the Miriam of *Sons and Lovers*. The rest of the early poems were written between 1908 and 1911, when Lawrence was teaching in Croydon. The best of them are distinguished by what Alfred Alvarez has called Lawrence's 'emotional realism'. Candour, truth and power of feeling often burst through the conventional frame in startling imagery: the voices of the parents in his childhood remembered as slender and thick lashes competing with the terrible whips of the ash-tree outside, shrieking in a storm at night; cherries hanging round the ears of a girl seen as blood-drops, thus linking her offer of love with the dead birds under the cherry tree; sex and violence again linked by potent imagery in 'Renascence', 'Snap-Dragon' and 'Cruelty and Love'; striking images of light and dark, colour and movement; images which presage the mature Lawrence – rainbows, dolphins, the long sea journey through 'the grandeur of night' to the amazing newness of dawn, resurrection, and the return to Paradise.

In 1913 Lawrence wrote to Edward Marsh:

> I have always tried to get an emotion out in its own course, without altering it. It needs the finest instinct imaginable, much finer than the skill of the craftsmen.... I don't write for your ear.... I can't tell you what *pattern* I see in any poetry, save one complete thing. (*2L* 61)

But Lawrence's instinct, at this stage of his career, worked fitfully, and there was little craftsmanship to fall back on. He had no ear for formal rhythm or rhyme, and when he attempted them was usually inept.

Occasionally, in these early poems, the rhythm briefly frees itself and springs to life:

> Rabbits, handfuls of brown earth, lie
> Low-rounded on the mournful grass they have bitten
> down to the quick.
> Are they asleep? – Are they alive? – Now see, when I
> Move my arms the hill bursts and heaves under their
> spurting kick.
>
> 'The Wild Common'

Sometimes he achieves the moving colloquial directness and simplicity of Brecht:

> But when I meet the weary eyes
> The reddened aching eyes of the bar-man with thin
> arms,
> I am glad to go back where I came from.
>
> 'After the Opera'

Particularly impressive are the four dialect poems, on the strength of which Pound proposed Lawrence for the Polignac Prize. Here Lawrence is able to forget Swinburne, Meredith and the Pre-Raphaelites and take his rhythms from the local speech he knew so well.

Lawrence never shied from sentiment for fear of

sentimentality. He had the courage of his emotions, whether grief for the dead mother, sexual frustration, nostalgia for childhood, or delight in the baby which ran across the lawn to him. He expressed them all with rare delicacy. But they were the emotions of a man who had not found himself and who was at odds with his life.

Lawrence came to maturity as a poet at the same time that he came to maturity as a man and a novelist, at the time of his marriage. It is as though the new life which he launched with Frieda in 1912 and his departure from England freed him from the pressures which had retarded his development and the conventions which had crippled so much of his verse. *'Look! We Have Come Through!'* is a record of his early years with Frieda, up to the war. It is also an epithalamium, a celebration of love and marriage, not omitting the conflict and occasional misery. Marriage, Lawrence claimed, 'sort of keeps me in direct communication with the unknown, in which otherwise I am a bit lost'. His vision becomes increasingly sacramental. He does not distinguish between the creativeness which brings him and Frieda through to 'some condition of blessedness', and the creativeness which issues in poetry; neither is an achievement of the deliberate self, both are products of the wind that blows through him to which he must open and attune himself:

> Oh, for the wonder that bubbles into my soul
> I would be a good fountain, a good well-head,
> Would blur no whisper, spoil no expression.
>
> 'Song of a Man Who Has Come Through'

The success of his marriage is achieved by breaking through old dead ideas and life-modes. In his art, too, he seeks to break down all the 'artificial conduits and canals through which we do so love to force our utterance', to allow the spontaneous, uniquely appropriate form to emerge. This technique produces, when successful (as it is increasingly to be), 'the perfect utterance of a concentrated spontaneous soul'. It is a far deeper and more demanding discipline than the discipline of the craftsman. Lawrence has no use for the word 'aesthetic'. The discipline is spiritual and emotional as well as linguistic. The poems are a by-product of 'that piece of supreme art, a man's life'. Some of the poems in *'Look!'* are personal in the restricting sense. But it is only through the wholeness and depth of personal experience that Lawrence is to create the impersonally authentic forms and universal meanings of *Birds, Beasts and Flowers.*

The horrors of the war, the moral debacle at home, the suppression of his splendid novel, *The Rainbow,* persecution, ill-health and poverty, all combined to destroy in Lawrence, during the war, his faith in humanity and a human future. He turned, to retain his sanity and faith in life, to the non-human world of birds, beasts and flowers.

Lawrence had an almost occult penetration into the being of other creatures. But in several of the best poems, the purpose is to reveal the sheer unknowable otherness of the non-human life and its strange gods. He goes to the very pale of his being, of human consciousness, and looks outward. Creatures, 'little living myths', bring him messages not only from out of the surrounding darkness, but also from the unknown depths of his own being:

> In the very darkest continent of the body there is God. And from Him issue the first dark rays of our feeling, wordless, and utterly previous to words: the innermost rays, the first messengers, the primeval, honourable beasts of our being, whose voice echoes wordless and forever wordless down the darkest avenues of the soul, but full of potent speech. Our own inner meaning . (*STH* 205)

Lawrence is here making his own raid on the inarticulate. And the messengers he comes nearest to understanding are the snake and the tortoise. *Tortoises* is one long poem in six sections, a metaphysical poem about the tragedy of man's sexuality, with all the suffering, dependence, exposure that implies, and yet, ultimately, the joy, for it is a means, like death, marriage with the universe.

There is no longer, in *Birds, Beasts and Flowers,* any sign of formal difficulty. Lawrence's demon, his daring visionary insight, speaks out clear and bold (though somewhat stridently in the less successful poems). Ostensibly about creatures, these poems explore a vast range of experience. They are dramatic confrontations between the human and non-human and potent evocations of the spirit of place. They are brimming with vitality and awareness, humour and wisdom.

Lawrence called his next volume *Pansies* because the poems are little thoughts like Pascal's *Pensées,* and because he wanted them to be thought of as unpretentious flowers blooming briefly, rather jauntily, not as monuments for posterity. He called them 'rag poems'. In the best of them we hear what Richard Hoggart has called 'the voice of a down-to-earth, tight, bright, witty Midlander.... slangy, quick, flat and direct, lively, laconic, sceptical, non-conforming, nicely bloody-minded'. The less successful are merely 'sketches for poems', or, like the pieces of soft fruit Ibsen gave his pet scorpion, something into which Lawrence could discharge his accumulated venom.

In *More Pansies* and *Last Poems* Lawrence's thoughts become poems much more consistently than in *Pansies.* Thought is 'a man in his wholeness wholly attending' and here the poet strives to make 'a new act of attention' and then give 'direct utterance from the instant, whole man' in language that will make us prick our innermost ear. His primary theme is life's tremendous characterization and man's capacity for wonder. Now, on the brink of death, he gives us the naïve opening of a soul to life. Despite his awareness of the desperate ills of our civilization and of his own impending death, he is no longer, as he often was in *Pansies,* flippant or exasperated or spiteful. His new-found insouciance brings assurance, playfulness, and a new joy in life, in 'the magnificent here and now of life in the flesh'. It is a kind of resurrection as the dying tree puts out new strange blossoms.

The clarity and splendour of these poems testify to the depth of vision they spring from – what Coleridge meant when he spoke of Wordsworth's 'sentiments':

> No frequency of perusal can deprive them of their freshness. For though they are brought into the full daylight of every reader's comprehension; yet are they drawn up from depths which few in any age are privileged to visit, into which few in any age have courage to descend.[2]

This courage manifests itself supremely in 'Bavarian Gentians' and the other poems about death. They are poignant, but never waver in their faith that death is only a part of life, the longest journey, perhaps the greatest adventure.

[2] Stephen Potter (ed.), *Coleridge: Select Poetry and Prose* (London: Nonesuch Press, 1950), 295.

Lawrence and Frieda: The Alternative Story

First published The D. H. Lawrence Review, *9 (1), 1976.*

All the biographers of Lawrence have given the same account of his first meeting with Frieda. This is not surprising, as it derives from Frieda herself:

> It was an April day in 1912. He came for lunch, to see my husband about a lectureship at the German University… Soon afterwards he wrote to me: 'You are the most wonderful woman in all England'.[1]

Frieda records two further visits by Lawrence to her home, on Easter Sunday and another Sunday, and one visit by herself and her little girls to Derbyshire, before she and Lawrence left for Germany together six weeks after their first meeting. This account is not at all full or accurate. If the first meeting was in April and they left for Germany on May 3rd, they could not have known each other for six weeks. Lawrence spent the period March 25-30 with his friend George Neville in Staffordshire, and wrote from there on 27 March 1912 to May Chambers Holbrook:

> I'll bring you Man and Superman on Sunday [March 31]. I suppose J.[essie] will be at the cottage. I said nothing to Mrs. Weekley about coming over. Will discuss it further with you. (*1L* 377)

Lawrence must have discussed with May the possibility of bringing Frieda to the Holbrook farm before his departure for Staffordshire. He therefore cannot have met Frieda later than the weekend of March 23-24. Frieda did subsequently visit Holbrook's farm, possibly during the weekend Lawrence

[1] Frieda Lawrence, *Not I, But the Wind.* (London: Heinemann 1935), 3-4.

spent with the Holbrooks when Jessie called on the Sunday morning and saw him for the last time. He told her of his plans to go to Germany 'within a few days'.[2] Jessie says that this weekend was 'some three weeks after Easter,' which fell on April 7. But Lawrence and Frieda spent the weekend of April 27-28, their last in England, at the Cearne, Edward Garnett's house in Kent. So the weekend at Holbrook's farm was probably that of April 20-21. Frieda's failure to mention this visit, or the weekend at the Cearne, in *Not I, But the Wind. . .*, could be put down to her unwillingness to implicate either the Holbrooks or Edward Gamett, though Lawrence's letters to Garnett about that weekend had already been published in Huxley's edition (with Frieda as 'Mrs. —').

If Frieda's estimate of six weeks between meeting and elopement is correct, they must have met just before Lawrence's departure for Staffordshire. In a letter dated May 9 (*1L* 394) Lawrence refers to 'eight weeks of acquaintance,' which puts the meeting a week earlier. Jessie Chambers remembered it as 'late February or early March'.[3] There is nothing in any of the primary biographical sources to throw any doubt upon a March meeting, except, perhaps, the 'coincidence' that both Lawrence and Frieda had been planning trips to Germany in May long before this. Lawrence first mentioned the idea on 12 January (*1L* 350). No one, to my knowledge, has ever suggested in print that Lawrence and Frieda may have met before 1912.

***

At the end of 1969 I had decided to try to find out a little more about the Pagans, a group of young Eastwood men and women of which Lawrence was a leading member. The

[2] Jessie Chambers, *D. H. Lawrence: a Personal Record* (London: Frank Cass, 1965), 214-5.

[3] Émile Delavenay, *D. H. Lawrence: L'Homme et la Genèse de Son Oeuvre, 1885-1919* (Paris: Librairie Klincksieck, 1969), 706.

Pagans turned out to be less subversive than the name suggests – they did little but organize rambles – but my enquiries led me to the home, in Eastwood, of the only surviving Pagan I could locate, Steve Bircumshaw. He was a man of amazing memory, not only about Lawrence but also about the whole life of Eastwood and the history of the mining industry in which he had spent his working life. All his recollections which could be checked have proved to be accurate to the smallest detail.

Lawrence, George Neville and Steve Bircumshaw were the effective leaders of the Pagans, which also included Ada Lawrence, Jessie and Alan Chambers, Louie Burrows (to whom Lawrence was engaged throughout 1911), Richard Pogmore and Kitty Holderness (both teachers at Albert St. School at the same time as Lawrence), Emmie and Mabel Limb, Polly Goddard, and the five Cooper sisters (four of whom were to die in their twenties of consumption). Steve's cousin Blanche Bircumshaw, who lived at 144 Lynn Croft (the Lawrences lived at 97) was a student-teacher at the same time as Lawrence; they helped each other with their homework. Steve's girlfriend Agatha Kirk (later his wife) also lived in Lynn Croft (109), was a close friend of Ada Lawrence and taught at the same school. She was born in the same month as Lawrence. Agatha Kirk and Steve Bircumshaw appear in *Mr. Noon* as Agatha Sharp and her 'best boy' Freddie.

There was no privacy in Lynn Croft. There could be no secrets. We can see, for example, in *A Collier's Friday Night*, how freely and frequently neighbours would come in and out and be drawn into the family's most intimate concerns. Anything that happened at 97 Lynn Croft would soon be known to the whole street, and hence to the whole town. Steve Bircumshaw and his wife were certainly in a position to know what they claimed to know. This is the story they told me in April 1970.

Lawrence began a two-year course at Nottingham University College in September 1906. He respected only one of his teachers, Ernest Weekley, Head of the Modem Languages Department. It did not take Weekley long to realize that he had a genius in his class. He invited Lawrence to his home for private tuition. There Lawrence met Weekley's German wife, fifteen years younger than her husband. Frieda decided she would have Lawrence at whatever cost. During the next few years she and Lawrence met regularly, and during Lawrence's holidays from teaching in Croydon, she made frequent visits to the Lawrence home, usually on Saturdays. The houses on that side of Lynn Croft overlooked a field anyone walking from the station would cross. Many a neighbouring family, including the Kirks, would watch Frieda, a striking figure in her Burberry coat and floppy tam-o'shanter with enormous pom-pom, a little girl on each hand (she never brought Monty) approaching the Lawrence house. Lawrence's sister Ada loved the little girls but hated Frieda. Ada would sulk all day at school, and Agatha would eventually get out of her: 'Frieda's coming again this weekend. How I hate her!' Mrs. Lawrence condoned the relationship because she saw it as more of a threat to Jessie than to herself. Lawrence was 'unofficially engaged' to Jessie Chambers at the time, and his mother was intensely jealous. Jessie knew of the relationship between Lawrence and Mrs. Weekley and spoke of her anxiety to her friend Mabel Thurlby, who was also a friend of Lawrence. Indeed, the whole of Eastwood knew of it. When it came to the attention of Thomas Wilson, headmaster of New Eastwood School where Ada taught, he told Ada: 'Miss Lawrence, I can't stop your brother coming to meet you and Miss Kirk outside the school, but please don't bring him on the premises again'.

Ada told Agatha that Ernest Weekley followed his wife one day. She met Lawrence and they went to Colwick Woods, a beauty spot near Nottingham. There Weekley confronted Lawrence and gave him a thrashing. Unable to ride his bicycle, Lawrence walked home, arriving in the early hours. He accounted for his bruises by claiming to have fallen off his bicycle. He stayed in bed for two or three days. But Frieda was not deterred. Her visits continued.

This story was told with great conviction and sincerity and was fleshed out with many fascinating details of Eastwood life at that time and stories about other people not directly involved. It was told mainly by Steve with occasional nods, prompts, and footnotes from his wife. It did not occur to me at the time to doubt the absolute truth and accuracy of everything they told me. It would have needed great cleverness and meticulous research to have concocted the story, and they had no motive for so doing.

My inclination to believe was reinforced when, later the same day, I visited Mabel Thurlby, then Mrs. Collishaw, at Beeston, a suburb of Nottingham. The Thurlby family had been very close to the Lawrences at one time. In the summer of 1897 the two families were packed into a carrier's cart in their Sunday best to be taken to Nottingham to have their photographs taken. The men went ahead on foot so that they could call for drinks. These photographs survive, and the Lawrence family photograph has been often reproduced. Mabel's father was a miner who, having lost an arm in a pit accident, was found a job as level-crossing keeper at Moorgreen crossing. On one occasion, while Mabel and Lawrence were waiting for a train to pass. Major Thomas Philip Barber, the local coal owner, rode up on horseback and demanded to be let through. Mr. Thurlby said: 'Are you going to make that horse's mouth bleed?' and made him wait. Many years later Lawrence used this incident in *Women in Love*. Mrs. Collishaw confirmed all the Bircumshaws had told me.

***

At this point I wrote up the story and sent copies to Frieda's children for their comments. All three disbelieved it, but Montague Weekley seemed a good deal less certain than his sisters. I continued to look for further evidence or testimony.

In October 1970 I met Enid Hilton, formerly Enid

Hopkin, who told me that Lawrence brought Frieda to meet her mother Sally 'considerably more than six weeks – perhaps several months' before the elopement. In that same month I obtained from the B.B.C. the script of a programme broadcast in 1961 called *Portrait of Frieda Lawrence*, devised and presented by Alfred Alvarez, who had married one of Frieda's grand-daughters. The programme included an interview with Ida Wilhelmy who had been nurse to the Weekley children from 1906. She recalled Lawrence's first visit, but mentioned no date. It seems strange that Ernest Weekley should speak of bringing (in Miss Wilhelmy's words) 'a young genius from the university' if Lawrence had left the university four years previously. Also there is Alvarez' puzzling statement that Lawrence appeared on the scene 'after eleven years of marriage' – i.e. in 1910.

George Henry ('Diddler') Neville was for several years Lawrence's closest male friend and was regarded as one of the family. An idea of their relationship and joint philandering is given by Lawrence's play *The Married Man*, written early in 1912. If Lawrence confided in anyone about his sexual life during the period 1907-1912 it was in George Neville. James G. Neville kindly allowed me to see, in 1972, his father's memoir of Lawrence. There Neville claims that he could have written the full story of those early days, but had refrained from doing so because living people might be hurt. But he does say, speaking of the year 1912: 'Lawrence knew the woman who was afterwards his wife long before that time'.

Though this story seems to me very convincing, so does the very different story told independently and consistently by Lawrence and Frieda. Perhaps decisive evidence will yet emerge.

The Strange History of *The Daughter-in-Law*

First published in The D. H. Lawrence Review, *11 (2), 1978.*

Intrigued by the sudden appearance of a previously unknown major Lawrence play , without a word of explanation, in the *Complete Plays* in 1965, and galvanized by the splendid production by Peter Gill at the Royal Court Theatre in 1968, I decided to try to discover more about *The Daughter-in-Law* . Once having made the connection with Walter Greenwood's 1936 adaptation *My Son's My Son,* I wrote to Greenwood's publisher, asking them to forward my letter to the agent of the Estate of 'the late Walter Greenwood'. I was most embarrassed to receive a reply from Greenwood himself beginning: 'I'm still my own agent'. (He was, in fact, only 66.) There followed a helpful correspondence.

I should like to thank Gerald Pollinger and the Estate of Mrs. Frieda Lawrence Ravagli for permission to quote from unpublished correspondence of Laurence Pollinger and Frieda Lawrence; Lindeth Vasey of the Humanities Research Center, University of Texas at Austin, for providing information from the Curtis Brown files; A. P. Watt & Son and Mrs. B. H. Evans for access to the files on *My Son's My Son* and for permission to quote from Walter Greenwood's letters; and the Librarian of the University of Salford for access to the prompt copy of *My Son's My Son* and Walter Greenwood's scrapbook; and the Theatre Museum of the Victoria and Albert Museum, London, for their press cuttings on the play.

On 12 January 1913 Lawrence wrote to Edward Garnett:

> I am going to send you a new play I have written. It is neither a comedy nor a tragedy – just ordinary. It is quite objective, as far as that term goes, and though no doubt, like most of my stuff, it wants weeding out a bit, yet I think the whole thing is there, laid out properly, planned

> and progressive. If you don't think so, I am disappointed. (*1L* 500-1)

This new play, which can only be *The Daughter-in-Law*, is never mentioned again in Lawrence's letters. But this description is enough to establish that the play was not in any way incomplete or unfinished. Lawrence felt that, if anything, it was too long and that further revision would have to take the form of 'weeding out'.

When Lawrence left Germany in September 1913 he left with Frieda's sister Else Jaffe several of his manuscripts including four plays *The Merry-Go-Round, The Married Man, The Fight for Barbara*, and *The Daughter-in-Law*. It seems he subsequently forgot about them, and so did Else, for she did not rediscover them until 1933, three years after Lawrence's death. She sent them to Frieda who was in London at the time for the court proceedings about Lawrence's estate. Interviewed in the *Daily Telegraph* (London), 24 March 1933, Frieda said: 'I had no idea the plays existed until the manuscripts were discovered in my sister's house in Munich'. When Frieda returned to Taos the following, month she left the MSS. behind, apparently in the keeping of Edward Garnett. In May 1933 they were typed (three copies) by Curtis Brown's office. The top copies (typed on identical paper, tied with identical ribbon, and bearing Curtis Brown's stamp) are now in the Humanities Research Center of the University of Texas at Austin. There is a set of carbons at Berkeley. The original holograph manuscript of *The Daughter-in-Law* is now at the Berg Library in New York. The play was first published in *The Complete Plays of D. H. Lawrence* in 1965 from the Berkeley carbon typescript. Apart from typing and printing errors, the text is the same in all its forms – holograph, typescript, and published text. In May 1934 Frieda copyrighted *The Daughter-in-Law* as a complete four-act play.

Curtis Brown's office was already actively trying to get the play either published or produced, and in October 1933 two copies had been sent to the theatrical impresario Leon M.

Lion. In January 1934 Lion returned one copy from which Laurence Pollinger (then working for Curtis Brown) wanted to have further copies made. A Miss Saville made two further copies of both *The Daughter-in-Law* and *The Married Man*. Lion's second copy had gone to Richard Hughes (the author of *A High Wind in Jamaica*) who, according to a Curtis Brown MS. transfer slip of 31 January 1934, was 'interested in making the adaptation'. Three weeks later contracts were exchanged between Frieda Lawrence and Richard Hughes. This contract was later cancelled and replaced by new contracts with Lion for a production and Hughes for an adaptation in April. These negotiations were conducted without reference to Frieda, the solicitor C. P. Medley signing for her on instructions from Laurence Pollinger. On 20 April 1934 Pollinger wrote to Frieda:

> It looks as though Leon M. Lion will be putting on The Daughter-in-Law in the near future. The final contract went to Medley to sign on your behalf a couple of days ago. All who have read the play since Richard Hughes has worked on it, think it very fine.

Medley signed, but commented that the royalty seemed to him very low. Curtis Brown noted: 'Royalty not at all bad, I think, considering uncommercial nature of the play'. But when Frieda received her copy of the contract she dug her heels in and wrote to Pollinger (6 May 1934):

> The Lion contract seems a rotten one – 5 per cent – Won't take it – where does Hughes come in? Did he *rewrite* Lawrence's play? What dodge is this? Is it Lawrence's play and I haven't even seen what Hughes did – He wrote he wanted 25% then straight away he asks for 50 – £.50 of the first 100£s – No, I wont do – It surely is *Lion*'s business to pay for any alteration he wants to make – I want 10 per cent or he can leave it. That play does not cost much to produce.

On 15 May 1934 Frieda wrote again reiterating her demand for a 10% royalty. Naturally enough, Frieda could not understand why the play needed any 'adapting' at all; but Lion clearly agreed with Curtis Brown that by the West End standards of the time, the play as it stood was not 'commercial'. On 31 May 1934 Richard Hughes was paid an advance of forty-five pounds. On 6 June 1934 Pollinger wrote to Frieda:

> Leon M. Lion's production of 'Daughter-in-Law' is now in rehearsal and the First Night will be in the course of the next few weeks.... I have no doubt but that Lion will do a distinguished production of the Play. While the terms he is paying are not extravagant, they are fair and reasonable as the Play might easily go down and not up. It was necessary that the Play should be revised in certain places if it were ever to be produced. Please don't lose sight of the fact that Lawrence wrote it many, many years ago, and times and conditions have considerably changed since then.

Frieda replied that she would stop the production if she did not get her 10%. This provoked from Pollinger a 'brutally frank' letter in which he said that the deal was consummated and nothing could be done to alter it: 'Lion's offer isn't a startling one but it is fair and reasonable and Hughes is certainly not being overpaid for all of the work he has put in on the play, so as to make it presentable on the stage'. But the anticipated production did not materialize, and cannot have been as far advanced as Pollinger had suggested. A year later we find him writing to Frieda that Hughes had done 'not a little work', but had not succeeded in adapting the play, and that now Lion was asking for a further free twelve-month option to give him time to find another dramatist.

I can find no evidence of what work Hughes actually did, if any, nor of why he found his task impossible. But Leon Lion persisted, and in April 1936 persuaded Walter

Greenwood to take over the job. On 29 April 1936 Lion wrote to A. P. Watt, the agent acting for Greenwood:

> What are the services which Mr. Greenwood proposes rendering in return for his taking 25% of the fees? … We definitely envisaged his overseeing at rehearsals in the general North country atmosphere of the play, and modifying any dialogue necessary. I made it quite clear that I could indicate the structural form of the elaboration for Act three, (on which I gave him two pages of notes) but that as I did not know the mining folk or their dialect, I should have to depend on him for that.

In his reply of the following day, Mr. Watt, referring to 'Mr. Lawrence's uncompleted play', quoted a letter from Walter Greenwood:

> Briefly, I'll have to rewrite the 3rd act of the play: this in itself will necessitate certain adjustments to the two preceding acts. As the play now stands it will be unintelligible to West End audiences because of its dialect. I propose to modify this into idiomatic English.

Greenwood had in fact already gone to the Lake District, and had nearly finished his work on the play there:

'Writing in Lake District', *News Chronicle* (London):

> In the peace and quiet of the Lake District Walter Greenwood, author of *Love on the Dole*, is now settling down to write the last act of an unfinished play by D. H. Lawrence. The manuscript of the play was found in a box of old papers, and is on the same theme as Lawrence's book *Sons and Lovers*.

The idea that the original play was unfinished was not just a journalistic aberration, but seems to have been actively fostered by Lion and Greenwood. A clause in the contract between them reads: 'The Adapted Play shall be announced as "An Unrevised Play by D. H. Lawrence Completed by Walter Greenwood"', and was indeed so announced in the press and in the theatre programme. The word 'completed' was clearly intended to suggest, without actually saying so, that the original play was not just 'unrevised' but unfinished.

The new third act was sent to Lion on 2 May 1936 with these comments by Greenwood:

> Here's the 3rd act of the Lawrence play. I feel I ought to protest about the way I've been rushed – I mean, it scarcely was fair to me: it didn't give me an opportunity to digest the play thoroughly. The first two acts need things doing to them, too. And I'd have liked to have opportunity to have done more to the enclosed. However, Mr. Lion wanted it quickly.

The play was in fact due to open on 26 May 1936. Lion replied that Greenwood had had more than a fortnight, and had produced 'less than three new pages' in the entire act:

> These embodied one of the new 'twists' which I outlined to Mr. Greenwood at our interview. The other one he has so far ignored – (and I shall have to complete it myself and have the dialect made right afterwards) the rest was merely Lawrence's original with some dialect phrases changed here and there – exactly the job that can most adequately be done at rehearsal.

It seems from Greenwood's prompt copy of *My Son's My Son* (now at the University of Salford) that he did no further work on Act III. But he did a few things to the first two acts, making numerous small cuts in Lawrence's dialogue and adding three new scene endings. For example, at the end of Act I of *The Daughter-in-Law* (which becomes Act II, Scene in *My Son's My Son*) Greenwood added this more 'theatrical' curtain:

> Joe: They tell me there's one down at Empire – where a chap breaks more plates nor what I do. Will that make yi laugh, Minnie, or cry – d'ye think?
> Minnie: Watch me – an' see. (She goes out)
> Joe: Tha'rt a comic – ain't tha? If tha' doesna take care tha'lt cry in th'end. Come on!

These lines do not simply give Joe a better exit; they transform him into the stock broken-hearted clown figure, and prepare us, in a heavy-handed way, for the blowing off of his legs at the end. The effect of the subsequent changes has been accurately analysed by Sylvia Sklar.[1]

It is not clear whether Lion or Greenwood was responsible for the new act division and new title. What is clear is that the amount of new material written by Greenwood adds up to no more than several pages, which a professional dramatist could have written in a day or two, and that though there is more Greenwood in the third act than in the other two, it is still, as Lion said, 'merely Lawrence's original' but for 'less than three new pages'. Nevertheless, the *News Chronicle* report that Greenwood was writing 'the last act of an unfinished play' was not an isolated aberration. Paper after paper repeated the story, obviously circulated in press releases and confirmed by Greenwood in interviews, that the original Lawrence play had consisted of two acts only, and that Greenwood had written the whole of the third.

'D. H. Lawrence Play', *Standard* (London), 21 May 1936:

> The play was found in a tin box in Berlin among other of Lawrence's effects, and is about twenty years old. Mr. Lion, knowing I was acquainted with Northern dialect, asked me to finish and revise it, and I have attended all the rehearsals, coaching the actors in their unfamiliar speech. The play deals with a fight between mother and

[1] Sylvia Sklar, '*The daughter-in-law* and *My son's my son*', *D. H. Lawrence Review*, 9, Summer 1976.

> daughter-in-law for possession of the son. It was originally called *The Daughter-in-Law*. The dialect is Derbyshire but it bears a strong resemblance to Lancashire.

The dialect is Nottinghamshire, which is quite different from Lancashire as Greenwood well knew.

All the reviewers told the same story:

Manchester Evening News, 29 May 1936: 'the play which Lawrence left incomplete'.

Sunday Referee (London), 31 May 1936: 'D. H. Lawrence's unrevised portion of a play'.

'Play Found in a Trunk', *Daily Herald* (London), 27 May 1936: 'D. H. Lawrence wrote the first two acts of the play, *My Son's My Son*, and Mr. Walter Greenwood obliged by writing the third act'.

Unidentified review: 'The manuscript of this play was left by the late D. H. Lawrence, completed as to two acts and roughly drafted as to the third'.

'Old Woman Dominates D. H. Lawrence Play', by D. B., *Evening Standard* (London), 27 May 1936: 'Two complete acts of a play and the draft of a third were found amongst D. H. Lawrence's papers in a box in Berlin'.

Unidentified review: 'The first two acts are played almost exactly as Lawrence wrote them. The third was in draft, and has been completed by Walter Greenwood'.

The similarity of these accounts can only be explained by assuming the existence of a press release deliberately propagating this wholly false story. Several of the reviewers based their reviews on it. James Agate (who claimed to know more about miners than Lawrence) wrote:

Sunday Times (London), 31 May 1936: 'Mr. Greenwood, the author of *Love on the Dole*, has finished the play. It is a pity he did not begin it. And that goes for the middle, too!'

And C. V. B., reviewing the revival at the Golders Green Hippodrome in August 1936 wrote, 'D. H. Lawrence Fragment':

> The play reflects D. H. Lawrence in every line of the first two acts and Walter Greenwood, who has more of the theatre in one of his little fingers than Lawrence could muster from a whole life's suppressed eructation, has contrived to make of the third act a living, breathing thing. A drama in one act with introduction by D. H. Lawrence.

Other reviewers preferred what they took to be Lawrence's contribution:

The Times (London), 27 May 1936:

> We can hardly help becoming aware, as the tale of sons and lovers nears its close, that its atmosphere has undergone a subtle change. There is still violence, but it is violence of a more familiar theatrical convention; there is still tension, but tension radically different from that which has bound together the rest of the play; there are odd incursions of sentimental comedy; and, perhaps unjustly, we attribute the change for the worse to Mr. Greenwood's natural failure to see life steadily from Lawrence's peculiar angle. But what else could a collaborator have done but give the tail of the situation left him at the end of the second act a melodramatic flourish?

Manchester Evening News, 29 May 1936:

> It was clever of Mr. Greenwood to solve the problems

> that had been built up dramatically but not tragically. His climax is ever so slick — and D.H. Lawrence, I felt, would have gone on to the logical tragedy. Slickness had no part in his genius.

Perhaps the best comment, in the circumstances, was that of H.H.:

The Observer (London), 31 May 1936:

> The sabotage in the mine, which placated the dark gods in the miner's blood, tore the fabric of truth, let in perfunctory melodrama, and procured a dubiously happy ending. Where Lawrence leaves off and stagecraft begins, is a question that need not detain us. Sufficient to say that, while the voice is the voice of Jacob, the hands are more like the hands of Esau.

Louise Hampton as the mother was generally admired, and there was praise for Giles Isham as Luther and Valentine Dyall as Joe, but D. B.'s reference in the *Evening Standard* (London), 27 May 1936, to the 'passages of pure Kensington which crept persistently in, and into which Miss Sarah Erskine, as Luther's wife, at last frankly relapsed', suggests that Walter Greenwood's dialect coaching had not been wholly successful. The August revival, though it boasted Dame Sybil Thorndike and her children, Christopher and Anne Casson, in the cast, seems to have sported accents ranging from Oxford to Blackpool, and even less care seems to have been taken with the costumes:

'D. H. Lawrence Fragment', by C. V. B.:

> Returning from work in a mine, covered with a layer of coal dust and sweat, he [Nicholas Phipps as Luther] amazed me by turning the soles of his boots to the audience as he sat down – white, virgin soles that could

> not possibly have been anything else but brand new. It seemed hardly consistent with a day's work in a mine.

There could be no such criticism of the play's next revival, at the Royal Court Theatre, London, 19 March 1967, a loving production of Lawrence's original text, which established it as one of our few English twentieth-century dramatic masterpieces.

The problem remains, why did Lion and Greenwood foster the myth that *The Daughter-in-Law* was not a complete four-act play, but an unfinished play of two acts with notes for a third? Was it just a publicity stunt? Why were they allowed to get away with it by Curtis Brown? In her article '*The Daughter-in-Law* and *My Son's My Son*', Sylvia Sklar wrote: 'At no time did Walter Greenwood lay claim to completing an unfinished Lawrence play'.[2] Walter Greenwood made that claim consistently in his every statement on the play from April 1936 to 24 February 1970, when he wrote to me:

> A Mr. Leon M Lion, theatrical manager, wrote to me in 1936 (c) to say that he or somebody had found 'in a box in an attic in Vienna' the MS of two acts of a play by D. H. Lawrence and would I write the missing third act. We agreed terms. He sent me the two acts which, if my memory serves was typewritten (blue ribbon?) on bank paper. I returned this together with the third act which I wrote. Therefore two acts of the play as performed then were Lawrence's, the other mine.

There seems no point in maintaining this myth thirty-four years later. Either Greenwood's memory served him very badly or he had come to believe his own fabrication.

Another puzzle is why *The Daughter-in-Law* should have

[2] '*The daughter-in-law* and *My son's my son*', *D. H. Lawrence Review*, 9, Summer 1976.

disappeared so completely from the ken of Lawrence scholars after 1936. Martin Secker published *A Collier's Friday Night* in 1934, and was negotiating at the same time with Curtis Brown for the publication of *The Daughter-in-Law.* Perhaps disappointing sales for *A Collier's Friday Night* deterred Secker. Lawrence Clark Powell's *The Manuscripts of D. H. Lawrence* of 1937 mentions three of the four plays found in Else's attic (now located in Heidelberg), but not *The Daughter-in-Law.* That he should erroneously describe *The Married Man* as having been produced in England in 1936 'from this manuscript' suggests some accidental conflation of his material. E. W. Tedlock, Jr., in *The Frieda Lawrence Collection of D. H. Lawrence Manuscripts, A Descriptive Bibliography* of 1948, compounds Powell's mistake by giving *The Daughter-in-Law* as an alternative title for *The Married Man.* Harry T. Moore, in *The Life and Works of D. H. Lawrence* in 1951, makes no mention of *The Daughter-in-Law*, but notes: 'Walter Greenwood's *My Son's My Son*, a Lawrence manuscript of an unfinished play completed by Greenwood – as yet unpublished – was produced in London in 1936'. In his definitive *A Bibliography of D. H. Lawrence* of 1963, Warren Roberts notes (probably taking his information from Moore): 'Walter Greenwood completed a play called *My Son's My Son* from an unfinished Lawrence manuscript'. He does not link *My Son's My Son* with *The Daughter-in-Law*, though he lists the Berkeley typescript of the latter.

Fortunately someone picked up that reference in time to get *The Daughter-in-Law* included in *The Complete Plays of D. H. Lawrence* (1965), where it came to most of us as a treasure conjured from thin air. In 1970 I established that *My Son's My Son* was a version of *The Daughter-in-Law* (Sagar 1971),[3] but, as I was thrown by all those references to an unfinished play, it has taken me until now to work out the exact relationship.

[3] Keith Sagar, 'D. H. Lawrence: dramatist', *D. H. Lawrence Review*, 4, Summer 1971. [My *D. H. Lawrence: Life into Art* (1985) contained an extended version of that essay.]

The Strange History of *The Daughter-in-Law*

The Daughter-in-Law was the sleeping beauty of Lawrence's works, locked in her dark attic for twenty years, unnecessarily tarted up for her two brief outings in 1936, then neglected for another thirty years. Now, at last, she has come into her own.

Beyond D. H. Lawrence

This paper was delivered at the Lawrence conference at Southern Illinois University in 1979, and first published in D. H. Lawrence: the man who lived, *ed. R. B. Partlow and H. T. Moore (Carbondale and Edwardsville: Southern Illinois University Press, 1980).*

Lawrence has been dead for half a century; I have been working on Lawrence for a quarter of a century; it is perhaps an appropriate moment to stand back from both the works and the life, and ask some large questions about Lawrence and the way we teach him and write about him. I sense a generation gap opening up, a certain resistance to Lawrence in our students and younger readers; or is it simply a resistance to the way we teach him and the assumptions we make about him? Why should we expect Lawrence to mean the same to young readers in the late seventies and eighties that he meant to us in those far-off fifties? Are we going to go on telling them that we cannot put them onto any other writer who can more adequately interpret their world, more appropriately voice their own aspirations, hopes, fears, needs, than one who was of the same generation as their great-grandfathers?

The excitement generated by Lawrence in his lifetime and for two generations of readers since has been something more than the recognition of great literary talent. For his own generation Lawrence was a prophet, obscure and erratic, but felt to be in touch, as no one else at that time seemed to be, with the sources of vitality and hence able to see more clearly than anyone else the sickness of his society. Every generation needs such a prophet. The next generation, whose consciousness and conscience he might have helped to shape, was too preoccupied with the turbulent politics of the thirties and the horrors of the forties to listen to Lawrence or to such voices in the wilderness as F. R. Leavis and Harry T. Moore.

Thanks largely to Penguin books, which published all his major works in 1950, the next generation, my generation, discovered Lawrence afresh in the fifties, adopted him as its spokesman, and attempted to shape itself in his image. It is not easy now to remember just what it was in Lawrence that we latched onto so avidly. He asked us the necessary questions, the questions St Mawr asks Lou: what is real? are you alive? He stood for 'the maximum of fearless adult consciousness, that has the courage even to submit to the unconsciousness of itself.'

In a world given over entirely to liberal rational humanism (that was how it looked at Cambridge), we felt that liberal values had not stood the test of recent history, that rationalism was false and sterile insofar as it claimed to be able, in time, to explain everything and jettisoned so many other human faculties, and that humanism made arrogant assumptions no more tenable than the medieval theory that the earth must be the centre of the universe because we live on it. We were all living under the mushroom cloud which we felt to be symbolic of the total divorce between man and nature and the irresponsibility of science. Germ warfare was being developed. A horrible, obscene disease, myxomatosis, was deliberately spread in an attempt to wipe out the rabbit population of England. DDT almost wiped out the birds. Industry was pouring pollution unchecked into our air and waters. Living communities were being razed and replaced by vertical slums in the name of progress. The education system was a process of elimination designed to produce an elite for government, management, and the professions.

Of course political solutions were being propounded for some of these problems, and Marxism was thriving in the universities up to 1956, but most of us felt that the search for political solutions was merely tinkering, or, in the case of Marxism, a belief that the great machine would work better if it were turned upside down. Materialism was the enemy. We wanted to redefine the term 'standard of living.'

Also we wanted to be rid of all that cant and hypocrisy, especially in sexual and religious matters, which was beginning to reassert itself after the war. Lawrence opened all the doors. He offered not only a damning analysis of what was false in society, but a new orientation, a whole new system of values whereby everything could be judged according to whether or not it is life-enhancing. There would be a bloodless revolution, for when a sufficient number of people came to make Lawrentian demands on their own lives and on society, society would have to change to accommodate them.

In some ways, to some extent, this has happened. Some of Lawrence's battles have been won. There is now less cant and hypocrisy. The education system is more open and child-orientated. Lawrence took women more seriously as independent beings, free souls, than any earlier English novelist and made a tremendous contribution to their emancipation (though precious little thanks he has had for it). But his most spectacular success was in the effect he had on our attitudes to sex ('a making free and healthy of this sex'). Perhaps younger readers need to be reminded of what it was like in the fifties. Here is the beginning of Philip Larkin's poem 'Annus Mirabilis':

> Sexual intercourse began
> In nineteen sixty-three
> (Which was rather late for me) –
> Between the end of the Chatterley ban
> And the Beatles' first LP.
>
> Up till then there'd only been
> A sort of bargaining,
> A wrangle for a ring,
> A shame that started at sixteen
> And spread to everything.

Other battles have been lost. Our society is even more materialistic and mechanized. Life is even more thoroughly secularized. Alternative societies have nearly all degenerated or fallen into the hands of frauds and fanatics. On other fronts the fight continues, but Lawrence's weapons and strategy have become outmoded, though he can still inspire the troops.

Lawrence was shaped by his time, region, and class. He directed his efforts to changing the world, especially England. The England of 1980 is completely different from the England of 1910 or even 1930. He did not live to see fascism rampant, the death camps, nuclear war, the dismantling of the British Empire, the Welfare State, the rise of the unions, the industrialization of the third world, worldwide terrorism, the breakdown of law and order at home, the decline of religion and marriage, permissive sexual morality, the contraceptive pill, the legalized slaughter of the unborn, feminism, the pop scene, television, space exploration, biological engineering, the control of many diseases, including tuberculosis — the list is endless. No writer dead half a century can be a spokesman for people born into this world. He can be a continuing source of standards and inspiration, a fund of life, but so can all great writers of the past. A writer's value to his contemporaries is bound to be rather different from his value to posterity. For his contemporaries the surface of his work will be directly applicable to their lives and time. The received values are being challenged in very specific ways. The way we live is wrong here and here and here. This has obvious advantages in terms of relevance and urgency, but there is the disadvantage of the temptation, both for the reader and for the writer himself, to turn the vision into a political program or a cult, and to deal with symptoms rather than root causes. This is why it is often necessary to wait some decades to be sure how great a writer is, to wait until that part of his achievement which can date has dated, so that we can see clearly what remains.

The primary and unique discipline for the imaginative writer is to find metaphors for his own nature. 'The Waste Land' is a great poem not because it is a clever analysis of Western civilization, but because, in drawing from the world around him metaphors for his own nature, his own psychic problems, Eliot was able to communicate an authenticated vision of alienation which, because it derived from those depths of the psyche at which all men are alike, was immediately recognized as expressing a common sense of alienation, and therefore as an 'objective' account. Kafka found metaphors for his own very peculiar nature, his psychic disturbances; they revealed and embodied, in an extreme and very pure form, common anxieties.

If metaphors are authentic and dredged from the depths, they translate the local and temporal experience into terms equally applicable to human experience at any time and any place. They fan outwards into vast perspectives of permanent realities, including those of the nonhuman world. Thus we go to Shakespeare to find out what it was like to live through that particular watershed of English history, but at the same time find ourselves journeying into ourselves, being changed, and seeing our distinctive twentieth-century situation rather differently.

All great writers are disturbed. Their inner conflicts are the source of their creative energies. Lawrence's favourite metaphors are generated by the stress between the opposing claims of his parents; between the male and female elements in his sexual make-up; between his Puritanism and anti-Puritanism; his need for rootedness and for freedom, for continuity and change. All these stresses and many others he was able to cope with by objectifying them as metaphors (in the large sense that a whole novel may be a metaphor). This process is of great value not only to the writer himself as auto-therapy; he is like the shaman who makes the dangerous journey into the spirit world again and again for the sake of his people, or the haruspex who examines the entrails of animals and birds for revelations. But the other world the writer enters is his own unconscious; the entrails he examines are his own. His metaphors are the clues he brings back of what he has found there. A conscious examination of himself and his experience would not take him far without such clues, nor could his findings be validated and communicated without them.

The imagination attends to both seen and unseen, strives to bring more and more of life into consciousness and to reach an inclusive vision within which the warring dualities of existence can be atoned. It has all other human faculties at its service, and so leaves behind all other disciplines in the pursuit of the deepest, most permanent truths. The vision of life, as inclusive as the writer can make it, and the provisional orientation towards life he takes up on the strength of it, Lawrence called his metaphysic. Every great writer must have a metaphysic; and every major new work is a new attempt to extend and test and substantiate it. The ultimate test of greatness in a writer is the adequacy of his metaphysic.

The most taxing challenge for the literary critic is the task of evaluating a great writer's metaphysic. 'Give me a lever and I will move the world.' There are no fixed criteria. Belief in a fixed criterion – Marxist, Christian, or whatever – seems to me to disqualify a critic. Some critics have offered an absolute standard we are all supposed to find unquestionable. Leavis based all his criticism on Lawrence's own aphorism 'Art for life's sake.' But 'life' is not an unquestionable good. Nietzsche tells of the wood-sprite Silenus who, if caught, had to answer any question truthfully. On one occasion he was caught and asked, 'What is man's greatest good?' He replied, 'Ephemeral wretch, begotten by accident and toil, why do you force me to tell you what it would be your greatest boon not to hear? What would be best for you is quite beyond your reach: not to have been born, not to be, to be nothing. But the second best is to die soon'.[1] What right have we to rule out in advance such a metaphysic? It has got to be 'Art for truth's sake'.

We can test a writer's 'reality' against our own sense of it, but this is very dangerous. It may prevent us from making that imaginative leap into another man's world which must

[1] Friedrich Nietzsche, *The birth of tragedy* (Garden City, N. Y.: Doubleday, 1956), 29.

precede any judgment. It may simply give us the opportunity to rationalize our inertia or discomfort at finding some of our cherished habits of thought and feeling under assault. We must bring the writer's reality into the closest possible contact with our own, but to take our own as a standard would be arrogant in the extreme, as the great writer is by definition larger than we are. We can test a writer's metaphysic against what we take to be common human experience. But what if the writer believes everybody's understanding of what common human experience is to be a huge misunderstanding or a conspiracy to believe things because we believe everyone else believes them?

One of Lawrence's own favourite methods was to pit his own metaphysic against that of some other great writer, Hardy, for example, at the beginning of his career, Tolstoy and Dostoevsky toward the end. Always he accuses the other writer of distortion, of putting his thumb in the balance. Hardy's form, he says, is 'execrable in the extreme,' 'for nothing in his work is so pitiable as his clumsy efforts to push events into line with his theory of being, and to make calamity fall on those who represent the principle of Love.' (*STH* 93) We can see the distortion very clearly in this well-known passage from *Tess of the D'Urbervilles*:

> The call seldom produces the comer; the man to love rarely coincides with the hour for loving. Nature does not often reply 'Here!' to a body's cry of 'Where?' till the hide-and-seek has become an irksome, outworn game.
>
> In the present case, as in millions, it was not the two halves of a perfect whole that confronted each other at the perfect moment; a missing counterpart wandered independently about the earth, waiting in crass obtuseness till the late time came. Out of which maladroit delay spring anxieties, disappointments, shocks, catastrophes, and passing-strange destinies. (Ch.5)

This is not the place to argue the justice of Lawrence's criticism of Hardy. The point I want to make is that, if it is cheating in a novelist thus to make things work out badly to fit a pre-existing pessimistic metaphysic, is it not equally cheating to make things work out well to fit a pre-existing optimistic metaphysic? In Lawrence the call always produces the comer (in the form of a Polish widow, a Ministry Inspector, an Italian circus-rider, a Mexican general, a gipsy, a gamekeeper, a Priestess of Isis) and Nature is always right on cue.

Lawrence would argue that he had *proved* that life can be great. He had known suffering and frustration, but in his moment of greatest need fate had given him Frieda, and everything which had gone before fell into place as a necessary prelude. From this he generalized that life actively concerns itself with the fulfilment of those who have the courage to submit wholly to it. But Hardy was not pessimistic out of sheer perversity. The prevalence in his work of betrayal and frustration, the succession of wasted lives, the close association of misery and marriage, testifies to a life which must have enforced such generalizations. This is what he had experienced, seen in his friends, heard in village gossip, and read in newspapers.

Lawrence says of Hardy's protagonists: 'They have not the necessary strength: the question of their unfortunate end is begged in the beginning'(*STH* 50). But Lawrence's decision to give his characters the necessary strength is equally question-begging. If we apply the thumb-in-the-balance test to *Anna Karenina* and *Lady Chatterley's Lover* (a comparison Lawrence himself invites), it is not Tolstoy who is pushing harder.

Putting one's thumb in the balance is only one way of cheating, favouring one's own preconceived interpretation of reality. What is in the other pan is, or ought to be, reality itself, raw, uninterpreted, complete — the inescapable facts. A more insidious, less easily detectable form of cheating is leaving certain facts out of account. Lawrence was well aware that he was leaving a great deal out of account, and had his defence:

> Realism is just one of the arbitrary views man takes of man. It sees us all as little ant-like creatures toiling against the odds of circumstance, and doomed to misery. It is a kind of aeroplane view. It became the popular view, and so today we actually are, millions of us, little ant-like creatures toiling against the odds of circumstance, and doomed to misery; until we take a different view of ourselves. For man always becomes what he passionately thinks he is; since he is capable of becoming almost anything. (*IR* 149).

Ursula 'believed more in her desire and its fulfilment than in the obvious facts of life.' So did Lawrence. His impatience with Hardy, Bennett, Chekhov, Mann, Tolstoy, and many other major writers was because they did not. They insisted on writing about men and women who do not despise life and yet are denied it. There is in Lawrence remarkably little undeserved suffering, loneliness, frustration, breakdown, loss, which is not merely a prelude to a resolution or resurrection. His metaphysic excludes a large part of what has traditionally been regarded as tragic experience.

Lawrence's vision was essentially utopian; it was almost idealistic. The usual distinction between the ideal and the real seems to me to blur an essential distinction. There are really three possibilities for the artist: to write of what is, what should be, or what could be. To write exclusively about what is Lawrence rightly saw to be a dead realism, a capitulation, a 'giving in before you start.' To write about what should be does not seem to me to be a particularly interesting or valuable or even adult activity; there can be no checks on the writer's self-indulgence, escapism, wish-fulfilment, if he is not obliged to pay any debts to reality.

That Lawrence thought of himself as writing of what could be is evidenced by the many attempts he made to translate his vision into life as well as art. Most of them were fiascos. He asked too much of his early girl-friends, and all those relationships were painful fiascos. He asked too much of his marriage, and was bitterly disillusioned. He asked too much of his friends, and found them all Judases. He asked too much of humanity, and had to write it off as an evolutionary dead end. There was the fiasco of the visit to Cambridge in 1915; of the proposed lecture-tour with Russell; of *The Signature* and Rainbow Books and Music; the whole series of fiascos resulting from his attempts to set up Rananim, culminating in the sick farce at the Café Royal in 1923. Only the long-dead Etruscans did not let him down, and the natural world, though he was very careful what aspects of that he looked at.

His works had to compensate for all these failures. He had a natural tendency to turn his back on aspects of reality he could not stomach and drift toward his desired image. He did not resist this tendency, but rationalized it: 'When one is shaken to the very depths, one finds reality in the unreal world. At present my real world is the world of my inner soul, which reflects on to the novel I write. The outer world is there to be endured, it is not real – neither is the outer life' (*1L* 610). By this means any facts he could not face could be easily disposed of, consigned to an 'unreal' world of madness or nightmare. According to this reasoning, the war, for example, 'never happened': 'Not to me or to any man, in his own self. It took place in the automatic sphere, as dreams do. But the actual man in every man was just absent – asleep – or drugged – inert – dream-logged' (*AR* 118). The job of the artist is to bring inner and outer realities together, not to escape from one into the other.

The testing of one man's metaphysic against another's can be extended in what I find to be a useful way by taking literally the metaphor I have used of orientation toward experience. Let us imagine all possible orientations toward life to be points on a compass. The bleak North is nihilism, the belief that life is unredeemable. Let us appoint Beckett as its literary representative. The opposite, the warm South, is Lawrence's position, the belief that life is not in need of redemption. In the East let us put the meliorists, who say that life can be reformed, improved by purely secular reorganization; Brecht can stand here. And in the West stands religion, the belief that life can be redeemed from outside itself, by transcendental means; the later Eliot can stand for this. Now we can test the relative adequacy of each position by subjecting it to the heaviest possible bombardment from the other three, and seeing what is left when the smoke clears.

There would not be much left of *Lady Chatterley's Lover* after prolonged exposure to Beckett's bombardment; not much left of Lawrence's infantile politics after exposure to Brecht; not much of his pseudo-religious terminology after exposure to Eliot. But Beckett, Brecht, and Eliot might well suffer even more from Lawrence's fire, might well be shown to leave even more than he does out of account, as if that were the price of their special insights.

Is there, then, any modern writer whose metaphysic can be set against Lawrence's who is genuinely more inclusive, who neither puts his thumb in the balance nor leaves a great deal out of account, who stands, as it were, in the centre of the circle, drawing together and attempting to reconcile what is irreducible in all the visions on the circumference (for he has been there too)? The writer who seems to me to have come nearest to achieving this is Ted Hughes.

At one end of the spectrum Hughes is very Lawrentian:[2] in his opposition to rationalism, humanism, and certain aspects of science; in his insistence on the sacredness, miraculousness of Nature; in his belief in the need for an ego-death and a resurrection in individuals; and in his belief in the ability of two people to reconstitute each other in marriage. At the other end of the spectrum he looks unflinchingly, especially through the eyes of his persona Crow, at all those aspects of Nature and human experience Lawrence turned a

[2] See my essay '"Straight oxygen": Ted Hughes' debt to D. H. Lawrence'. *Journal of D. H. Lawrence Studies*. 2. i.

blind eye to.

Lawrence, dazzled by the glamour of the universe, failed to notice a great deal of the evidence, evidence meticulously noted by Crow. For example, Crow quickly recognized war as a characteristic human activity:

And when the smoke cleared it became clear
This had happened too often before
And was going to happen too often in the future
And happened too easily
Bones were too like lath and twigs
Blood was too like water
Cries were too like silence
The most terrible grimaces too like footprints in mud
And shooting somebody through the midriff
Was too like striking a match
Too like potting a snooker ball
Too like tearing up a bill
Blasting the whole world to bits
Was too like slamming a door
Too like dropping in a chair
Exhausted with rage
Too like being blown to bits yourself
Which happened too easily
With too like no consequence.

'Crow's Account of the Battle'

Crow's own characteristic activity is predation, a central activity of Nature which Lawrence chose to pay little attention to.

In their ruthless quest for personal fulfilment Lawrence's protagonists refuse to be distracted by the death-cries of others. Lawrence is callous in his insistence on the total existential freedom of every individual. Even Frieda compared him to the little boy who said, 'I'll teach you to be a toad!' as he stamped on the toad.

Hughes does not pay for these insights, as so many

modern writers do, by losing his grip on the essential Lawrentian positives. In the epilogue to *Gaudete* he performs the incredible feat of holding together in a single all-embracing vision the bleak realities and black negatives of *Crow* and the joyful affirmations of *Season Songs*.

Lawrence achieved far more than we have any right to ask of any man in a full lifetime, let alone half a lifetime. For almost half a century he has stood alone as a beacon of sanity. But we do him no service to claim that he had all the answers or that all the answers he had to the wants of his day are as relevant now as they were then. His life and thought-adventure took him deep into new continents, but there is still infinite darkness beyond his farthest vision to be explored. He believed he was participating in a process of evolving human consciousness, and that future explorers would go much farther. He would have wished us to strive to go beyond those frontiers where he reached the limit of his vision, to try to construct a metaphysic adequate to our world, with the help of the greatest writers of our own time — 'for brave men are for ever born, and nothing else is worth having'.

Introduction to *Sons and Lovers*

First published in D. H. Lawrence, Sons and Lovers *(Harmondsworth: Penguin, 1981).*

In 1966 the Penguin English Library was inaugurated as a sister series to the Classics. Apart from aiming to provide a lively critical and historical introduction and notes to clarify the texts, the main concern was to provide authoritative text.s, which certainly did not exist at that time where Lawrence was concerned. I had established a good relationship with Penguin through the success of my Lawrence Selected Poems and two collections of his short stories I had edited for them, and they invited me to be the general editor of all Lawrence titles in the series, with the freedom to choose both titles and editors. Seven titles appeared between 1981 and 1983. I chose Sons and Lovers *for myself.*

> He [Lawrence] said that Borrow had mingled autobiography and fiction so inextricably in *Lavengro* that the most astute critics could not be sure where the one ended and the other began. From his subtle smile I felt he was wondering whether he might not do something in the same fashion himself.[1]

Sons and Lovers is, on the face of it, a very straightforward book. It tells a simple story simply, with none of the artistic self-consciousness we find in, say, Joyce's *Portrait of the Artist as a Young Man*; with none of the obvious symbolic density, complex structure, strained language (and other 'modernist' techniques) of, say, *Women in Love.* Yet *Sons and Lovers* has aroused as much critical dissension as any Lawrence novel, dissension which shows no sign of being resolved. The question is whether Lawrence was in sufficient command of his experience, had come to a sufficient understanding of it, to be able to present it adequately in a novel. The charge against him is that, consciously or unconsciously, he distorted the story in order to make Paul and his mother come out of it

[1] Chambers (1935) 110.

better than they should, at the expense of Miriam and his father. That is, that Lawrence had not realized, at the time of writing *Sons and Lovers*, the extent to which his mother had been in the wrong, had been responsible for both the failure of her own marriage, and Paul's inability to make a satisfactory relationship with any other woman. There is clearly some truth in this charge. But the amount of weight it carries will depend very much on whether we read the novel as autobiography or fiction.

If we judge it as autobiography, and know the facts, we can easily catch Lawrence lying; but what is great imaginative fiction if not the telling of lies which are truer than facts? We have to try to get clear to what extent Lawrence was trying to tell the truth about his early life, as auto-therapy ('we shed our sickness in our books'), and to what extent he was trying to write a novel with a more general relevance and significance. In order to do this, it seems to me helpful to know something about the genesis of the novel.

Lawrence's first novel, *The White Peacock*, had not been autobiographical. Though the narrator Cyril is clearly Lawrence himself, Emily is Jessie Chambers, and most of the other characters are based on real people, Lawrence largely avoided confronting overtly the problems which, as we know from *Sons and Lovers*, were central in his life during the years 1906-9, when *The White Peacock* was being written. The characters are transposed to a purely rural setting; most of them are transposed upwards socially. Thus Lawrence's own home life is evaded altogether. Sexual matters are dealt with very obliquely as in the mid-nineteenth-century novel. There is much purple prose, many descriptions of the natural world for their own sake. The novel, as Lawrence himself recognized even before he had finished it, reads like the efforts of a callow but precocious youth (or young lady, as some of the reviewers surmised) to do something along the lines of George Eliot's *The Mill on the Floss* or early Hardy. His second novel, *The Trespasser*, was based entirely on the experiences of Helen Corke, not his own.

By 1909 Lawrence had written at least one purely autobiographical work (discounting poems), his first play *A Collier's Friday Night*. But it seems that when he embarked on *Paul Morel* (Lawrence's working title for *Sons and Lovers*), he did not at first contemplate giving it anything like that degree of realism and authenticity. He obviously intended from the first to put very much more of himself into Paul than into Cyril, and to make his own home in Eastwood the focal point of the novel. But in many ways his story was to be highly fictionalized. It is Paul's younger brother, Arthur, who goes to Nottingham High School and University College. He quarrels with his father, who throws a steel at him, killing him. The father is then imprisoned, and dies of grief shortly after his release. Jessie Chambers (Miriam) appears in the novel, but conflated with another of Lawrence's friends (but never his girl-friend) Flossie Cullen. Miriam's family (called Staynes, of Belfast House) is closely modelled on the Cullen family. Miss Wright, the Cullen family governess, whom Lawrence much admired, becomes Miss May, a major character in the novel, who marries Mr. Revell, the incompetent Congregational minister of whom Mrs. Morel has tired. They go to live at the Haggs, taking Miriam with them. When her father dies she inherits some money. She proposes to become a nurse, but becomes a peripatetic music teacher instead. All this Cullen material disappeared later from the novel, but reappeared in 1912 in *The Insurrection of Miss Houghton*, an early draft of *The Lost Girl*, and again in 1920 in *The Lost Girl* itself.

One of the major impulses behind *Paul Morel* was Lawrence's desire to pay tribute to his mother, to pay her some fictional compensation, posthumously, for her suffering and wasted life. On the 6th December 1910, three days before his mother died of cancer, Lawrence wrote to his new fiancée Louie Burrows:

> Mother has had a devilish married life for nearly forty years — and this is the conclusion — no relief. What ever I

> wrote, it could not be so awful as to write a biography of my mother ... She is my first, great love. She was a wonderful, rare woman — you do not know; as strong, and steadfast, and generous as the sun. She could be as swift as a white whip-lash, and as kind and gentle as warm rain, and as steadfast as the irreducible earth beneath us ... My mother has been passionately fond of me, and fiercely jealous. She hated J[essie] — and would have risen from the grave to prevent my marrying her. (*1L* 195-7)

In a sense Lydia Lawrence did rise from the grave, as Gertrude Morel, and Lawrence handed her the laurels of victory over Miriam, as he had done in real life over Jessie. How could he do otherwise if she were sun, rain and earth to him, and he had loved her 'like a lover'?

If his mother is to be revealed to the world as a 'wonderful, rare woman', then her faults must be hidden, not least from Lawrence himself. First, her husband must bear the blame for that 'devilish married life'. Mrs. Lawrence had taught young Bert to pray that his father should either become a chapel man or die. In the novel Lawrence can play God and make that prayer come true. Paul plans to poison his father slowly with verdigris in his tea, but is saved from having to carry out his murder by the incident with the steel (which actually happened to an uncle of Lawrence's). Lawrence's attitude to his father had changed little by the time he began *Paul Morel*. A month after the death of his mother he wrote to his Congregational minister that his father was 'disgusting, irritating, and selfish as a maggot. Yet I am sorry for him: he's old, stupid, and very helpless and futile' (220). The passages in *Sons and Lovers* where Walter Morel is described in very different terms from these must have been written much later.

The standards by which Walter Morel is judged, even in the final *Sons and Lovers*, are largely those of his wife, because Lawrence's were still largely those of his mother. By Lydia Lawrence's standards, Arthur Lawrence was simply irresponsible. He had, for example, before their marriage, described himself to her as a mining contractor. This was strictly true, as mining contractor was the official term for butty; but he well knew that Lydia would take it to be something rather grand, far above a face worker. The first time he returned home from work, she did not recognize him. She thought he was a Negro. She loved reading and talking more than anything, but she could not talk to him. He could hardly write, and his reading never went beyond the newspapers, of which he understood little. He was inarticulate (at least at home). She thought she could make him teetotal, but he could not keep it up for long. She conditioned her children to regard drunkenness as a form of extreme moral degradation. In *Sons and Lovers* Lawrence himself occasionally lapses into the language of the Temperance tracts:

> She knew that the man who stops on the way home from work is on a quick way to ruining himself and his home. (*SL* 86)

There were two Arthur Lawrences. The one known to his friends was gentle, generous, easy-going, good-humoured – the ideal work-mate or drinking companion. A miner loses several pints of body fluid every shift. If he did not replenish it, he would die. That particular culture dictated that it should be replenished with beer, and that the intense comradeship built up between the men underground should be continued in the pub. Hence the need for all that intense temperance activity in the mining areas. As he was treated as a stranger in his own home, the pub was Arthur Lawrence's home from home. He was not, by the standards of his mates, a heavy drinker, and was even more convivial when slightly tipsy. This Arthur Lawrence was generally respected and loved, but his family saw little of him. It is difficult to remain genial when confronted by systematic ostracism. The transformation when Arthur Lawrence arrived home has been graphically described by Ada Lawrence:

> Mother would wait up for him at night, her rage seething, until on his arrival it boiled over in a torrent of biting truths which turned him from his slightly fuddled and pleasantly apologetic mood into a brutal and coarse beast.[2]

Unable to match his wife in verbal abuse, he would occasionally resort to violence. The children blamed the beer, not their mother. No one outside the family ever saw this Arthur Lawrence. Consequently people were outraged when they heard toffee-nosed Bert, who would never make half the man his father was, insult his father in public.

Though *Sons and Lovers* contains several scenes where our sympathy goes out to Walter Morel, as he tells stories to his children, makes fuses, cooks his rasher of bacon in the early morning when he has the kitchen to himself, nevertheless the novelist's condemnatory tone is close to that of Mrs. Morel. A more mature Lawrence would have been able to analyse the failure of this marriage in terms of the completely different values and attitudes into which each had been conditioned by class and culture. Instead we are simply given the mother as right, the father as wrong: 'He had denied the god in him'.

Second, the mother must bear no blame for the failure of Paul's relationship with Miriam. On the contrary, she is praised for providing him with standards of normality and wholeness by which he can judge both Miriam and Clara to be, in their opposite ways, wanting. This despite the fact that in May 1911 Lawrence could write to Jessie:

> They [meaning his mother and sisters] tore me from you, the love of my life. It was the slaughter of the foetus in the womb. (*1L* 268)

The evasions extended to the handling of Paul himself. Why

[2] Edward Nehls, *D. H. Lawrence: A Composite Biography*. Vol. I (Madison: University of Wisconsin Press, 1957), 11.

is he presented as an artist rather than a writer? Why does his brother, not he, go to university? These were sensitive areas. Mrs. Lawrence had taken an interest in Bert's painting; it was a harmless enough recreation, conventional and second-hand. But his creative writing had to be hidden from her, written in college note-books so that she would think he was 'working'. She had scrimped and saved to send him to college to work hard and pass examinations and get a good job and get on in the world, not to fritter his time away writing about things he could not possibly understand. By 1910 Lawrence had completely lost his mother's admiration for learning and 'getting on', so that area of discord had to be avoided.

In the autumn of 1911 Lawrence sent the entire manuscript of *Paul Morel* to Jessie:

> He had written about two thirds of the novel and appeared to have come to a standstill. In reading the Ms. I felt oppressed by a sense of strain, as though he had had to force himself to write it. There was no spontaneity, no sparkle. It was his mother's story, told rather sentimentally; a young non-conformist minister whose sermons she composed was there as a set-off to the brutal husband. Our household of Willey Farm was not there at all, and the character he calls Miriam was placed in a suburban atmosphere in Eastwood. In my reply to Lawrence I suggested that he should relate the story of his mother's married life as it had actually happened, and include his brother Ernest, whose story was omitted in the first draft. It seemed to me that the reality was so much more poignant and interesting than his semi-fictitious account. Not only that, I felt that if he could work out artistically and within himself all the issues of his mother's life and their implications, not only would he write a magnificent novel, but he would rid himself of his obsession with regard to his mother, and be a free and a whole man.[3]

[3] Jessie Chambers, 'The Collected Letters of Jessie Chambers'. Ed. G. Zytaruk. *D. H. Lawrence Review*, Spring-Summer 1979. 65-6.

Lawrence took Jessie's advice, and even incorporated several passages written by her. But the new version he passed to Jessie a dozen pages at a time through February and March 1912 hurt her deeply. It seemed to her a betrayal, not just of herself, but of 'the truth', to justify the mother.

Jessie Chambers was later to write her own version of 'the truth' in *D. H. Lawrence: A Personal Record.* Many critics, assuming *A Personal Record* to be accurate in its facts and truthful in its interpretation of them, have used it as a means of locating distortions in Lawrence's account in the novel. It is certainly an invaluable book; particularly for the picture it gives us of that remarkable culture, whose pivots were the Congregational Church and the Mechanics' Institute Library, at that moment in history. It tells us what the young Lawrence was reading and discussing and painting and singing, and what these things meant to him, and that it was not so much the activities themselves which distinguished him from the other young people of his generation as the vitality and enthusiasm and intelligence he brought to them. It is where *A Personal Record* is most personal that it is least reliable – in its account of the relationship between Jessie and Lawrence.

Jessie no doubt gives her version in good faith, but she cannot help putting herself always at the centre of the stage, sometimes excluding the rest of her family completely, and casting herself in the role of betrayed maiden, tragic heroine. Jessie's elder sister May, who was not emotionally involved, also left a record of many of the same incidents which are described by her sister in *A Personal Record* and by Lawrence in the novel. More often than not, May's account is nearer to Lawrence's than to Jessie's.[4]

Nevertheless, one's sympathy goes out to Jessie. She loved Lawrence deeply. Given her upbringing, the moral climate of the time, Lawrence's own hang-ups, it is difficult to see how she could have behaved otherwise than she did. And it seems

[4] Nehls, *op. cit.,* vol.III (1959), 552-620.

grossly unfair to load so much of the responsibility for the failure of Paul and Miriam onto Miriam. Several critics have chivalrously leapt to the defence of Jessie/Miriam against Lawrence/Paul and his mother. But it seems to me that in doing so they have distorted the novel as much as Lawrence, in the opposite direction. Let us suppose that Paul's mother had been not at all possessive and had positively encouraged his relationship with Miriam. Can we imagine that the novel could have ended with Paul and Miriam happily married? Surely such a marriage could only have been, for Paul, a capitulation.

Lawrence and Jessie Chambers shared much of real value, but it is clear that a marriage would have been disastrous. Years later Lawrence said: 'It would have been a fatal step. I should have had too easy a life, nearly everything my own way, and my genius would have been destroyed'.[5] He needed a woman not only free herself from that puritanical inheritance, but also strong enough to shake him out of his own narcissistic Puritanism and priggishness. He needed Frieda. If his mother ensured that in 1912 he was not married to Jessie Chambers or to Louie Burrows, but free and ready for Frieda, then he had much to thank her for.

Mrs. Lawrence's dislike of Jessie did not spring entirely from selfish possessiveness. Lawrence was irritated by aspects of Jessie's character without any prompting from his mother. Jessie was not well liked, even within her own family. Her brother David Chambers wrote of her 'rhapsodical moods' and 'inflexible will':

> She knew what was right – in taste as well as in conduct; she did what was right and expected to receive what was due to her for her universal rightness.[6]

Jessie recorded one occasion when she visited the Lawrence home:

[5] Nehls, vol.I, 71.
[6] Nehls, vol.III, 537.

> The talk was lively, and Mrs. Lawrence seemed to be the pivot on which the liveliness centred. She struck me as a bright, vivacious little woman, full of vitality and amusingly emphatic in her way of speaking.[7]

Such a tribute, by someone who had every reason to resent Mrs. Lawrence, indicates that the qualities Lawrence ascribed to his mother in the letter to Louie, and gave to Mrs. Morel in the novel, were not entirely in his own imagination.

Nevertheless, if we were to judge *Sons and Lovers* as autobiography, we should have to agree with Jessie that it was a cruel betrayal of her, and of 'the truth'. For in the novel Lawrence ignores many of the good things he had shared with Jessie, presenting Miriam as almost totally dependent and destructive. But Lawrence strenuously denied the charge:

> I could hear in advance Lawrence's protesting voice: 'Of course it isn't the truth. It's an adaptation from life, as all art must be. It isn't what I think of you; you know it isn't.'[8]

Throughout his life Lawrence had the same problem. All his novels (except his two collaborations, *The Trespasser* and *The Boy in the Bush*) draw heavily on his own experience and relationships. He did not see the point of inventing anything if he could draw on reality. Most of his characters are amalgams of two or three real people, and, of course, aspects of himself. Often his friends would recognize themselves in unsympathetic characters, and feel betrayed. Two of them, Philip Heseltine and Compton Mackenzie, even threatened legal action. Yet it seems that Lawrence could not create characters in any other way than by 'adaptation from life'. Usually he refused to accept that his characters were 'portraits', insisting that, though certain immediately

[7] Chambers (1965), 24.
[8] *Ibid.*, 204.

recognizable features of real people might have been incorporated into his characters, their inner significance was quite different from his real-life judgements of those people. There was a good deal of truth in this. For example, the figure of Hermione in *Women in Love* was already created in her essentials before Lawrence had ever met Lady Ottoline Morrell, of whom it was widely assumed to be a portrait. And Lawrence himself, as much as Compton Mackenzie, was the man who loved islands.

Jessie Chambers was well aware that Lawrence used this method:

> The character of Clara is a clever adaptation of elements from three people, Miss Burrows, Miss Corke, and Mrs. Dax. The external resemblance to Mrs. Dax is the strongest. At any rate, she regarded herself as the original because I received a letter from her some years after the publication of *Sons and Lovers* in which she said – 'I have read *Sons and Lovers* and I swear that it is not true.'….As the novel was nearly finished before Lawrence made the acquaintance of Mrs. Weekley, it is a little difficult for her to claim a place there. There is one incident, however, that may refer to her – where Paul Morel goes to the theatre with Clara. From the description of her dress I guessed at once Mrs. Weekley, and they actually did see *Man and Superman* here at Nottingham, together. You see how life went straight into his work.[9]

It is difficult to see much of either Louie Burrows or Helen Corke in Clara. What Jessie did not see, could hardly have seen given the strong 'external resemblance' between Miriam and herself, was that Miriam was also an adaptation of elements from at least three people, herself, Louie Burrows, Helen Corke, and, perhaps, Agnes Holt.

Lawrence's creative motivation was always a matter of

[9] Chambers (1979), 67.

attempting to deal imaginatively with urgent and immediate problems. When he wrote *Paul Morel* his relationship with Jessie Chambers was effectively over. His current relationships were with Louie Burrows, his official fiancée, Alice Dax, his mistress, Helen Corke and Agnes Holt. His problem with all of them except Alice was essentially the same as his problem with Jessie. What Lawrence wrote to Blanche Jennings in January 1910 about his latest girl-friend Agnes Holt, he might equally have said of any of them:

> She still judges by mid-Victorian standards, and covers herself with a woolly fluff of romance that the years will wear sickly. She refuses to see that a man is a male, that kisses are the merest preludes and anticipations, that love is largely a physical sympathy that is soon satisfied and satiated. She believes men worship their mistresses; she is all sham and superficial in her outlook, and I can't change her. (*1L* 153)

Helen Corke was another such 'dreaming woman', who, shortly before she met Lawrence, had driven her lover to suicide by trying to impose on him a purely spiritual relationship and making him hate his own ungovernable body. She drove Lawrence similarly into 'an extremity of mental torture':

> How we hate one another to-night, hate, she and I
> To numbness and nothingness; I dead, she refusing to die.
> The female whose venom can more than kill, can
> numb and then nullify.
>
> 'Repulsed'

The same doomed struggle was resumed with Louie, the

> Betrothed young lady who loves me, and takes good care
> Of her womanly virtue and of my good name.
>
> 'The Hands of the Betrothed'

All Lawrence's sense of the destructiveness of the dreaming woman, his intense hatred of her, went into his work. In his first novel, *The White Peacock*, it had been Lettie, who destroyed George; in *The Trespasser* Helena, who destroyed her lover; in *Sons and Lovers* it is Miriam, who would have destroyed Paul had his mother not saved him.

So Lawrence was caught between two needs, the need to 'tell the truth' in Jessie's sense, and avoid hurting her yet again, and the need to produce art rather than reproduce life, that is, to attempt a wider significance than the exclusively personal. So the novel evolved towards autobiography in that it became less evasive, but towards art also in that it became more 'restrained' and 'impersonal' (*1L* 184), speaking for a whole generation of young men:

> It is a great tragedy, and I tell you I've written a great book. It's the tragedy of thousands of young men in England – it may even be Bunny's [David Garnett's] tragedy. I think it was Ruskin's and men like him. – Now tell me if I haven't worked out my theme, like life, but always my theme. (477)

To do this Lawrence had to draw on all his experience, not just the triangle of himself, his mother and Jessie.

The form he now had in mind for the novel was that the mother would function as stable centre, pivot, source of vitality and standards of normality and wholeness. (It had not yet occurred to Lawrence that she too might belong to the class of destructive women.) Paul would be baptized into life by her. As a young man he would begin to move away from her, but would keep her standards to prevent him from throwing himself away as his elder brother had done. He has two relationships, one with a dreaming or spiritual woman, one with a passionately physical woman. Neither proves satisfying in the long run because neither meets the standard of wholeness set by the mother. The physical relationship is good as far as it goes, but limited; the spiritual relationship is deadly. That, presumably (the manuscript of this intermediate version has not survived), is the form the novel still took when Lawrence met Frieda Weekley in March 1912.

At Walbrol in May, waiting for Frieda to join him to begin their life together, he revised the novel, and on 9 June sent it to Heinemann. Edward Garnett, already Lawrence's friend and adviser, was a reader for Heinemann. Lawrence knew the novel was too long, and offered to make what alterations Garnett suggested. Garnett sent detailed notes. Frieda made more radical criticisms. In September 1952 she wrote to Garnett:

> I think L. quite missed the point in *Paul Morel*. He really loved his mother more than anybody, even with his other women, real love, sort of Oedipus; his mother must have been adorable. He is writing P.M. again, reads bits of it to me and we fight like blazes over it, he is so often beside the point. (449)

Elsewhere she recorded:

> Towards the end of *Sons and Lovers*, I got fed up and turned against all this 'house of Atreus' feeling, and I wrote a skit called: 'Paul Morel, or His Mother's Darling'. He read it and said, coldly: 'This kind of thing isn't called a skit'.[10]

The rewriting took from the end of July to the middle of November. In the absence of manuscript evidence, we can only deduce what changes it contained.

The point that Lawrence had missed, according to Frieda, was that the relationship between Paul and his mother was psychologically unhealthy; a classic case of what Freud had called the Oedipus complex. Lawrence had probably never heard of Freud, but Frieda and her sisters had long been

[10] Frieda Lawrence, *op. cit.,* 74.

familiar with some of the leading psychologists of central Europe. Indeed Frieda had been the mistress of Otto Gross, a disciple of Freud. Lawrence's acknowledgement of the truth of Frieda's analysis was registered in his decision, in October 1912, to change the name of the novel from *Paul Morel* to *Sons and Lovers*.

On 19 November Lawrence sent Garnett his well-known synopsis of the novel:

> It follows this idea: a woman of character and refinement goes into the lower class, and has no satisfaction in her life. She has had a passion for her husband, so the children are born of passion, and have heaps of vitality. But as her sons grow up, she selects them as lovers — first the eldest, then the second. These sons are urged into life by their reciprocal love of their mother — urged on and on. But when they come into manhood, they can't love, because their mother is the strongest power in their lives, and holds them. As soon as the young men come into contact with women, there's a split. William gives his sex to a fribble, and his mother holds his soul. But the split kills him, because he doesn't know where he is. The next son gets a woman who fights for his soul — fights his mother. The son loves the mother — all the sons hate and are jealous of the father. The battle goes on between the mother and the girl, with the son as object. The mother gradually proves the stronger, because of the tie of blood. The son decides to leave his soul in his mother's hands and, like his elder brother, go for passion. He gets passion. Then the split begins to tell again. But, almost unconsciously, the mother realizes what is the matter, and begins to die. The son casts off his mistress to attend to his mother dying. He is left at the end naked of everything, with the drift towards death. (*1L* 476-7)

As several critics have pointed out, this does not describe the novel we actually have; rather, the novel Lawrence would have written had he begun again at this moment. But Lawrence's insights had come too late to allow him to reshape *Sons and Lovers* in terms of them. He would have had to start all over again. But, at the outset of his marriage and his career, penniless, he was not in a position to jettison all the work he had already put into the novel.

In January 1913 Lawrence wrote:

> The old son-lover was Oedipus. The name of the new one is legion. And if a son-lover take a wife, then is she not his wife, she is only his bed. And his life will be torn in twain, and his wife in her despair shall hope for sons, that she may have her lover in her hour. (*SL* 473)

That same month he wrote *The Daughter-in-Law* which dramatizes that very situation with an objectivity far beyond the novel. In the 'Parent Love' chapter of *Fantasia of the Unconscious* Lawrence summed up his mature position:

> The son gets on swimmingly for a time, till he is faced with the actual fact of sex necessity. He gleefully inherits his adolescence and the world at large, without an obstacle in his way, mother-supported, mother loved. Everything comes to him in glamour, he feels he sees wondrous much, understands a whole heaven, mother-stimulated. Think of the power which a mature woman thus infuses into her boy. He flares up like a flame in oxygen. No wonder they say geniuses mostly have great mothers. They mostly have sad fates. (*PU* 127)

According to Frieda, Lawrence said in later life:

> I would write a different *Sons and Lovers* now; my mother was wrong, and I thought she was absolutely right.[11]

[11] *Ibid.*, 74.

That would surely have been a lesser *Sons and Lovers* than the one we have, where, almost by accident, the mother is presented as neither absolutely right nor absolutely wrong. The version we have holds in creative tension the opposing attitudes. Lawrence's earlier love and gratitude towards his mother had not yet turned to resentment and bitterness ('all self-righteous women ought to be martyred' (Brewster 1934: 255)), though there are signs of his embryonic awareness that she had damaged him, broken his father, given Jessie no chance. The relationship between Paul Morel and his mother is not rendered uncritically, but is not distorted to make it fit a crude psychological theory; it is immediate and authentic and true to the essential paradox of all mother-son relationships.

On 19 November Lawrence sent off what he took to be the final version of the novel to Garnett. He had slaved 'like a Turk' at it, and felt that he had made it 'heaps better – a million times' (*1L* 466): 'I want to defend it, quick. I wrote it again, pruning it and shaping it and filling it in. I tell you it has got form – form: haven't I made it patiently, out of sweat as well as blood' (476). But Garnett was still not satisfied. He saw that it still needed extensive cutting, not only because it was too long to suit the publishers, but because there were still many passages of irrelevant, slack, sometimes embarrassingly bad writing. Apparently his letter to Lawrence pulled no punches, for Lawrence replied:

> I sit in sadness and grief after your letter. I daren't say anything. All right, take out what you think necessary – suppose I shall see what you've done when the proofs come, at any rate. I'm sorry I've let you in for such a job – but don't scold me too hard, it makes me wither up. (481)

Lawrence had by this time had enough of *Sons and Lovers*. He was anxious to write FINIS under that part of his life it represented, and to embark on new work, either his semi-autobiographical novel to be based on the life of Robert

Burns, or *The Insurrection of Miss Houghton*, his return to the story of Flossie Cullen. Thus he was glad to be able to leave to Garnett such `pedgilling' work as still needed to be done on the *Sons and Lovers* manuscript.

Garnett removed about a tenth of the novel. He did his work very skilfully, as can be seen from the California facsimile of the manuscript. In his introduction to that facsimile edition, Mark Schorer writes:

> Every deletion that Garnett made seems to me to have been to the novel's advantage. Nothing important is lost, ineptitudes disappear, and the novel emerges as tighter and more smoothly paced than it would otherwise have been. A final interesting fact about these deleted passages, a fact that suggests that they were indeed extraneous, is that they could simply be lifted out, almost never involving Lawrence in the necessity of writing in little transitional bridges.[12]

Garnett was not in any way censoring the novel. Of the seventy-odd cuts he made, only one can have had anything to do with propriety. Much of the deleted material is about Paul's insufferable elder brother William – his athletic prowess, his irresistible knees (in a kilt), and the succession of 'brazen hussies' who are 'gone on him'. There are also several passages where Lawrence tells us again and again in almost identical terms why Paul cannot kiss Miriam. These passages had been much revised by Lawrence himself without making much difference, as though he were nervously picking at a sore.

When Lawrence saw the proofs, he wrote to Garnett:

> You did the pruning jolly well, and I am grateful. I hope you'll live a very long time, to barber up my novels for me

[12] Mark Schorer (ed.), *Sons and Lovers: A Facsimile of the Manuscript.* (Berkeley, Los Angeles, London: University of California Press.1977), 9.

> before they're published. I wish I were not so profuse – or prolix. (*1L* 517)

He did not restore any of Garnett's cuts. He dedicated the novel to Garnett. When he received his first copy on 19 May 1913 he was 'fearfully proud' of it, and wrote to Garnett: 'Thanks a hundred times'(551). He was soon to leave Garnett behind, as he left behind every other critic except Frieda, but he could hardly have found a better barber for *Sons and Lovers*.

Sons and Lovers was published on 29 May 1913. The Lawrences were living in Germany at the time. A friend sent Lawrence an unsigned review from *Standard*, which was so favourable that Lawrence thought it must be by Garnett:

> In description of incident, even more than in revelation of character, Mr. Lawrence shows that he is a master, and in reading his book we feared always to miss a line containing the touch which shows the mark of genius and inspiration as distinct from that of talent and invention. No other English novelist of our time has so great a power to translate passion into words, but that is neither the beginning nor end of his art.[13]

Garnett did not in fact review the book, but published his assessment of it in 1916, where he compared it as a family epic and social history with Balzac and Flaubert:

> This novel is really the only one of any breadth of vision in contemporary English fiction that lifts working-class life out of middle-class hands, and restores it to its native atmosphere of hard veracity. (*Ibid.*, 117)

In mid-June the Lawrences returned to England and went straight to Garnett's house, the Cearne, in Kent. There,

[13] R.P. Draper (ed.), *D. H. Lawrence: The Critical Heritage.* (London: Routledge and Keegan Paul, 1970), 58.

waiting for Lawrence, was a batch of reviews which delighted him. *The Standard* was by no means alone in acclaiming him as a major writer. Nearly all the reviewers recognized and praised the sincerity, authenticity, vividness and vitality of the novel. There was almost universal admiration for Lawrence's rendering of the early married life of the Morels. Several reviewers felt that Lawrence had succeeded in making the mother admirable without being always likeable. The father, too, they recognized, escaped easy judgements. *The Nation* reviewer commented perceptively: 'Our sympathy with the sentimental, violent miner-husband is deeper than (we imagine) it was intended to be' (70). Lascelles Abercrombie concluded his review in the *Manchester Guardian:*

> Life, for Mr. Lawrence, is a coin which has both obverse and reverse; so it is for most people, but his unusual art consists in his surprising ability to illuminate both sides simultaneously. The scope and variety of the life he describes, his understanding and vivid realizing of circumstances and his insights into character, and chiefly his power of lighting a train of ordinary events to blaze up into singular significance, make *Sons and Lovers* stand out from the fiction of the day as an achievement of the first quality. (68)

Some reviewers detected a falling away in the novel as it begins to be about Paul and his sexual problems. *The Westminster Gazette* reviewer thought it would have been a better novel if Lawrence had 'been able to keep the whole of his story within the bounds of Mrs. Morel's experience'. He found 'an implicit acquiescence in Paul's super-human selfishness in his relations with the two women whom he tries to love' (60). Harold Massingham in the *Daily Chronicle* thought that 'Paul can never get far enough away from his creator to solidify into a self-sufficient person' (63). Several reviewers complained at the lack of plot or obvious formal shaping; but the *Nation* reviewer saw the lack of plot as an advantage: 'How would a "plot" have torn through this fine web of poetry, realism, and shrewd or tender analysis!' (69), while others, though feeling that they ought by all the rules to be bored, admitted that they were not, but could not account for what held them and gave the book its coherence except by vague gestures towards something 'poetic'. Some meant by this word simply that the novel had lyrical passages or passages of 'high' style which to us now seem merely pretentious. But some were clearly groping towards some expression of the way in which they felt Lawrence was able to handle apparently realistic scenes in such a way that they acquire a resonance and significance far beyond mere scene-painting. Apparently the word 'symbolism' had not yet entered the vocabulary of novel-reviewers.

The presence in this novel of a number of inarticulate, taciturn, or paralysingly self-conscious characters meant that there were severe limits on what could be conveyed by dialogue. A stream of authorial commentary would have deprived the novel of all objectivity. Lawrence therefore developed what was to become, in *The Rainbow*, his characteristic stylistic device, the organic symbol. He creates numerous scenes and incidents which are perfectly natural and appropriate and convincing on the surface, but are rendered in such terms that, without our realizing it, they reverberate, open out into larger significance, link up with other such symbols to provide a matrix which is both a formal grid for the novel and also a source for its value judgements. I am thinking of such scenes as the night-communion, when Mrs. Morel, pregnant with Paul, looks out into the rich world he is to enter:

> The night was very large, and very strange, stretching its hoary distances infinitely. And out of the silver-grey fog of darkness came sounds vague and hoarse: a corncrake not far off, sound of a train like a sigh, and distant shouts of men. (*SL* 35)

She returns to the house with a blessing of pollen on her face. Other symbolic moments are the scene with Paul and Miriam on the swing, which prefigures so much of what follows, and the description of Paul and Clara making love by the Trent in flood. It is there in the use of colours (especially golden), flowers, bird-songs. In comparison with *The Rainbow* Lawrence's use of this method is perhaps sketchy here, but it makes an important contribution to the transformation of autobiography into art.

[The views I expressed here on Garnett's deletions were subsequently modified. I came to feel that the loss of this material changed the nature of the novel away from the more general issue announced by its title, towards the merely autobiographical.]

Introduction to *The Complete Short Novels*

First published in D. H. Lawrence, The Complete Short Novels *(Harmondsworth: Penguin, 1982).*

Having married another Lawrence specialist, Melissa Partridge, in 1981, I suggested to her that we should edit The Complete Short Novels together, allocating her the earlier tales and myself the much juicier later ones.

Lawrence's discovery of the short novel form in 1921 seems to me to have been disastrous for his art. In a short story there is little room for anything but story-telling. In a full-length novel there are checks and balances, the obligation to pay one's debts to reality. But the short novel form enabled Lawrence to conceive stories as mere vehicles for his current ideas – ideas which were, at that particular phase of his life, misanthropic and desperate – or, in the case of 'The Ladybird', the merest wish-fulfilment, arrogating to himself in his fictional underworld the power he had so completely failed to achieve in the real world, with a surrogate Lady Cynthia Asquith as his resistless bride in place of the all too resistant Frieda. The 1921 novelettes are doctrinaire, ruthless, and humanly thin, by Lawrence's own best standards.

The phase of Lawrence's belief in leadership, male supremacy, and the sexually passive role of women lasted from the end of the war until about 1924. It reached its culmination in *The Plumed Serpent*, the first version of which was written in the early summer of 1923, where Lawrence attempted to develop those ideas into a full-blown religious and political system preached by Don Ramon Carrasco, Lawrence's representative in the novel: 'I do believe what Ramon means – for all of us' (Lawrence 1989: 318).

In the second version of the novel, however, written at the end of 1924 and beginning of 1925, we find many hints of reservations and scepticism which, the following year, were to grow into a repudiation of Don Ramon (and with him

Hepburn, Henry and Count Dionys):

> The hero is obsolete, and the leader of men is a back number. After all, at the back of the hero is the militant ideal: and the militant ideal, or the ideal militant, seems to me also a cold egg. We're sort of sick of all forms of militarism and militantism... The leader-cum-follower relationship is a bore. And the new relationship will be some sort of tenderness, sensitive, between men and men and men and women, and not the one up one down, lead on I follow, ich dien sort of business. (*6L* 321).

***

Lawrence returned to the short novel form in the summer 1924 (that is, between the two drafts of *The Plumed Serpent*), at his ranch in New Mexico, to write *St Mawr* and 'The Princess'. Fortunately, having got his 'hero' theme out of his system in *The Plumed Serpent*, he felt free to take up other themes in these stories. *St Mawr* is about a woman who does not meet a man capable of transforming her life, but who manages, nevertheless, to bring about its transformation, with the help of first a horse, then a landscape. No other Lawrence heroine is denied her saving man. Lou's phrase 'since the mystic new man will never come to me' gives her story a dimension lacking in all those where Lawrence is able to take the easy option of resolving his heroine's problems by producing a 'mystic new man' for her out of his hat. Here, for the only time in his major fiction, Lawrence denies himself the opportunity to approach his religious vision of the truly human and therefore truly religious life – through sexual metaphor.

Lou Carrington, like so many Lawrence heroines, is living in a world so empty, false and trivial that she cannot believe it is real. It can only be a bad dream from which she waits to be woken. The style of the opening is ironic, flippant, undercutting, its life all on the surface. The arrival of St Mawr changes everything. He seems to inhabit a different world and cannot be accommodated in Rico's world of 'attitude'. To describe him, a language other than that appropriate to Rico is demanded of Lawrence, a highly charged poetic language which erupts through the brittle irony:

> She could not bear the triviality and superficiality of her human relationships. Looming like some god out of the darkness was the head of that horse, with the wide, terrible, questioning eyes. And she felt that it forbade her to be her ordinary, commonplace self. It forbade her to be just Rico's wife, young Lady Carrington, and all that. (*SM* 31)

The questions St Mawr silently asks her are: 'What is real?' and 'Are you alive?' and 'What in you can answer to my horseness?' He challenges her to meet him half-way – 'half-way across from our human world to that terrific equine twilight'. St Mawr's role in the story is exactly that of Evangelist in Pilgrim's Progress, who awakens Christian to the realization that he inhabits the city of destruction, strengthens his resolve to sever all the ties which bind him to it, and shows him the way towards the new life. Once Christian has begun his spiritual journey, Evangelist's role is done, and we hear no more of him. Lawrence, too, uses the archetypal myth of the spiritual journey, and once Lou is embarked upon it, St Mawr can lapse back into being an ordinary horse, rather than a messenger from the gods.

Why should Lawrence cast a splendid and dangerous stallion in the role of Evangelist? The image of Major Thomas Philip Barber, the local coal-owner, making his horse's mouth bleed as he forced it to stand at Moorgreen crossing while a colliery engine clanked past, had imprinted itself on Lawrence's imagination as a child, so that horse and rider became for him a symbol of the human will bullying the body, or the instincts, or the life of nature, long before he knew what a symbol was. The Bible confirmed the symbol:

'Be ye not as the horse, or as the mule, which have no understanding: whose mouth must be held in with bit and bridle'.[1] His early acquaintance with Plato's dialogues would have given him the same symbol developed into an allegory of the soul as charioteer (intellect) driving a team of horses, one white and compliant (spirit), the other black and hardly to be controlled (passion). There comes a point where the black horse, long frustrated and reined in, 'takes the bit between his teeth and pulls shamelessly':

> The driver, however, experiences even more intensely what he experienced before; he falls back like a racing charioteer at the barrier, and with a still more violent backward pull, jerks the bit from between the teeth of the lustful horse, drenches his abusive tongue and jaws with blood, and forcing his legs and haunches against the ground reduces him to torment.[2]

His acquaintance, through Frieda, with the work of European psychologists no doubt gave Lawrence further understanding of horse symbolism. There is no space here to survey the rich use he made of it in *The Rainbow* and *Women in Love*. Certainly he already knew much of what he was to read in Jung's *Psychology of the Unconscious* in 1918:

> Legend attributes properties to the horse which psychologically belong to the unconscious of man: there are clairvoyant and clairaudient horses, path finding horses who show the way when the wanderer is lost, horses with mantic powers ... Horses also see ghosts. All these things are typical manifestations of the unconscious. We can therefore see why the horse, as a symbol of the animal component in man, has numerous connections with the devil ... The sexual nature of the devil is imparted

[1] Psalms xxxii, 9.
[2] Plato, *Phaedrus* (Harmondsworth: Penguin, 1973), 63.

> to the horse as well, so that this symbol is found in contexts where the sexual interpretation is the only one that fits ... Lightning, too, is represented theriomorphically as a horse.[3]

The first version of Lawrence's essay on Fenimore Cooper's Anglo-American novels was published in February 1919. Here Lawrence writes:

> It is quite certain that the pre-Christian priesthoods understood the process of *dynamic* consciousness, which is pre-cerebral consciousness. It is certain that St John gives us in the Apocalypse a cypher-account of the process of the conquest of the lower or sensual dynamic centres by the upper or spiritual dynamic consciousness (*SCAL* 205).

One of the most important cyphers in that account is the horse. It was probably his reading of this essay which prompted Frederic Carter to write to Lawrence about his own work, in December 1922, and to send him, the following April, a manuscript of his unpublished *Dragon of the Alchemists*. On his next visit to England Lawrence spent two days, 3-5 January 1924, visiting Carter at Pontesbury in Shropshire, discussing Apocalyptic symbols, including the four horsemen, and walking several miles into the hills:

> Lawrence liked the name – the Devil's Chair – for the stone on which we stood. And there we talked of the great hilltop rocks with similar names that are found all over Europe as seats of the changeful gods.[4]

[3] Carl Jung, *Psychology of the unconscious*, now called *Symbols of Transformation* (London: Routledge and Kegan Paul, 1952).
[4] Frederick Carter, *D. H. Lawrence and the body mystical* (London: Denis Archer, 1932), 40.

Whether or not Lawrence had already conceived *St Mawr*, this landscape, the place-names, the house in the churchyard looking over gravestones, the good-natured curate, and Carter himself, all were fixed in his memory and ready for use in the novel.

A week later Lawrence wrote his 'London Letter' to Spud Johnson for the periodical *The Laughing Horse*. Here Lawrence associates the horse with the centaur and with Pan, dead in Europe, but alive and kicking in the blue air of the Rockies:

> In modern symbolism, the Horse is supposed to stand for the passions. Passions be blowed. What does the Centaur stand for, Chiron in any other of that quondam four-footed gentry? Sense! Horse-sense! Sound, powerful, four-footed sense, that's what the Horse stands for. Horse-sense, I tell you. That's the Centaur. That's the blue Horse of the ancient Mediterranean, before the pale Galilean or the extra-pale German or Nordic gentleman conquered. First of all, Sense, Good Sense, Sound Sense, Horse Sense. And then, a laugh, a loud, sensible. Horse Laugh. After that, these same passions, glossy and dangerous in the flanks. And after these again, hoofs, irresistible, splintering hoofs, that can kick the walls of the world down. (*MM* 138)

In March Lawrence escaped from the 'dreadful mummy sarcophagus of Europe' back to New Mexico, where he knew the horse in us was not dead:

> In Lobo, in Taos, in Santa Fe the Turquoise Horse is waving snow out of his tail, and trotting gaily to the blue mountains of the far distance, And in Mexico his mane is bright yellow on his blue body, so streaming, with sun, and he's lashing out again like the devil, till his hoofs are red. (*Ibid.*)

In May the Lawrences moved two thousand feet higher up Lobo mountain to a new ranch, which Lawrence described to his niece:

> Forty years ago a man came out looking for gold, and staked here. There was some gold in the mountains. Then he got poor, and a man called McClure had the place. He had 500 white goats here, raised alfalfa, and let his goats feed wild in the mountains. But the water supply is too bad, and we are too far from anywhere. So he gave up ... So we leave the ranch quite wild — only there's abundant feed for the five horses. And if we wanted to take the trouble, we could bring the water here as McClure did, and have a little farm. … If we ride two miles, we can get no farther. Beyond, all savage, unbroken mountains. … We went to get Frieda's grey horse – the Azul – shod. They call him in Spanish el Azul – the Blue….I want a Mexican to come and live here while we are away, to keep the place from going wild, squirrels and bushy-tailed pack-rats from coming in, and to see the water doesn't freeze for the horses. (*5L* 110-11)

The first thing Lawrence wrote at the new ranch was 'Pan in America'. Here he defines his pantheism as 'a vivid relatedness between the man and the living universe that surrounds him' (*MM* 160):

> The contact between all things is keen and wary: for wariness is also a sort of reverence or respect. And nothing, in the world of Pan, may be taken for granted. (164)

There was indeed real danger up there. Three horses on the neighbouring ranch were killed by lightning.

There was much work to be done at the ranch that summer, but Lawrence found time in June to write 'The Woman Who Rode Away' and, in July and August, *St Mawr*.

It can be seen from this skeletal account of the genesis of *St Mawr* how the horse came to focus so many of Lawrence's deepest and most lasting preoccupations; how, with a minimum of overt reference to mythology or psychology or any abstract ideas imported from outside the novel, rather through vivid scenes and through the perfect control of evocative language, Lawrence is able to endow his stallion with such a range and depth of significance. Yet this account of the genesis of the novel has left out a whole cluster of themes every bit as central to it. It is a measure of the complexity of the story, not as story but as pattern of meanings, that its genesis could be described convincingly in terms which have nothing to do with horses.

Lawrence had always been highly ambivalent about the monastic ideal, which fascinated him. Despite his allegiance to the body, he led a relatively ascetic life, and his hatred of the human world often led him to explore various possibilities of withdrawal from it. On 31 July 1915, thanking Viola Meynell for the loan of her cottage at Greatham, he had written:

> I feel as if I had been born afresh there, got a new, sure, separate soul: as a monk in a monastery, or St John in the wilderness. Now we must go back into the world to fight. We must set about cleaning the face of the earth a bit, or everything will perish (*2L*: 374).

A year later he wrote:

> I have been reading St Bernard's *Letters,* and I realize that the greatest thing the world has seen, is Christianity. (633)

Throughout this period Lawrence consistently thought of his projected ideal community – Rananim – as overtly monastic. By 1917 he was already locating it in the American west:

> And what I want is for us to have sufficient to go far west, to California or the South Seas, and live apart, away from the world. I hope in the end other people will come, and we can be a little community, a monastery, a school – a little Hesperides of the soul and body (*3L* 70).

This recurrent imagery of monasticism was brought into clear focus for Lawrence by his visit to an actual monastery, the Abbey of Monte Cassino, the birthplace of European monasticism, in February 1920. Lawrence's account of that visit, in his introduction to the Maurice Magnus memoirs, reveals how closely his response to the monastic ideal was bound up with his sense of the past and of the spirit of place: 'That hill-top must have been one of man's intense sacred places for three thousand years' (Lawrence 1968: 326).

As soon as Lawrence arrived in Taos in 1922, the Indian pueblo affected him 'like one of the old monasteries': here he recognized another of those 'choice spots of the earth, where the spirit dwelt'. It reminded him of what happened in Europe in the Dark Ages:

> Then those whose souls were still alive withdrew together and gradually built monasteries and convents, little communities of quiet labour and courage, isolated, helpless, and yet never overcome in a world flooded with devastation, these alone kept the human spirit from disintegration, from going quite dark, in the Dark Ages. (*IR* 34)

In January 1924, in the essay 'Books', Lawrence returned to the theme:

> The flood of barbarism rose and covered Europe from end to end. But, bless your life, there was Noah in his Ark with the animals. There was young Christianity. There were the lonely fortified monasteries, like little arks floating and keeping the adventure afloat. There is no

> break in the great adventure in consciousness. Throughout the howlingest deluge, some few brave souls are steering the ark under the rainbow ... But now I live in 1924, and the Christian venture is done. The adventure is gone out of Christianity. We must start on a new venture towards God. (*RDP* 199-200)

Lou in *St Mawr* starts out on just such a new venture. In 1922 Lawrence had written:

> I think one must for the moment withdraw from the world, away towards the inner realities that are real: and return, maybe, to the world later, when one is quiet and sure (*4L* 175).

In the New Mexico Rockies Lou is face to face with those realities. They are not wholly beautiful. If Lou allows herself to be dazzled by the glamour, she will be crushed like the New England woman before her. They are also sordid and destructive: 'The gods of those inner mountains were grim and invidious and relentless, huger than man, and lower than man'. You do not serve these gods and expect them to love you. You fight them 'to win from the crude, wild nature the victory and the power to make another start'. (*SM* 150-1)

Lawrence's new venture, in which Lou is his and our representative, is in a sense a return to paganism, or more particularly, Pantheism. His primary effort, from now on, is to resanctify the world, to reawaken in his readers their long-lost power to recognize and respond appropriately to the sacred in themselves and the living environment on which they totally depend. It was a Herculean undertaking in 1924, when nature seemed to be disappearing under 'the century-deep deposits of layer upon layer of refuse: even of tin cans'; when the machine seemed to have triumphed utterly; when H. G. Wells and the vast majority for whom he spoke could complacently and arrogantly assume that history was man's progress towards the triumph of 'mind' over both nature and human nature. Pantheism, at that time, had come to mean nothing more than the Wordsworthian pieties. It was not a serious option as a religion for the twentieth century. Lawrence took it upon himself to make it so; not just an option, but a necessity for sanity and survival.

Up to this time, Lawrence's thinking had been thoroughly dualistic. He had been torn by contradictory impulses and mutually exclusive needs. In 'The Crown' he saw all creation in the image of the lion of the body (Plato's black horse) and the unicorn of the spirit (Plato's white horse) fighting for the crown of life, never to be reconciled. He could not at that time have reconciled in himself that which identified itself with everything we have seen to attach to the image of the horse, and that which identified itself with everything attaching to the image of the monk. In a central passage in his friend E. M. Forster's novel *Howards End*, the author had spoken of 'the rainbow bridge that should connect the prose in us with the passion. Without it we are meaningless fragments, half monks, half beasts, unconnected arches that have never joined into a man'.[5] In *St Mawr* Lawrence attempts to connect and reconcile the monk and the beast in us. He finds there a perfect fictional vehicle for drawing together these two hitherto diverse currents of his thought into a single stream.

That Lawrence knew exactly what he was doing is evident in his choice of the name St Mawr for his stallion. It is a strange name for a horse. St Mawr comes from Wales, and his name is first pronounced in the story 'with a Welsh twist'. 'Mawr' in Welsh is the masculine form of the adjective meaning 'big' or `great'; but according to Dorothy Brett, who was living with the Lawrences at the time and typed out *St Mawr* page by page as Lawrence wrote it, Lawrence himself pronounced the name 'Seymour'. 'Seymour' is a common English surname which derives from the Norman French 'de

[5] E. M. Forster, *Howards End* (Harmondsworth: Penguin, 1941), 174.

St Maur'. The village of St Maur in Normandy is named after St Maur or Maurus, the disciple of St Benedict. Chaucer's monk ('a good man to horse') has no time for the traditional monastic life: 'The Rule of good St Benet or St Maur / As old and strict he tended to ignore'.[6] St Benedict, the father of western monasticism, established his great monastery at Monte Cassino in 529. The monk at Monte Cassino with whom Lawrence had become particularly friendly on his visit there in 1920, and to whom he had later sent a copy of *The Lost Girl*, was called Don Mauro Iguanez.

St Mawr represents not only the life of the body and the senses, but also the life of the spirit which modern barbarism seeks to extinguish. The whole meaning of the story is encapsulated in its title.

***

`The Princess', which Lawrence wrote immediately after *St Mawr*, is in a way its shadow or negative.

During their stay in London the previous December and January, the Lawrences had stayed with Catherine and Donald Carswell, whom they had met before the war. Catherine told Lawrence of a novel she had in mind:

> The theme had been suggested to me by reading of some savages who took a baby girl, and that they might rear her into a goddess for themselves, brought her up on a covered river boat, tending her in all respects, but never letting her mix with her kind and leading her to believe that she was herself no mortal, but a goddess.[7]

[6] Geoffrey Chaucer, *The Canterbury Tales* (Harmondsworth: Penguin, 1951), 30.

[7] Catherine Carswell, *The savage pilgrimage* (London: Chatto and Windus, 1932), 201.

Lawrence was fired by the idea, and offered to collaborate. Indeed, he sketched an outline the same day. Catherine felt inadequate, and left the story to Lawrence, who later completed it as 'The Princess'.

According to his original outline, Lawrence had at first intended to begin with the story of the girl's parents – material he later dropped. After the death of the mother, leaving a baby girl, the outline continues:

> Then it seems to him [the father] the mother was not mortal. She was a mysterious woman from the faery, and the child, he secretly believes, is one of the Tuatha De Danaan.[8] This idea he gradually inculcates into the people round him, and into the child herself. It steals over them all gradually, almost unawares.The girl accepts from the start a difference between herself and the rest of people. She does not feel quite mortal. Men are only men to her: she is of another race, the Tuatha De Danaan. She doesn't talk about it: nobody talks about it. But there it is, tacit, accepted. Her father hires a poor scholar to be her tutor, and she has an ordinary education. But she has no real friends. There is no one of her race. Sometimes she goes

[8] 'In the epics of ancient Ireland, the Celtic warrior kings and their brilliant chariot fighters move in a landscape beset with invisible fairy forts, wherein abide a race of beings of an earlier mythological age: the wonderful Tuatha De Danaan, children of the Goddess Dana, who retired, when defeated, into wizard hills of glass. And these are the very people of the *sidhe* or Shee, the Fairy Host, the Fairy Cavalcade, of the Irish peasantry to this day. "Who are they?" asks the poet Yeats. And he gives a trilogy of answers: "Fallen angels who were not good enough to be saved, nor bad enough to be lost," say the peasantry. "The gods of the earth," says the Book of Armagh. "The gods of pagan Ireland," say the antiquarians, "the Tuatha De Danan, who, when no longer worshipped and fed with offerings, dwindled away in the popular imagination, and now are only a few spans high." [Campbell (1974), 40-41].

> to Glasgow, to Edinburgh, to London with her father. The world interests her, but she doesn't belong to it. She is a little afraid of it. It is not of her race.
>
> When she is seventeen her father is suddenly killed, and she is alone, save for her tutor. She has an income of about three hundred a year. She decides to go to London. The war has broken out – she becomes a nurse. She nurses men, and knows their wounds and their necessities. But she tends them as if they were lambs or other delicate and lovable animals. Their blood is not her blood, their needs are not the needs of her race.
>
> Men fall in love with her, and that is terrible to her. She is waiting for one of her own race. Her tutor supports her in the myth. Wait, he says, wait for the Tuatha De Danaan to send you your mate. You can't mate with a man. Wait till you see a demon between his brows.
>
> At last she saw him in the street. She knew him at once, knew the demon between his brows. And she was afraid. For the first time in her life, she was afraid of her own nature, the mystery of herself. Because it seemed to her that her race, the Tuatha, had come back to destroy the race of men. She was terrified of her own destiny. She wanted never again to see the man with the demon between his brows.
>
> So for a long time she did not see him again. And then her fear that she would never see him any more was deeper than anything else. Whatever she wanted, she wanted her own destiny with him, let happen what might. (*Ibid.*, 203-4)

It is not at all clear from this outline whether the woman's destiny is to be an escape into a more real world, 'the man with the demon between his brows' being the 'mystic new man' who will perform for her the function performed for Lou by St Mawr, or whether it is to be suicidal, like that of the Princess or the woman who rode away. Certainly, the other world from which St Mawr is a messenger could easily have been linked to that of the Tuatha De Danaan, the pre-Christian nature deities of Ireland, as it is linked by Lewis to Celtic folklore. The outline could have gone either way, towards rebirth or madness.

In August 1924 Lawrence was away for ten days on his trip to see the Hopi Snake Dance. During his absence a neighbour, Bill Hawk, took Brett riding much further into the mountains behind the ranch than she or Lawrence had ever been. On his return Lawrence needed little persuading to make the same journey, with Brett and Rachel Hawk. Brett records the trip with great enthusiasm:

> We reach a flat spot and dismount. Around and about us are the mountain ridges, running hither and thither in wild, strange lines. It is immense and fierce and dynamic. The pink and white rocks of Red River shine across the valley; and below, far below in the valley, lies a tiny green lake, blue green and dark: Columbine Lake, round which the drama of your story 'The Princess' is written.[9]

It seems not to have occurred to Brett how much of herself Lawrence had put into the character of his princess, brilliantly fusing what he knew of Brett's life with the princess he had inherited from Catherine Carswell. It was the identification with Brett which determined the final negative outcome.

Thus Catherine Carswell's story could be seen as the germ of all three stories Lawrence wrote in the summer of 1924. In Lou Carrington it is given its most positive development. Her sense of what makes her different from other people is her sanity, her openness to life, her deep need for a meaningful relationship with the living universe. But the story itself is open to life: we cannot predict what will happen to Lou. In a sense, however, the very fact that she has answered the call is her salvation, although Lawrence was well aware of the

[9] Dorothy Brett, *Lawrence and Brett: a friendship* (Santa Fe: Sunstone Press, 1974) 151.

dangers of cutting oneself off from one's fellow men and retiring to some wilderness place. It could be escapist. It could be a temptation to egotism, narcissism or solipsism; a way of closing oneself to life until one becomes a sealed monad and goes mad like the Princess, or dies of it like the man who loved islands.

***

In September 1925, Lawrence left America for the last time, to spend the remaining five years of his life in Europe. At last he was reconciled with Frieda's daughters. Barby, in particular, stayed often with the Lawrences in Spotorno, and told Lawrence many stories of her life in the Weekley household. In January 1926 he wrote *The Virgin and the Gipsy*, based largely on those stories.

The Virgin and the Gipsy is more like a conventional novel than the other short novels, full of 'characters', family and social relationships presented in 'scenes', and moral judgement evinced through a finely modulated ironic tone, like a more direct, barbed and colloquial Jane Austen. The mode is realistic, with no dominant symbol, emblem or myth, except insofar as the gipsy himself may be regarded as a symbol. Indeed, he functions on two levels, like St Mawr. He is a real gipsy, hawking his brooms, saucepans and copperware, with several brats to maintain; but for Yvette he is much more than that, much more than any mere man. He is messenger from a world free from all the stifling hypocrisies of her home, class and religion, a projection of her hope of a fulfilled life as a woman free from guilt. Having given her the courage to assert her independent womanhood, he reverts to being just the semi-literate Joe Boswell.

The integrity of the story can be measured by the extent to which it does not fulfil the expectations aroused by its perhaps unfortunate title. The relationship between virgin and gipsy never becomes overtly sexual. We do not know, and it does not matter, whether at the end she is still a virgin or not. Nor is the gipsy blown up to figure as a 'mystic new man', a man with a demon between his brows or a noble savage, except to a slight degree in Yvette's adolescent imagination. Lawrence beautifully captures that phase of a girl's life – the infuriating selfishness, the sulks and outbursts of revolt, the general vagueness and wryly romantic longings.

Again, the ending is open. It is unlikely Yvette will ever see her gipsy again; certainly she pins no hopes upon him. There is no doubt much conflict and suffering ahead for her; but she has found the courage to live her own life, and is unlikely to let go of that.

***

Lawrence had for several years been fascinated by the Etruscans. In March 1927, in the company of his American Buddhist friend Earl Brewster, he undertook a tour of several of he major Etruscan sites, ending at Volterra on Easter Sunday, 10 April:

> I was really happy looking at Etruscan tombs by the coast north of Rome – Cerveteri, Tarquinia etc. No rush there! Even the ass brays slowly and leisurely, and the tombs are far more twinkling and alive than he houses of men. (*6L* 28)

He returned home to the Villa Mirenda, near Florence, but not to write *Etruscan Places*. What he wrote first was 'a story of the Resurrection – what sort of a man "rose up", after all that other pretty little experience' (40). Earl Brewster recalled:

> My memory is that Easter morning found us at Grosseto [in fact Volterra]: there we passed a little shop, in the window of which was toy rooster escaping from an egg. I remarked that it suggested a title – *The Escaped Cock* – a story of the Resurrection. Lawrence replied that he had been thinking about writing a story of the Resurrection.[10]

[10] Brewster, *op. cit.,* 124.

Thus *The Escaped Cock* is a direct product of Lawrence's Etruscan experience. In the tombs the egg was also a frequent resurrection symbol. The man who has died 'holds up the egg of resurrection, within which the germ sleeps as the soul sleep in the tomb, before it breaks the shell and emerges again' (*SEP* 53). The shell, in Lawrence's interpretation, is the old dead life, hardened into habit and egotism. The 'germ' which emerges is 'the soul itself, the conscious spark of every creature' (63). It is also life itself, inextinguishable, 'the fiery spark of procreation' (60). Resurrection for Lawrence, is as always a metaphor for a spiritual death and rebirth, which is envisaged as a recovery, through the body, of a lost connection with everything else that lives.

The cock in Lawrence's story escapes not from a shell, but from the cord which ties him by the leg. He represents the dauntless life-urge – 'resplendent with arched and orange neck by the time the fig trees were letting out leaves from their end tips' – denied its full expression. He crows for the kingdom power and glory which is his birthright:

> Body, soul and spirit were tied by that string. Underneath, however, the life in him was grimly unbroken. It was the cord that should break. (*VG* 124)

His crow wakes the man who had died. Again, he is a messenger, crowing from the world Christ had denied, as he had denied 'the greater life of the body':

> The world, the same as ever, the natural world, thronging with greenness, a nightingale singing winsomely, wistfully, coaxingly calling from the bushes beside a runnel of water, in the world, the natural world of morning and evening, forever undying, from which he had died. (126)

The bird, herald of a new day, is already risen. The man, recognizing in the cock 'the necessity to live, and even to cry out the triumph of life', must rediscover and re-establish his connection with the phenomenal world, must learn to ride the 'wave of life of which the bird was the crest' (130). His earlier denial of that world he now sees was an evasion of the life issue, leading inevitably to the Crucifixion.

Lawrence summarized *The Escaped Cock* to Earl Brewster in these words:

> I wrote a story of the Resurrection, where Jesus gets up and feels very sick about everything, and can't stand the old crowd any more – so cuts out and as he heals up, he begins to find what an astonishing place the phenomenal world is, far more marvellous than any salvation or heaven – and thanks his stars he needn't have a 'mission' any more. (*6L* 50)

In *Etruscan Places* Lawrence takes up the contrast between the preacher and the nightingale:

> And before Buddha or Jesus spoke the nightingale sang, and long after the words of Jesus and Buddha are gone into oblivion the nightingale will sing. Because it is neither preaching nor teaching nor commanding nor urging. It is just singing. And in the beginning was not a Word, but a chirrup. (*SEP* 36)

In the story, as in the travel book, the villains are the Romans, who trample on the rose of life and burden the earth with their monuments:

> Because a fool kills a nightingale with a stone, is he therefore greater than the nightingale? Because the Roman took the life out of the Etruscan, was he therefore greater than the Etruscan? Not he! Rome fell, and the Roman phenomenon with it. (*Ibid.*)

Lawrence recognized in the Etruscans a people who 'lived their own lives, without wanting to dominate the life of others' (*6L* 33). Jesus, in his way, had wanted to dominate as much as the Romans. Both conquering and saving are forms of domination. The man who had died does not see his crucifixion as a triumph:

> My triumph is that I am not dead. I have outlived my mission and know no more of it. It is my triumph. I have survived the day and the death of my, interference, and am still a man ... The teacher and the saviour are dead in me; now I can go about my business, into my own single life ... For my reach ends in my finger-tips, and my stride is no longer than the ends of my toes. Yet I would embrace multitudes, I who have never truly embraced even one. (*VG* 132)

He is rediscovering the Etruscan insouciance. The Etruscans knew the gods 'in their very finger-tips'; they danced to the very ends of their fingers and toes; they entered into the flow of touch which comes not from pawing and laying hold, but 'from the middle of the human being' (*SEP* 54-5).

The Escaped Cock is the story of how Jesus becomes an Etruscan. At the end he is letting the current carry him, and smiling the enigmatic Etruscan smile.

Lawrence wrote only the first part of *The Escaped Cock* in the spring of 1927. It was almost a year before he had the idea of adding a second, and this was actually written in Switzerland in the summer of 1928. The cock had now fulfilled his role of messenger and pointer of the way. The challenge remaining for Lawrence was to imagine Christ's resurrection in the flesh and atonement with his own body, with woman, and with the natural world. It seems likely that Lawrence had been reading Frazer yet again. In any case, he was already familiar with *The Golden Bough,* where Frazer's accounts of the mutilation, death and resurrection of the pagan fertility gods, particularly Adonis, Attis and Osiris, cannot fail to impress the reader with their similarity to the story of Christ. Frazer himself trod warily here, but allowed himself to say that 'Christians and pagans alike were struck by the remarkable coincidence between the death and resurrection of their respective deities'.[11] Starting from this hint of Frazer's, Lawrence brilliantly saw how he could solve his problem by completing the identification of Christ with Osiris. Christ is crucified, and resurrected as a young fertility god at the hands of the priestess of Isis in Search.

It was a daring undertaking in 1928, risking blasphemy, and indeed it caused much outrage at the time. But such is the tact and sensitivity with which it is carried through that many Christians have subsequently responded warmly to it as a corrective to the tendency of orthodox Christianity to be life-denying, and to evade the implications of the phrase 'the resurrection of the body'.

It would perhaps have been an even greater challenge to Lawrence to follow his hero still further, and imagine a life for him wherever he is heading at the end. Lawrence had only six months to live, and wrote no more fiction.

[11] J. G. Frazer, *The golden bough* (London: Macmillan, 1957) 475.

D. H. Lawrence: the Man and the Artist

First published in The Modernists: Studies in a Literary Phenomenon: Essays in Honor of Harry T. Moore *(Rutherford, Madison, Teaneck: Fairleigh Dickinson University Press; London and Toronto: Associated University Presses, 1987.*

Of the many assessments of Lawrence published at the time of the fiftieth anniversary of his death in 1981, one of the best was by Philip Larkin. Larkin spoke on the assumption that 'the age of proselytizing is over. We are all Lawrence converts nowadays'. It was on that same assumption that, the previous year, I had given a talk called 'Beyond D. H. Lawrence' to a gathering of the faithful in Carbondale, Illinois. I had felt that after twenty years of preaching and praising Lawrence, it would be a salutary exercise for me, and perhaps a useful shock to the complacency of the assembled Lawrenceans, to talk, for a change, about his deficiencies and limitations, especially for us fifty years on. I did not try to put myself in the position of his enemies and detractors; indeed, I assumed that he no longer had any, not in the academic world and the informed literate public at any rate. I felt that he no longer needed to be defended, that his status as the greatest English writer of the century was assured; but that we did him no real service by idolatry, by taking him to be all-in-all sufficient and all subsequent literature supererogatory. I felt that by recognizing his weaknesses we should be better able to appreciate his strengths. That talk was, I know, a disappointment to some of those who heard it, particularly to George Zytaruk and Harry T. Moore.

A year later I knew that they were right, and Larkin and I were wrong. 'The spirit of homage and affection' in which Larkin responded to the 'sane and healthy spirit' of Lawrence was conspicuously absent elsewhere in all the thousands of words published and broadcast about Lawrence in England in 1980. There was scarcely another voice speaking up boldly for him; rather voice after voice niggling, belittling, vilifying. Instead of proselytizing, Larkin asked for a 'balanced assessment, a sorting out of the acceptable from the unacceptable'. Unfortunately, in the present state of English literary criticism, this is a recipe for just the sterile waste of trees Larkin himself obviously deplored. If criticism is to count for anything, the job of the critic is to proselytize for all he is worth on behalf of every great writer who ever lived, and there will never be a great writer who does not need to be fought for again and again, every generation, against those who, afraid to meet his challenge, deny his greatness. It was heartening to hear Henry Miller say, in an interview just before his death, that the business of the Lawrence critic is 'to love him, absorb him, and make others love him'.

Lawrence's enemies are still numerous, perhaps even still a majority in the literary establishment. They kept a low profile in the sixties and seventies. Perhaps the death of F R. Leavis gave them the courage to come into the open again. The phenomenon forced me into some radical new thinking, not only about Lawrence, but also about the teaching of literature in our universities, the business of criticism, the nature of the creative imagination, and the purpose of literature. Some of my first thoughts went into the essay that follows, intended as a counterweight to 'Beyond D. H Lawrence'. I hoped that Harry Moore would read it and approve. At least he heard a little of it in Santa Fe in 1980, the last time I saw him. But perhaps, as Lawrence said, 'The dead don't die. They look on and help'.

'Lawrence the Man'– the phrase carries the implication, 'as opposed to Lawrence the Artist'. Yet in fact no such distinction is possible. If T. S. Eliot is right in his claim that 'the more perfect the artist, the more completely separate in him will be the man who suffers and the mind which creates',[1] then Lawrence is a most imperfect artist, yet in good company, as, by the same criterion, Eliot judges *Hamlet* to be an artistic failure. Lawrence created directly out of his living, and his work draws its vitality directly from his engagement with life. All his works are attempts to tell the truth about life as he was currently experiencing it.

Lawrence met, and dismissed, the Eliotic position early, in the works of Flaubert and Thomas Mann. In his essay on Mann he wrote:

[1] T. S. Eliot, *Selected Essays* (London: Faber, 1951) 18.

> He has never given himself to anything but his art ... But then there are other artists, the more human, like Shakespeare and Goethe, who must give themselves to life as well as to art. And if these were afraid, or despised life, then with their surplus they would ferment and become rotten. Which is what ails Thomas Mann. He is physically ailing, no doubt. But his complaint is deeper: it is of the soul. (*IR* 208)

Lawrence, like Keats, saw life as a vale of soul-making, and literature as a record of and contribution to that process.

In 1915 Lawrence was saddened by reading the letters of Van Gogh. Van Gogh, it seemed to Lawrence, had destroyed himself by failing to reconcile, 'the artistic life' with 'real life'. The best, Lawrence says, is to

> *be the artist creating a man in living fact* . . . – and where the art was the final expression of the created animal or man – not the be-all and being of the man – but the end, the climax. And some men would end in artistic utterance, and some men wouldn't. But each one would create the work of art, the living man, achieve that piece of supreme art, a man's life. (*2L* 299)

In a life that is an achieved work of art one would expect to find unusual significance and coherence. Nothing will be accidental or trivial. Every place and person, every choice, act, experience, will be symbolic, drawing universal significance from the fact that he acts and chooses from a depth of his own humanity at which we can recognize him as our representative or prototype, going naked into the unknown as both hero and scapegoat (like Prometheus, to whom Lawrence frequently compares himself).

Lawrence's life story, told simply and dramatically, allowed to find its own shape and follow its own rhythms, will be found to have the form, impetus, resonance, centrality, and inevitability of a work of art. More than anything, else, what gives Lawrence's life these qualities is that it takes one of the oldest and most potent of all mythic forms, that of the quest. The hero ventures out from the visionless world of common reality, fights his demon., suffers an ego-death, is reborn into a world cleansed and re-spiritualized, returns to make his health-bringing visions available to his fellow men. This is a metaphorical account of the life of any great artist: but it is a literal account of Lawrence's.

The quest began with Lawrence's early rejection of Puritanism, industrialism, and materialism. He diagnosed that these and many other characteristics of the modern world were symptoms of a disease he came to call 'the mental and spiritual Consciousness'; and he knew that the only cure was imagination, which, like Blake, he defined as the only true vision. As early as February 1913 he wrote to Ernest Collings:

> One needs something to make one's mood deep and sincere. There are many little frets that prevent our coming at the real naked essence of our vision. . . . I often think one ought to be able to pray, before one works and then leave it to the Lord. Isn't it hard, hard work to come to real grips with one's imagination – throw everything overboard. I always feel as if I stood naked for the fire of Almighty God to go through me – and it's rather an awful feeling. One has to be so terribly religious, to be an artist. (*1L* 519)

What does Lawrence mean by throwing everything overboard and standing, naked before God? What must be jettisoned is everything that works against the deepest sincerity – against what Birkin calls'the old effort at serious living': everything egotistical, cowardly, frivolous, superficial, self-indulgent, secondhand, inauthentic. What must be got out from under is the suffocating pillow of convention, especially in England. Conventional morality and conventional art are both manifestations of the same inauthentic social being that

Lawrence was to castigate in his last substantial piece of literary criticism, his essay on Galsworthy in 1928:

> Satire exists for the very purpose of killing the social being, showing him what an inferior he is and, with all his parade of social honesty, how subtly and corruptly debased. Dishonest to life, dishonest to the living universe on which he is parasitic as a louse. By ridiculing the social being, the satirist helps the true individual, the real human being, to rise to his feet again and go on with the battle. For it is always a battle, and always will be. (*STH* 213)

And how are we to recognize 'the true individual,' 'the real human being'?

> While a man remains a man, a true human individual, there is at the core of him a certain innocence or naïveté which defies all analysis, and which you cannot bargain with, you can only deal with it in good faith from your own corresponding innocence or naiveté...
> It is the essential innocence and naiveté of the human being, the sense of being at one with the great universe-continuum of space-time-life, which is vivid in a great man, and a pure nuclear spark in every man who is still free. (210-11)

Lawrence comes extraordinarily close here not only to the ideas, but even to the terminology of existentialism. The existentialist hero is also involved in a lifelong battle against the social beings who deny life in the name of conformity and fixed moral principles, and the battle to create an area of freedom within which individuals can recover their own naïveté (an openness to life, an innocence on the far side of experience) and out of that relate to others in good faith.

The England of Lawrence's time was riddled with bad faith – Church and State, politics, the arts, public and private morality:

> The English seem as if they can't help themselves. A lily-livered lot: that's where all their purity lies. Alas, that they should be a nation of poltroons in the face of life! But that's what they are: bossed by the witless canaille and off sweepings of a dead 19th century. (*3L* 425)

Every Great writer has the obligation, the price of his gift, to keep up the fight with all the weapons at his disposal. The artist must always be an outlaw and troublemaker. His job, in Fiedler's phrase, is 'to give valuable offence'. He says 'No! In thunder' to the most cherished beliefs of his society. He mercilessly exposes its falsehoods, sophistries, hypocrisies, and complacencies – and that means most of what we live by. Hence the hatred he aroused and still arouses. In *No! In Thunder*, Fiedler says:

> When the writer says of precisely the cause that is dearest to him what is always and everywhere the truth about all causes – that it has been imperfectly conceived and inadequately represented, and that it is bound to be betrayed, consciously or unconsciously, by its leading spokesmen – we know that he is approaching an art of real seriousness if not of actual greatness.
>
> The thrill we all sense but hesitate to define for ourselves – the thrill of confronting a commitment to truth which transcends all partial allegiances – comes when Dante turns on Florence, Molière on the moderate man, de Sade on reason, Shaw on socialists, Tolstoy on the reformers, Joyce on Ireland, Faulkner on the South, Graham Greene on the Catholics, Pasternak on the Russians, and Abraham Cahan or Nathanael West on the Jews.[2]

[2] Leslie Fiedler, *No! In thunder* (London: Eyre and Spottiswoode, 1963) 7.

Surely Lawrence on England should have been in that list. Lawrence did not hate England. He hated 'their' England, what the liars had made of it and were making of it. If he had not loved England so much, he would not have cared so much. But a man cannot be free and a true individual simply by repudiating society and his fellow men and becoming a hermit in his cell or an artist in his ivory tower.

Lawrence believed that man is essentially a social animal, that the societal instinct is stronger than the sexual or even survival instincts. By this he meant that man has a biological drive to involve himself in some communal creative activity – exploring, pioneering, building, shoulder to shoulder with the best men of his generation:

> It is the desire of the human male to build a world… It is the pure disinterested craving of the human male to make something wonderful, out of his own head and his own self, and his own soul's faith and delight, which starts everything going… That is, the essentially religious or creative motive is the first motive for all human activity. (*PU* 671: 6)

But that describes a perfect world. In reality it is only the brave few who keep up the great adventure. And they must fight for survival against the majority who have sold out or chickened out of the struggle toward consciousness and creativity in favour of power or possessions or comfort, or who, inadvertently, through loss of vision, are living without faith or in bad faith. Art is a means of keeping the spark alive, keeping the ark afloat, even 'throughout the howlingest deluge': 'Once all men in the world lost their courage and their newness, the world would come to an end' (*RDP* 200).

But the artist cannot perform his task of initiating 'a new venture towards God' alone. Lawrence wrote to Bertrand Russell:

> If I know that humanity is chained to a rock, I cannot set

> forth to find it new lands to enter upon. If I do pretend to set forth, I am a cheating, false merchant, seeking my own ends. And I am ashamed to be that. I will not. (*2L* 284)

For the Christian idea of salvation Lawrence substitutes fulfilment. Fulfilment involves wholeness, and wholeness involves relationships, connections, interdependencies. Therefore the hermit life is not available to him, nor the ivory tower. He will withdraw from the world occasionally, but only temporarily, *pour mieux sauter*, to refresh himself at the source prior to a further effort in the world of men.

The great need, even more urgent now than in Lawrence's day, is to get the human race back into a viable vitalizing contact with the sources of life in the depths of the human psyche and in the nonhuman world. Evil, Lawrence's version of the Fall, is the denial of this larger, essentially religious life, and the attempt, almost completely successful now, to replace it with a sealed-off, airless, energyless, sterile world of the exclusively human – rational, secular, and mechanical. We have corrupted our own powers, spawned reptiles of the mind, and now spew out poison over the whole earth.

The artist is a healer, but what is the healer to do when confronted with a body wholly diseased: 'Everything lies in being, although the whole world is one colossal madness, falsity, a stupendous assertion of not-being' (593). The artist becomes destroyer. The old, false world must be destroyed before a new world can come into existence: 'The old world never tumbles down except a young world shoves it over, heedlessly' (575). But the young world cannot come into being without root-room or in poisoned earth. So the priority has to be to clear the ground, to raze the temples of arrogance, greed, and hypocrisy, to fight their guardians tooth and nail: 'One must be an outlaw these days, not a teacher or preacher. One must retire out of the herd and then fire bombs into it' (546). Frieda called Lawrence 'the only revolutionary worthy of the name'. But every great artist, as truth-teller (and art-speech, in Lawrence's words, is only the truth about the real world), is a revolutionary of a radical and total kind, committed to destroying not just institutions and governments and economic systems, but the falsity of our very thinking and feeling. The bombs are not just polemics and satires ('only satire is decent now') and tendentious books like *Lady Chatterley's Lover*. Every true word, every creative thought, every energizing image is a bomb fired into a false world.

Even within a living and respected tradition, even within a community of equally brave and dedicated souls, it is a daunting task, perhaps even a doomed one now, to take on the world in this way. But to be condemned to function in isolation and exile, with no sustaining comradeship and help, a voice in the wilderness, at best misunderstood, at worst hounded, is to put one's very sanity at risk. The prototypes here are Blake and Nietzsche. It is the central paradox of the role of the artist in the modern world. As with Cassandra, the god-given gift of prophesy carries with it the curse of never being heeded. In the very act of standing up for sanity and fullness of life, the artist is driven by rejection, by the gap between the urgency of his message and the general deafness to it, to wild extremes, eccentricities, cruelties.

Three things saved Lawrence's sanity during the worst times. He had Frieda to expend his rages against. He had nature to hold on to as a source of unfailing sanity: 'It isn't my disordered imagination. There is a wagtail sitting on the gatepost. I see how sweet and swift heaven is' (331). And he never lost his faith that the world in which the war was taking place was not as real as the world of his own imagination: 'I know it is true, the book [*Women in Love*]. And it is another world, in which I can live apart from this foul world which I will not accept or acknowledge or even enter' (659).

For an artist to rest in resignation before 'the facts' is escapism, as what is usually taken to constitute 'reality' is merely the product of a local and temporal tendency to believe to be real whatever you believe that other people believe to be real:

> Realism is just one of the arbitrary views man takes of man. It sees us all as little ant-like creatures toiling against the odds of circumstance, and doomed to misery. It is a kind of aeroplane view. It became the popular outlook, and so today we actually are, millions of us, little ant-like creatures toiling against the odds of circumstance, and doomed to misery; until we take a different view of ourselves. For man always becomes what he passionately thinks he is; since he is capable of becoming almost anything. (*IR* 149)

***

Lawrence recognized his isolation as 'meaningless', and committed himself to a vision of the good life that would be communal, and the effort to set up an actual community, Rananim, to embody it. His efforts were all fiascos, partly because there was nothing more than an assumption of goodwill (which tended to mean willingness to be acolytes) in the members, and their dedication to a simple-minded utopian and prelapsarian dream: 'The only way is the way of my far-off wilderness place which shall become a school and a monastery and an Eden and a Hesperides – a seed of a new heaven and a new earth' (*3L* 71-72).

In spite of the fiascos, Lawrence clung to his dream, and embarked on his pilgrimage in 1919 partly in the hope of finding, somewhere on earth, a living people who would prove the dream to be a possibility. He thought he had found, and to a degree did find, what he sought in the New Mexico Indians. There was a community held together by a common deeply religious consciousness. And for Lawrence it was the only true religion – a religion not of theology or morality, but simply of contact with everything else that lives:

> For the whole life-effort of man was to get his life into direct contact with the elemental life of the cosmos, mountain-life, cloud-life, thunder-life, air-life, earth-life,

> sun-life. To come into immediate felt contact, and so derive energy, power, and a dark sort of joy. This effort into sheer naked contact, without an intermediary or mediator, is the root meaning of religion, and at the sacred races the runners hurled themselves in a terrible cumulative effort, through the air, to come at last into naked contact with the very life of the air, which is the life of the clouds, and so of the rain. (*MM* 180)

Yet even here, where Lawrence goes as far as he was able to go in entering the spirit of the Indian dances, there are still hints, in the 'terrible' effort and 'dark' joy, of a final step Lawrence was never able or willing to take into identification with them; there is still a residue of the categorical statement he had made in 'Indians and Entertainment':

> The Indian way of consciousness is different from and fatal to our way of consciousness. Our way of consciousness is different from and fatal to the Indian. The two ways, the two streams are never to be united. They are not even to be reconciled. There is no bridge, no canal of connection. (*MM* 61)

Though he tried to do so, especially in *The Plumed Serpent*, Lawrence never quite overcame his initial spontaneous distaste for certain overtones in the Indian dances: '…the diabolical, pre-human, pine-tree fun of cutting dusky throats and letting the blood spurt out unconfined… Just the antithesis of what I understand by jolliness: ridicule. Comic sort of bullying. No jolly, free laughter' (117). Lawrence was too honest a writer not to put the same reservations into the mind of Kate in *The Plumed Serpent*. She detects behind everything a certain malevolence, 'something dark, heavy and reptilian in their silence and their softness': 'They did not belong to the realm of that which comes forth' (*PS* 121). Kate feels that she belongs, as they do not, to 'the upper world of daylight and fresh air' (148).

It was a relief to Lawrence to get back to Europe, to the Mediterranean, in November 1925. He found there at once 'a deep insouciance, which really is the clue to faith'. Looking back at America in 1929 he wrote:

> The spirit and the will survived: but something in the soul perished: the softness, the floweriness, the natural tenderness. How could it survive the sheer brutality of the fight with that American wilderness, which is so big, vast, and obdurate! (*IR* 119).

In contrast, when Lawrence first entered the Etruscan necropolis at Cerveteri, he experienced at once the feeling that it was good for his soul to be there. In tombs, of all places, he met 'a living, fresh, jolly people'; in those dark underground chambers he found daylight and fresh air:

> You cannot think of art, but only of life itself, as if this were the very life of the Etruscans, dancing in their coloured wraps with massive yet exuberant naked limbs, ruddy from the air and the sea-light, dancing and fluting along through the little olive trees, out in the fresh day. (*SEP* 48)

The American Indians had not quite embodied Lawrence's dream. His attempt to adapt their religion and culture to the needs of a modern state with white leaders in *The Plumed Serpent* had led him into horrors. The Indian way, he had reluctantly decided, was right for them, but wrong, or not available, for him. He abandoned the leadership principle. He abandoned, it seems, Rananim. Yet he continued to travel, and travelling itself implied a residual hope. In November 1926 he wrote:

> We do not travel in order to go from one hotel to another, and see a few side-shows. We travel, perhaps, with a secret and absurd hope of setting foot on the

> Hesperides, of running our boat up a little creek and landing in the Garden of Eden. (*IR* 294)

In the Etruscan tombs Lawrence felt he had come face to face with unfallen man. His long pilgrimage brought him at last to these tombs, and in them he found the vivid human life he had been seeking, a life of perfect awareness and relatedness, without the crippling dualism of mind versus body, human versus nonhuman, physical versus metaphysical, life versus death.

Lawrence's early dualism, his belief in the blood as wiser than the intellect, has now disappeared. The crude choice between the spiritual and intellectual on the one side and the emotional and physical on the other is no longer to be found in Lawrence's writings at this date. Nor is he searching for happiness – that is a desirable but not inevitable by-product of what he is seeking, which is wholeness. He wishes to reinstate the body and its emotions not because he values it more highly than the life of the spirit and of consciousness, but because he now knows that to pursue the life of the spirit or of the mind in opposition to the life of the body and to Nature, is to alienate, stultify, or pervert the spirit and to turn the mind into a sterile mechanism or juggling act. It is because they had a rich physical life that the Etruscans were able to have a rich spiritual life, or vice versa. To distinguish between them at all is part of the Socratic sickness.

Lawrence's effort, in these last years, is to respiritualize the world. The Etruscans confirmed for him what he had always known, that it is futile hubristic perversity to seek the life of the spirit apart from the given world; for God is in everything that lives and nowhere else.

The grail Lawrence sought and found in his quest was wholeness. Wholeness means atonement. And atonement means imaginative vision. Only literature speaks the whole truth, because only literature speaks from the whole man. The imagination is simply a charge that links up again and makes operative those senses and powers of perception which our rationalistic culture has allowed to atrophy. 'The mind is non-religious,' Lawrence said.

The imagination is necessarily religious. Any genuine act of attention – 'a man in his wholeness wholly attending' ('Thought') – yields a revelation:

> All it depends on is the amount of true, sincere, religious concentration you can bring to bear on your object. An act of pure attention, if you are capable of it, will bring its own answer. And you choose that object to concentrate upon which will best focus your consciousness. Every real discovery made, every serious and significant decision ever reached, was reached and made by divination. The soul stirs, and makes an act of pure attention, and that is a discovery. (*SEP* 62)

This, for Lawrence, is the only valid way of thinking. He brought himself to a pitch of internal discipline that enabled him to channel life through his pen almost whenever he put it to paper. His genius is just as likely to manifest itself in a letter, or a little newspaper article, as in a poem or major novel.

Starting from the narrow world we all inhabit, with its hubristic human perspectives and habitual complacencies, the imagination reaches inward toward the roots of our being in the psyche and outward toward the powers of the nonhuman world. Its goal is atonement, the healing of the split between the mind and the rest of our faculties which has brought us to our present chronic, perhaps terminal, condition. The analytical reason, operating in a void, is absurd. It has no validating or vitalizing contact with either inner or outer realities. If thought were a matter of mind only, man would be a windowless monad, an ego-bound obscenity:

> ... thought is an adventure, and not a practice. In order to think, man must risk himself. He must risk himself doubly. First, he must go forth and meet life in the body.

> Then he must face the result in his mind. … Today men don't risk their blood and bone. They go forth panoplied in their own idea of themselves. Whatever they do, they perform it all in the full armour of their own idea of themselves. Their unknown bodily self is never for one moment unsheathed. All the time, the only protagonist is the known ego, the self-conscious ego. And the dark self in the mysterious labyrinth of the body is cased in a tight armour of cowardly repression… And inside the armour he goes quite deranged. (*RDP* 213, 217-8)

All the great writers are visionaries and see this. They are not just busybodies and do-gooders. They see that this almost universal madness makes real living impossible for anyone, that it is responsible for most of the crime, war, and suffering in the world, and that it degrades the world with blasphemous living.

What is normally thought of as thinking, all those methods of 'thinking' that have been developed and systematized over the centuries in Western civilization under the name of philosophy or science or mathematics, and whose methods and assumptions have been built into the very structure of our language, have been techniques for separating things from each other and the parts of things from each other, atomizing, vivisecting, labelling, and compartmentalizing. We have completely lost the capacity for thinking in a way that puts things together again, perceives relationships and patterns and wholes. We no longer have the language for it, except those few who have the language of the imagination, poetry, at their disposal.

And this is why poetry, imaginative speech, is so unremittingly metaphorical. The metaphor is the linguistic equivalent of touch. It is the link, the bridge, the meeting, the marriage, the atonement, bit by bit reconstructing the world as a unity, blissfully skipping over the supposed chasms of dualism. When God needed a token of his atonement with man after the flood, he made a metaphor, a rainbow, a visible sign of the harmony behind all apparent dualities.

Lawrence's use of sex, for example, is metaphorical or symbolic. He always insisted that *Lady Chatterley's Lover* was a phallic not a sexual novel. A phallus is a penis seen in its impersonal and symbolic aspect. For Lawrence it symbolized that life in us which even now resists or ignores the conscious mind, taking its orders from elsewhere: 'It is far deeper than sex. It is the self which darkly inhabits our blood and bone, and for which the ithyphallus is but a symbol' (*Ibid.*, 216). The phallus is also a bridge between the self and the other, an explorer into the darkness of the unknown, a way for the soul to escape from the ego without death.

If the language of the imagination makes connections, reveals patterns and interdependencies, strives to see wholes, the language of current criticism breaks down, divides into categories and sub-categories that can be neatly labelled and then dealt with by formulae. A writer sacrifices his ease, his freedom, perhaps even his life, in order to make his testimony, for the race, for the truth. A critic then takes up this work written in blood and plays the game with it of deciding whether it should be labelled modernist, anti-modernist or post-modernist.

> Man is always, all the time and for ever, on the brink of the unknown. The minute you realize this, you prick your ears in alarm. And the minute any man steps alone, with his whole naked self, emotional and mental, into the everlasting hinterland of consciousness, you hate him and you wonder over him. Why can't he stay cosily playing word-games around the camp fire? (*IR* 233)

Most academics are hostile to great literature; it bursts their carefully constructed pigeon-holes. It challenges their cherished habits, and makes greater demands upon them than they are willing to meet. If it is old and established, it becomes a 'classic', which means that it need not be responded to at all, just taught and examined. If it is new, it is mocked, belittled, or ignored. They prefer the familiar and predictable. The great new work is always offensive, both morally and formally; but mediocrity doesn't rock the boat. Hence the approval of the critical establishment is the kiss of death. Thus the more effectively art is doing its job, the more hostility it will arouse in the defenders of the status quo, the Establishment, the social beings, the ideologists, the *laches*, and the *salauds* – that is, in the great majority which is always wrong. It is a measure of the extent to which Lawrence is still alive as man and artist that he can still offend and sting the defenders of civilized, liberal, and academic values, of reason and tolerance and impartiality and objectivity. They are against Lawrence not just as a quirky individual with obsessions and blind spots, but against him as archetypal artist and truth-teller. The fight for Lawrence is the fight for art, for the life of the imagination, which is our only hope of redemption.

Mr Noon

My proposal to Penguin/Viking for D. H. Lawrence: Life into Art *listed twelve chapters. As the deadline approached, it became obvious that I could not complete it in time. Deadlines for critical works are not usually inflexible, but in this case the book was planned for publication in 1985, to commemorate the centenary of Lawrence's birth, and could not be delayed. I managed to complete only nine chapters. As it happened, the three unwritten chapters were all on the later fiction: chapter 6, 'The Withering Vision', on* Aaron's Rod, The Lost Girl *and* Mr Noon, *chapter 8, 'The Dark Gods', on 'The Ladybird',* Kangaroo, The Boy in the Bush *and* The Plumed Serpent, *and chapter 10, 'The Phallic Vision', on* Lady Chatterley's Lover. *Subsequently I began to revise and extend the book with a view to a possible second edition. I wrote chapter 6 in about 1988. In 2007 I took the only copy with me to the Eastwood Lawrence conference, where I managed to lose it. I have since found another copy of the section on* Mr Noon.

We must beware of the temptation to treat *Mr Noon* as part of the Lawrence canon. Though Lawrence did try to publish Part I in serial form, his motive was probably, as in the case of *The Lost Girl*, purely financial, He never finished the draft of Part II, nor revised what he had written of it. Part III, which was to have taken the story up to 1919, was never begun, and it seems likely that some of the material he had in mind for it was used in *Aaron's Rod* and in the 'Nightmare' chapter of *Kangaroo*. Lawrence's last reference to the novel in the letters is in October 1922, when he wrote to Mountsier; 'I doubt if I want to finish *Mr Noon*. One day I might'. (*4L* 319) Had he done so, he would no doubt have improved or dropped most of the slack or arch passages, and developed the themes and symbols which are latent in the first draft. For example, very little is made of the fact that Gilbert is a composer. If Lawrence could not find a way to make this significant (as Aaron's music is significant), perhaps he would have made him a writer. – How strange that no Lawrence hero is a novelist!

As Lawrence never returned to *Mr Noon*, one might argue that in publishing it at all the Cambridge University Press was hardly respecting his 'final intention', which was to consign it to oblivion. On the other hand, there is plenty of evidence, internal and external, to suggest that it was the crisis in his relationship with publishers, critics and readers, rather than any dissatisfaction with the work in progress, which caused Lawrence to abandon the novel. In October 1921 be wrote to Mountsier: 'I don't know whether I shall finish *Mr Noon*, I get so annoyed with everybody that I don't want to tackle any really serious work. To hell with them all. Miserable world of canaille' (107).

In Part II he had undertaken to describe his most intimate experiences, deepest feelings, most cherished beliefs, to readers who must, he felt, be continuously cajoled into not taking him seriously, as to do so would inevitably lead to disgust and outright rejection. The reviews of *The Lost Girl,* which arrived just as Lawrence was beginning Part II, no doubt undermined what little faith he had in the enterprise. Edward Garnett's review had warned 'people who do not appreciate the analysis of the forces of sensuous passion or the delineation of the feminine surrender to the spells of Eros' that the novel was not for them.[1] Yet he also praised the novel for its 'aesthetic charm' and 'a dexterous lightness of touch that is irresistible'. Here was Lawrence embarking on a far more brutally frank and unsentimental delineation of those forces. He felt obliged therefore to strive for an even more ingratiating lightness of touch. The 'really serious work' has to be undermined with frequent injections of flippancy. Never can lightness of touch have been applied more heavy-handedly, The attempt to write with heart on sleeve and tongue in cheek simultaneously was self-defeating. Lawrence feels more and more humiliated by the cap and bells, and his humour, which had begun as a kind of mock-eighteenth-

[1] Draper, *op. cit.,* 146.

century geniality (often relapsing into the grotesque self-consciousness and social insecurity of his early letters to such upper-class, novel-reading young ladies as Grace Crawford), becomes more and more defensive, then more and more aggressive, until the final outburst against the 'rather cowardly and imbecile reader' (*MN* 292) before whom he cannot continue to cast his pearls.

It is not that Lawrence is incapable of writing in a comic or ironic vein. There is a good deal of successful comedy in *Mr Noon*, comedy which is necessary to the vision and structure of the work. This comedy comes when Lawrence's eye is on the scene, not the reader, when he is neither evading the serious and often painful implications nor overstating them with bluster, but maintaining a just sufficient ironic distance to avoid total identification with Gilbert. This distance is not imposed on principle, but the natural result of the passage of time. To the Lawrence of 1920 the Lawrence of 1912 cannot but appear as a rather foolish figure, (as, it seems, he had often appeared at the time to Frieda). The story is, after all, about Gilbert's rapid progress from the clown caught with his trousers down in Part I, through the innocent abroad of the early chapters of Part II, to the mature man who has at last 'cracked the womb' and come through all the trials and tribulations, the pitfalls and pratfalls, to an achieved marriage and a home in Italy at the end. His ultimate achievement is more impressive, more valid, than it would have been had he been given heroic stature from the outset.

This slightly wry perspective on Gilbert is achieved more successfully and consistently than the similar perspective Lawrence had tried to give us on Birkin. It is a perspective which might have transformed *Sons and Lovers* into a seriously comic novel (more like Joyce's *Portrait of the Artist as a Young Man*) had Lawrence written it a decade later than he did.

We must also beware of treating *Mr Noon* as a biographical treasure-house. Though Part II is closer to autobiography than any other novel, there are, as in *Sons and*

Lovers, major departures from the facts for novelistic purposes. As Peter Preston has pointed out, Gilbert has had no problems with his mother, and Johanna has none with her children. Nor is Gilbert a writer.

The novel has been widely criticized for the discontinuity between Parts I and II. It is assumed that Lawrence first created Gilbert Noon as a portrait of his friend George Neville, but having reached an impasse with that story in Emmie's bedroom, suddenly and arbitrarily transformed Gilbert into himself. There seem to me to be several things wrong with this account. First, every Lawrence protagonist, male or female, is, at least in part, Lawrence himself. He might have written a short story about Neville, but in a novel whatever Lawrence draws on from Neville is much more likely to be but one element in a composite character. Peter Balbert describes the Gilbert Noon of Part I as a 'decidedly unLawrencean lover'.[2] Of course one knows what Balbert means; but Gilbert, even as expert spooner, is very close to a character who is unmistakably Lawrence – Billy Brentnall in *The Married Man.* Here the Neville character, George Grainger, is a married philanderer, but is not shown as spooning. It is Billy who reduces two girls to squealing by kissing them under the ear. On the second occasion he is caught in the act by Elsa (Frieda) who accuses him of being just as bad as Grainger.

The virtuoso description of spooning in the novel certainly does not suggest that Lawrence's knowledge is second-hand. Lawrence had no doubt, like his elder brother Ernest, served his sexual apprenticeship if not in the Eastwood Co-op entry, then in some other cul de sac. The whole point about spooning is that its perfected and controlled titillations serve as a substitute for real sensuality; 'Nothing earthy, not we. All in mid-air, our goings on' (*MN* 23). Gilbert Noon has to unlearn all that with Johanna: 'And

[2] Peter Balbert, 'Silver spoon to devil's fork: Diana Trilling and the sexual ethics of *Mr Noon*', *D. H. Lawrence Review* 20 (2), 1988, 238.

as for the leaping into the chasm of pure connection with the woman, that needs a basic courage and a strange concerted unison between the two protagonists, which life alone can give' (191).

Spooning is typical of all Anglo-Saxon attitudes: 'But now alas the English adventure has broken down. There is no going on. There is cul de sac and white-livered fawning' (191). 'It is sickening, this cats-pawing', Lawrence had written to Helen Corke in March 1911 (*1L* 239). And he found equally sickening the attitude to art which holds life at arm's length. Flaubert, he said in 1913, 'stood away from life as from a leprosy':

> And Thomas Mann, like Flaubert, feels vaguely that he has in him something finer than ever physical life revealed. Physical life is a disordered corruption, against which he can fight with only one weapon, his fine aesthetic sense, his feeling for beauty, for perfection, for a certain fitness which soothes him, and gives him an inner pleasure, however corrupt the stuff of life may be. (*IR* 211)

Gilbert Noon has his own version of this: 'Life is incompatible with perfection, or with infinity, or with eternity. You've got to turn to mathematics, or to art' (*MN* 12). Lawrence had himself flirted with a similar aesthetic in 'Art and the Individual' in 1908, quoting Hume with approval:

> The chief triumph of Art is to insensibly refine the temper, and to point out to us those dispositions which we should endeavour to attain by constant bent of mind and by repeated habit. (*STH* 142)

He also claimed that Beauty is an absolute: 'If a thing is in bad taste it is so absolutely, just as a sum in mathematics is either wrong or right' (141). According to Jung, it is a male characteristic to pursue perfection, which is a cul de sac, whereas the female strives for the much healthier, saner goal of completeness.

Structurally, *Mr Noon* is no different from the other two novels of the period, *The Lost Girl* and *Aaron's Rod.* In all three the protagonist is, at the beginning, locked into Eastwood and its mores, described in a style of exaggerated realism. In all three he or she makes a sudden break, a leap in the dark, out of that reality, which is called in question, towards another, deeper, more fulfilling reality. Each ends in Italy. Is there any more discontinuity between the Gilbert Noons of Parts I and II than between the Alvina of Manchester House and the Allaye who accompanies Ciccio to Califano? These are stories of rebirth, and there is no point in a rebirth if the reborn hero is not radically different from his former self.

We are told in no uncertain terns that the spoony Mr Noon of Part I is to be re-incarnated in Germany as Mr Now: 'That is, he is at his zenith' (99). The rebirth begins when Gilbert first surveys the great Isar valley, and for the first time in the novel, Lawrence takes his tongue from his cheek:

> It was a lovely, ringing, morning-bright world, for the Englishman vast and glamorous. The sense of space was an intoxication for him. … The bigness: that was what he loved so much. The bigness, and the sense of an infinite multiplicity of connections. … Many magical lands, many magical peoples, all magnetic and strange, uniting to form the vast patchwork of Europe. The glamorous vast multiplicity, all made up of differences, mediaeval, romantic differences, this seemed to break his soul like a chrysalis into a new life. (107)

For the first time Gilbert's vision is not limited to the cul de sac. From this perspective he can perceive the parochialism of England. He becomes 'unEnglished':

> His tight and exclusive nationality seemed to break down in his heart. ... it was so nice to be one among many, to feel the horrible imprisoning oneness and insularity collapsed, a real delusion broken, and to know that the universal ideals and morals were after all only local and temporal. (107-8)

The experience is comparable to Ursula's fall from the oak tree in *The Rainbow*. He is opened to receive whatever life might have in store for him, without seeking to impose his own ready-made judgments or submitting to those of others. He is ready to admit the strange woman who now knocks at the door of his being:

> Since he had been with her, and his old closed heart had broken open, he knew that she and he were fate and life to one another. She was his one connection in the universe. (228)

And Lawrence simultaneously opens his heart to give us unselfconscious prose of great freshness, simplicity and sensitivity:

> By the side of a little white shrine they sat in the sun, listening to the Alpine gurgling of running waters, smelling the tang of ice and bog in the sunshine, and eating the black bread, which is so very good with mountain butter, and the slices of rare good sausage, and sipping the Schnapps from a tiny shilling bottle, and hearing the cow-bells tong-tong-tong, behind the fir-trees at the back, and seeing the mountains in heaven pale and radiant. (131)

It needs great courage to write like this. There is no insulation of form or impersonality. It is exposed and vulnerable. As Lawrence was to write in his essay on Galsworthy:

> While a man remains a man, a true human individual, there is at the core of him a certain innocence or naïveté which defies all analysis, and which you cannot bargain with, you can only deal with it, in good faith, from your own corresponding innocence or naïveté. (*STH* 210-11)

But what happens when an artist knows, from bitter experience, that his work will not be so received, that there is no reciprocal good faith in his readership, that all responses and judgements will be governed by the fixed prejudices of the cul de sac? Here is another paragraph written in good faith:

> A bright, roused look was on her face. She lifted her eyelids with a strange flare of invitation, like a bird lifting its wings, And for the first time the passion broke like lightning out of Gilbert's blood: for the first time in his life. He went into her room with her and shut the door. The sultriness and lethargy of his soul had broken into a storm of desire for her, a storm which shook and swept him at varying intervals all his life long. (*MN* 136)

But Lawrence cannot muster the confidence to leave it at that or to continue in that vein. He lapses into excruciating self-consciousness, self-parody, forced flippancy, and petulant side-swipes at the reader:

> I am busy apostrophising Jupiter Tonans, Zeus of the thunder-bolt, the almighty Father of passion and sheer desire. I'm not talking about *your* messy little feelings and licentiousnesses either. I'm talking about desire. So don't interrupt. Am *I* writing this book, or are you? Let me tell you, even if, gentle reader, you happen to be a wonderful, chirping, gentle, soft-billed gosling of a critic, gentilissimo, *I* am writing this book, and it is *not* being chirped out by you. (137)

And so on.

In revision, Lawrence might have got rid of such passages, of which there are many. Or he might have taken further the experiment of conducting a dialogue with the reader which parallels the running battle between Gilbert and Johanna: 'Let us have a continual risk and tumble and the unceasing spur of jeopardy on our flank to make us jump and fly down the wind' (152). He could attempt to make the whole novel a battleground between the en-trenched, habituated, conventional sentimentality and prudery (and the covert prurience) of the reader's expectations, and the demands actually made by the novel. Lawrence seems to have made a start along these lines. There are, within the story, three models for the 'gentle' (that is, imprisoned by gentility) reader, models from three ages and three social classes, Emmie Bostock (in her twenties and working-class), Patty Goddard (in her forties and middle-class), and the Baroness (in her sixties and upper-class). All live in bad faith and are satirically exposed. And there is one model for liberated womanhood, openness, generosity and candour. Johanna. Gilbert is in the position of the ideal reader, who resists, fights back, but does so in good faith and is gradually, to his own infinite gratitude, won over.

The demands Johanna makes on Gilbert, the constant readjustments she requires of him, make him often ridiculous, but ultimately heroic. Johanna meets Gilbert in the first place because an adventure with a Japanese stranger on the train has caused her to miss her station. The chapter is called, ironically, 'Snowflower':

> 'I'm not a white snowflower. Don't you think it's absurd? When I'm a born dandelion. I was born to get the sun. I love love . . . There are lots of men in the world – such lovely men, I think'. (125)

She startles Gilbert with a full account of her love life, and her totally amoral views on sex: 'Marriage and all those things are based on fear. How can love be wrong? It. is the jealousy and grudging that is wrong' (127). Gilbert, though familiar with these arguments, finds them hard to controvert: 'He was troubled, and depressed. It all saddened him, and he did not agree, but did not know what to say'. On the other hand, Johanna's freedom from convention, her naïveté, her generosity and candour, are a large part of her attraction and inseparable from the rest of her character. Gilbert never comes to agree with her on these matters, but he is unsure of his own moral bearings, recognizing that there is an element of jealousy and grudging in his own preference for exclusivity. When he commits himself to Johanna he does so for better and for worse. She is not a woman to be moulded, like Emmie, to her husband's or society's requirements. He must love her and trust her for what she is, not what he would wish her to be. She makes no vow of sexual faithfulness and does not regard a casual affair as a serious betrayal of a permanent relationship. The acid test is her deliberately provocative admission of her casual unfaithfulness with Stanley. Both Johanna and the reader expect a violent explosion. It could easily have put an end to their relationship. Gilbert is shaken to the depths. But he refuses to respond out of hurt pride. He refuses to judge. As Blake said: 'One law for the lion and the ox is oppression'. He holds on to what is irreducible in their relationship:

> If he had married some really nice woman ... then he would never have broken out of the dry integument that enclosed him. He would have withered with the really nice woman inside the enclosure. For the act of birth, dear reader, really is not and cannot be a really nice business. It is a bloody and horrid and gruesome affair. And that is what we must face. (291)

For two reasons I believe Lawrence could not have made a success of such an experiment in the dialogic education of the gentle reader. It is in the same paragraph that Lawrence suggests a parallel between ' the incalculable fight such as he [Gilbert] fought, unconscious and willy-nilly, with his German Johanna' (291-2) and his own fight with the reader, that he characterizes that reader as 'rather cowardly and imbecile', which could certainly not be said of Gilbert. His fight with Johanna may have been incalculable, but it has certainly been creative, whereas Lawrence's relationship with his reader seems to have gone from bad to worse, and the fight is abandoned just a few lines later. Had it continued, the dialogue would have continually degenerated into diatribe. In any case, it is difficult to see how any reader unable to respond to the imaginative content of a novel could be argued or cajoled into doing so.

Second is the fact that self-conscious stunts were simply not what Lawrence was good at: 'But primarily I am a passionately religious man, and my novels must be written from the depth of my religious experience. That I must keep to, because I can only work like that' (*2L* 165). When, in 1923, he asked himself if the novel had a future as a supreme art form, he concluded that if it did, the novelist would have to ignore his audience:

> The novel has got a future. Its future is to take the place of gospels, philosophies, and the present-day novel as we know it. It's got to have the courage to tackle new propositions without using abstractions; it's got to present us with new, really new feelings, a whole new line of emotion, which will get us out of the old emotional rut. Instead of snivelling about what is and has been, or inventing new sensations in the old line, it's got to break a way through, like a hole in a wall. And the public will scream and say it is sacrilege; because, of course, when you've been jammed for a long time in a tight corner, you get really used to its stuffiness and its tightness, till you find it absolutely stinkingly cosy; and then, of course you're horrified when you see a new glaring hole in what was your cosy wall. You're horrified. You back away from

> the cold stream of fresh air as if it was killing you.
>
> But gradually first one and then another of the sheep filters through the gap, and finds a new world outside. (*STH* 155)

A few months before beginning *Mr Noon* Lawrence had written to Compton Mackenzie; 'Damn the world, why is one such a fool as to offer it anything serious *di cuore*. I've finished forever – wish I'd never begun. Henceforth my fingers to my nose –and my heart far off' (3L 491). But in 1920 writing saleable fiction seemed the only way to make a living. Without that pressure, Lawrence might have turned exclusively to poetry. The audience, such as it was, for poetry, could be assumed to be more judicious than that for fiction. In any case, the poet does not have the same obligation as the novelist to allow his work to be determined by market forces. A poem is addressed to the 'unseen witnesses'. In poems Lawrence can plumb the depths of the heart, and even break the womb of the exclusively human, issuing forth into the fresh, sacred and resonantly symbolic world of birds, beasts and flowers.

D. H. L and R. L. S

First published in the D. H. Lawrence Review, *24 (2), 1992.*

Treasure Island was one of Lawrence's favourite boyhood books. He re-read it with Jessie Chambers in adolescence, together with *Kidnapped* and *The Master of Ballantrae*.[1] By 1912 he knew something of Stevenson's life, recalling while convalescing in Bournemouth, that Stevenson had also gone to Bournemouth as an invalid (*1L* 361). In fact each had been plagued since early childhood with bronchial troubles which later developed into tuberculosis. They had convalesced in Bournemouth at the same age, Stevenson in 1885, the year of Lawrence's birth.

So many more similar coincidences were to follow in Lawrence's later life that D. H. Lawrence, might almost have been deliberately following in the footsteps of Robert Louis Stevenson. Each rebelled against a puritanical upbringing, against such conventional pieties as respectability and 'getting on'. Each fell in love with an older married woman with children and threw up everything to live abroad with her. Each was penniless and lived with great austerity. Each wrote in several genres and with great speed. Each was extremely responsive to children, animals, and the spirit of place. Each enjoyed, and in spite of recurrent illness found time and energy to do a great deal of walking and physical work. Each travelled widely and restlessly, in search of a comfortable climate and altitude. Lawrence was to visit several Mediterranean resorts which Stevenson had visited. Each visited Ceylon, and lived in America. Stevenson's visit to Samoa had been en route for Australia, though in the event he made only a brief visit to Sydney. Yet each would probably have made a similar pilgrimage in perfect health, partly to escape from a hated (though also deeply loved) native land, partly for love of travel, partly in search of sunshine and of an earthly paradise, or at least a people unspoiled by civilization.

[1] Chambers (1965), 96.

When Robert Louis Stevenson was twenty-four, a visiting New Zealander strongly recommended Samoa, and told him 'of beautiful places, green for ever; perfect shapes of men and women, with red flowers in their hair; and nothing to do but to study oratory and etiquette, sit in the sun, and pick up the fruits as they fall'.[2] Later, on the San Francisco waterfront, Stevenson listened to seamen's tales of the South Seas, of islands with:

> precipitous shores, spired mountain tops, the deep shade of hanging forests, the unresting surf upon the reef, and the unending, peace of the lagoon; sun, moon and stars of imperial brightness; man moving in these scenes scarce fallen, and woman lovelier than Eve; the primal curse abrogated, . . . the boat urged, and the long, night beguiled with poetry and choral song'.[3]

Lawrence sought to find blessedness, prelapsarian innocence, and atonement with nature in an actual place that one might reach by boat: 'If only it will all end up happily, like a song or a poem, and we live blithely by a big river, where there are fish, and in the forest behind wild turkeys and quails; there we make songs and poems and stories and dramas, in a Vale of Avalon, in the Hesperides, among the Loves' (*2L* 452). In Lawrence's case he was encouraged by Fenimore Cooper to locate that paradise in the American West. But he too was attracted by the South Sea Islands. Though he never actually lived there, he did live, for a while, at Thirroul (like Stevenson at Vailima), in sight of the Pacific. Each, despite his romantic notions about native dark-skinned people, refused to sentimentalize them in actuality.

In June 1920, when Lawrence was enthusiastically planning a voyage to the South Seas with Compton

[2] Robert Louis Stevenson, *The works of Robert Louis Stevenson*. Ed. L. Osbourne (London: Heinemann, 1922-3) vol.20, 319.
[3] *Ibid.*, vol. 7, 201.

Mackenzie, he wrote to him: 'I read some of Stevenson. Idiot to go to Samoa just to dream and get thrilled about Scotch bogs and mosses. No wonder he died. If I go to Samoa, it will be to forget, not to remember' (*3L* 549). This remark is misleading and unkind. Stevenson in Samoa was very involved in local politics (much more so than Lawrence in Taos). Nostalgia for Scotland is no more common in Stevenson's letters than for England in Lawrence's, and I can find no reference to Scotch bogs or mosses. Though both the novels Stevenson wrote in Samoa, *Catriona* and the unfinished *Weir of Hermiston*, are set in Scotland (the novella 'The Beach at Falesa' is set in Samoa), and Stevenson spent a lot of time trying to trace his ancestry (and therefore re-establishing contact with distant members of the family), he seems to have had no regrets about living there. He sounds very like Lawrence when he writes, 'It amazes me how people can live on in the dirty north'.[4]

Stevenson had expressed so little nostalgia in his long monthly letters to Sidney Colvin, that in September 1891 Colvin asked him if he was ever homesick for the Highlands and the Isles. Stevenson replied that for the last month he had been living there, in his grandfather's diaries and letters: 'Now, imagine if I have been homesick for Barrahead and Island Glass, and Kirkwall, and Cape Wrath, and the Wells of the Pentland Firth; I could have wept'.[5] A year later Stevenson wrote to J.M. Barrie: 'It is a singular thing that I should live here in the South Seas under conditions so new and so striking, and yet my imagination so continually inhabit that cold old huddle of hills from which we come'.[6] In August 1893, the penultimate year of his life, Stevenson invited Colvin to visit him:

[4] *Ibid.*, vol.22, 363.
[5] *Ibid.*, 396.
[6] *Ibid.*, vol.23, 169.

> And then you could actually see Vailima, which I *would* like you to, for it's beautiful and my home and tomb that is to be; though it's a wrench not to be planted in Scotland – that I can never deny – if I could only be buried in the hills, under the heather and a table tombstone like the martyrs, where the whaups and plovers are crying!! Did you see a man who wrote the Stickit *Minister* and dedicated it to me, in words that brought the tears to my eyes every time I looked at them. 'Where about the graves of the martyrs the whaups are crying. *His* heart remembers how'. Ah, by God, it does! Singular that I should fulfil the Scots destiny throughout, and live a voluntary exile, and have my head filled with the blessed, beastly place all the time![7]

These quotations would seem to confirm D. H. Lawrence's comments, but they give a false impression, as they are almost the only instances in hundreds of letters, and seem to be to some extent a result of Stevenson fulfilling the expectations of his Scottish correspondents.

***

The only other reference to Stevenson in Lawrence's letters came just a few weeks after finishing *Kangaroo*, when Lawrence described San Francisco as having still a bit of 'R.L. Stevenson unfinished "West" about it' (*4L* 290). This implies that Lawrence knew *The Silverado Squatters*, Stevenson's account of the summer he and his wife spent squatting in Silverado, a deserted silver-mining settlement high in the California Sierra Nevada. A few days earlier, just after leaving the South Sea Islands, Lawrence had written: 'Travel seems to me a splendid lesson in disillusion' (286), which may be an echo of a sentence in *The Silverado Squatters*: 'Sightseeing is the

[7] *Ibid.*, 315.

art of disappointment'.[8]

There is a chapter titled 'The Scot Abroad' where Stevenson describes his mixed feelings about his semi-voluntary exile:

> There is no special loveliness in that grey country, with its rainy, sea-beat archipelago; its fields of dark mountain; its unsightly places, black with coal; its treeless, sour, unfriendly-looking corn-lands; its quaint, grey castled city, where the bells clash of a Sunday, and the wind squalls, and the salt showers fly and beat. I do not even know if I desire to live there; but let me hear, in some far land, a kindred voice sing out, 'O why left I my hame?' and it seems at once as if no beauty under the kind heavens, and no society of the wise and good, can repay me for my absence from my country. And though I think I would rather die elsewhere, yet in my heart of hearts I long to be buried among good Scots clods.[9]

'The happiest lot on earth is to be born a Scotsman' reminds us of Lawrence's vow never to 'go back on my Englishness and myself'. He swung between planning to 'go to the ends of the earth' (*3L* 516) and, having got there, to 'return to England':

> I do think, still more now I am out here [Ceylon], that we make a mistake forsaking England and moving out into the periphery of life. After all, Taormina, Ceylon, Africa, America – as far as we go, they are only the negation of what we ourselves stand for and are… I really think that the most living clue of life is in us Englishmen in England. (*4L* 219)

[8] Robert Louis Stevenson, *The amateur emigrant & the Silverado squatters* (London: Folio Society, 1991), 158.
[9] *Ibid.*, 164.

In the early pages of *Kangaroo* Lawrence describes his alter-ego hero pining for Europe, for England, even for London, with Stevenson-like ambivalence:

> He felt he would have given anything on earth to be in England. It was May – end of May – almost bluebell time, and the green leaves coming out on the hedges. ... Oh God, in be in Europe, lovely, lovely Europe that he had hated so thoroughly and abused so vehemently, saying it was moribund and stale and finished. The fool was himself. (*K* 19-20)

We are four pages into *Kangaroo* before we learn our hero's name R.L. Somers. That form of the name and the full name Richard Lovat Somers are used several times in the first chapter, so that the reader cannot possibly fail to register the initials RLS and any literate reader in 1922 would make an instant connection with R.L. Stevenson. As it is hard to detect any other possible significance in the name, it seems certain that this connection was intentional.

There are few parallels between *Kangaroo* and *The Silverado Squatters.* Both books give a strong sense of a frontier, a landscape still largely untouched by man. Lawrence would have liked Stevenson's sentence: 'There is no foreign land, it is the traveller only that is foreign'.[10] There is no inner conflict in Stevenson, nor conflict with his wife, nor involvement in politics (that was to come in Samoa). A gentle easy-going humour pervades the book, with wonderful brief portraits of people, places, natural phenomena. Unlike Lawrence, Stevenson kept autobiographical material and his political involvement out of his fiction, and kept his marriage and his inner life largely out of his more autobiographical writings too.

Why did Lawrence make the connection? Perhaps, having read *The Silverado Squatters* shortly before beginning *Kangaroo*,

[10] Stevenson (1921), 182.

he had reacted to it with warm sympathy, and felt like acknowledging that fellow-feeling, and a wider sense of kinship and a parallel life as a novelist in semi-voluntary exile at the other side of the world, by his choice of initials for his alter-ego hero. There may be no further significance. But readers with a greater knowledge of Stevenson may spot parallels I have missed.

When Lawrence returned to Italy and the Riviera, he spent most of his time writing about the English midlands, in *The Virgin and the Gipsy*, *Lady Chatterley's Lover,* several short stories, and several essays including 'Return to Bestwood' and 'Nottingham and the Mining Countryside'. From the Villa Mirenda Lawrence sent Rolf Gardiner a letter as nostalgic as any of Stevenson's, for 'the country of my heart' (*5L* 592). In autumn 1928 he wrote to David Chambers, after a paragraph of pure nostalgia for the Haggs:

> Son' tempi passati, cari miei! quanto cari, non saprete mai! [They are times past, my dears! how dear, you will never know!] – I could never tell you in English how much it all meant to me, how I still feel about it. (*6L* 618)

What Lawrence did not yet know was that he would himself die the following year, at forty-four, the same age at which Stevenson had died.

How to Live? The End of Lawrence's Quest

New Mexico has meant a great deal to me. I spent time there every year from 1968 to 1981, but I had not been there for twenty-four years when I was invited to give the keynote speech at the Lawrence conference in Santa Fe in 2005. The theme of the conference was 'Lawrence and the Frontiers'. It was New Mexico, Lawrence said, that liberated him from the present era of civilization. With an hour at my disposal, I wanted to take on a wide topic, which would not be dwarfed by that 'vast amphitheatre of lofty, indomitable desert'. The talk was first published in Windows to the Sun: D. H. Lawrence's Thought Adventures, *eds V. Hyde and E. Ingersoll (Fairleigh Dickinson University Press, 2008).*

'Dare to be a Daniel. Dare to stand alone.'[1] The fiercely independent spirit of non-conformism was so thoroughly absorbed by Lawrence (and so closely fitted his temperament) that by the time he was twenty-two he was refusing to conform to any organized religion, writing to the Eastwood Congregational minister Robert Reid that every man had an obligation to formulate his own religion, slowly and painfully, subjecting it to constant modification. He remained true to that belief throughout his life. His works are that process of constant modification.

The pre-war novels could all be said to be about the process Jung called 'individuation'. Ursula in *The Rainbow* calls it discovering how the life that is in you wants to be lived. *The Rainbow* and *The Lost Girl* in particular are existentialist novels. The individual must struggle to live authentically, which means to resist the constant pressures of the extant social world to impose inauthentic, second-hand life-modes.

After Lawrence's death Frieda called him 'the only rebel worthy of the name'. We can see what she means. It is easy to describe Lawrence in these terms, and it is true as far as it goes. But it does not go very far. It leaves out of account at

[1] The title and chorus of a popular Sunday School song by Philip P. Bliss (1838-76).

least three other Lawrences, which we can think of as, first, Lawrence the married man and Priest of Love, second, Lawrence the Utopian Socialist, and third, Lawrence the Pantheist.

Though we admire Lawrence as free spirit, thought-adventurer, traveller, challenger, fore-runner, lonely explorer always forging ahead at the frontiers ... we must remember that these are the very terms Lawrence himself used, with heavy irony, for his baby tortoise. The arrogant baby tortoise is doomed to discover all too soon that isolation is not its birthright. By the time he wrote that letter to Robert Reid, Lawrence had already been 'crucified into sex':

> Doomed, in the long crucifixion of desire, to seek his
> consummation beyond himself.
> Divided into passionate duality...
>
> 'Lui et Elle'

Though he eventually found a worthy mate, became a 'priest of love', and gave a high place to sex in his personal religion, he never lost sight of the cost, the humiliation, entailed:

> Doomed to make an intolerable fool of himself
> In his effort toward completion again.

Is not a large part of *Women in Love* Birkin's doomed attempts, through his 'star-equilibrium' and what-not, to have his cake and eat it, to admit his absolute need for the woman while desperately, rather absurdly, trying to hang on to his 'free, proud singleness'. As Connie Chatterley was to reflect, 'if one wanted to be so tremendously free, one must evaporate into nothingness' (as the man who loved islands was to do).

If the second Lawrence is Lawrence the married man, who would, as he himself claimed, have been nothing without Frieda, a third Lawrence is the Lawrence who believed, with Birkin, that marriage cannot be an end in itself, is no more than 'égoïsme a deux' unless it involves at least 'a few other people'. While writing *Women in Love* Lawrence wrote:

> My individual self is all right, but it seems quite cut off and isolated, as if it had no connection and no relation with anybody, beyond Frieda. ...There is a gnawing craving in oneself, to move and live not only as a single, satisfied individual, but as a real representative of the whole race. (*3L* 63)

Birkin and Ursula cut themselves off from family, community, jobs, nation, culture, civilization itself, and find themselves at the end of *Women in Love* isolated in an icy wilderness. This problem was still unresolved by Mellors and Connie.

Lawrence was gregarious. As a youth he had always been the life and soul of the party, the leader of the Pagans in their excursions into the surrounding countryside, bringing more life, greater awareness, to others through his ability to communicate his own enthusiasms, knowledge and insights, as later through his school- teaching and his works. This is the Lawrence who, living through the dehumanization of the industrial system in the days before unions, imbibed an idealistic utopian socialism that led him to Willie Hopkin as his mentor.

Lawrence told Reid that his own religion would involve an awareness of the sufferings of 'multitudes of brothers', and that 'true Socialism' *was* religion. The constitution of Rananim was to be that of a socialist utopia. In 1918 Lawrence told Koteliansky that he wanted to make contact with several of the leading members of the Independent Labour Party, to escape from his 'rather meaningless isolation'. For a few years Lawrence's utopianism was diverted into the cul-de-sac of leadership, but he seems to have left that behind him when he returned to Europe from America in 1925. On his last visit to England in 1926 he wrote:

> Curiously, I like England again, now I am up in my own regions. It braces me up: and there seems a queer, odd sort of potentiality in the people, especially the common people. One feels in them some odd, unaccustomed sort of plasm twinkling and nascent. They are not finished. And they have a funny sort of purity and gentleness, and at the same time, unbreakableness, that attracts one. (*5L* 519-20)

It was this feeling which generated the first version of *Lady Chatterley's Lover*. In May 1929 Lawrence cheered the victory of the Labour Party in the General Election, and a few weeks later he wrote:

> And though the pomegranate has red flowers outside
> the window
> and oleander is hot with perfume under the afternoon
> sun
> and I am 'il Signore' and they love me here,
> yet I am a mill-hand in Leeds
> and the death of the Black Country is upon me
> and I am wrapped in the lead of a coffin-lining, the
> living death of my fellow men.
>
> 'We Die Together'

There remains a fourth Lawrence, a Lawrence who would not have been satisfied even had he found perfect 'self-effectuation' within a perfect marriage within a perfect community. Such a life would require for its completeness a larger context still, the context of Nature, of birds, beasts and flowers, and the wheeling cosmos. For those of us who live in cities, especially in that tight little island across the Atlantic, simply coming to New Mexico gives us a glimpse of what Lawrence called the Greater Day, a landscape of huge horizons which dwarfs humanity, and a landscape bristling with its own untamed vitality, which Lawrence also called Pan.

These, then, are my four Lawrences. Like his baby tortoise, perhaps like all male human beings, Lawrence had a 'cross-wise, cloven psyche'. The four corners are in perpetual conflict with each other. The striving for self-effectuation comes into conflict with the demands of sexual love for self-abnegation, culminating in the 'little death', the ego-death of coition. Self-effectuation and marriage both come into conflict with what Trigant Burrow called 'the societal instinct'. Lawrence firmly believed that the instinct to work shoulder-to-shoulder with one's fellow men in building a civilization, or at least a model of one, was as basic as the sexual and survival instincts. And all of these come into conflict with the attractions of the non-human world. In 1917 Lawrence wrote:

> As for republics, they are the imaginary chickens of an addled egg. Nothing will save us now; we must lapse sheer away from the extant world, reject it all, become indifferent, and listen beyond. (*3L* 139)

He told Kot that his Rananim idea was 'the true one. Only the people were wrong. But to go to Rananim *without* the people is right' (23). During his wartime 'nightmare' this split caused him not only to envisage a colony without people, but a world without people, just, in Birkin's words, 'the long grass waving, and a hare sitting up'.

It seemed that humanity and nature could not be reconciled. The Great Goddess or the Great God Pan demand that man should suspend what seems to define him as human in order to comply with their laws. As Ted Hughes wrote:

> The ego's extreme alternatives are either to reject her and attempt to live an independent, rational, secular life or to abnegate the ego and embrace her love with 'total, unconditional love', which means to become a saint, a holy idiot, possessed by the Divine Love. ... Man will

> always choose the former, simply because once he is free of a natural, creaturely awareness of the divine indulgence which permits him to exist at all, he wants to live his own life, and he has never invented a society of saints that was tolerable.[2]

***

In my first book, *The Art of D. H. Lawrence,* forty years ago, I spoke of Lawrence's work as falling into four phases, roughly corresponding to the four Lawrences I have just described. Now I think it is probably more accurate to speak of these not as consecutive phases, but as coexisting, from his adolescence onwards. The tension between them generates those phenomenal creative energies. His lifelong quest is to try to reconcile them so that these energies can be directed into a coherent and constructive life mode and 'metaphysic'. The vocation of the great writer is to be a healer, to bring gifts of healing truths. But before he can perform this task, he must heal himself. The work enacts or re-enacts the struggle for atonement and completion, and the reader's participation in this struggle is itself a healing experience.

Ursula's perception of the self as a 'supreme gleaming triumph of infinity' in *The Rainbow* has to be painfully superseded by her recognition of the self's total dependence on the whole spectrum of relationships, human and non-human, material and spiritual, symbolized by the rainbow itself, a symbol which adumbrated for Lawrence, as it had for Blake, the complete life which was his ultimate goal.

***

As L. D. Clark demonstrated in his beautiful book *The Minoan Distance,* by far the most important image in relation to

[2] Ted Hughes, *Shakespeare and the Goddess of Complete Being* (London: Faber, 1992), 392-3.

Lawrence's life or work is that of travel – travel, of course, as quest. The quest is simultaneously an inner quest for the idea of a complete life, and an outer quest for a real place in which such a life might be found or founded. The fact that England, possibly the whole of Europe, is rotten does not necessarily imply that there is nowhere in the wide world where men live saner lives, in good faith. Lawrence's 'savage pilgrimage' was a search for such a place.

Virtually imprisoned in England during the war, Lawrence was obliged to look for some alternative to travel as the main enacting of his quest. He chose during his 'nightmare' to write off all existing societies and cultures, and to start a new one with a few hand-picked, like-minded souls. In his recent biography of Lawrence John Worthen argues that Lawrence was never wholly serious about Rananim, never really intended to put it into practice. I disagree. His reluctance seems to me to signify quite the opposite – that the idea was so precious to him that he feared to put it to the test. Had he ever got so far as to set up his community we can have little doubt that it would have collapsed for the same reason such experiments almost always collapse, the inability of people to subject their own egos to the higher needs of a community. When the candidates included such sizeable egos as those of Murry, Russell, Huxley and Heseltine, the idea was a non-starter. And of course Lawrence's own ego would have been the main problem, as he assumed that every community had to have a leader, and that he himself would automatically fill that role. Gonzalo's commonwealth in *The Tempest* abolishes kingship, yet could be instituted only if he were king. Half of Lawrence alerted him to these dangers, and deeply frustrated the deep desire of the other half to take the plunge.

After the war the Brewsters persuaded him to try Ceylon, but it nauseated him. In Australia he responded very strongly to the bush, but felt that to 'go bush' would be to betray his Englishness. The South Sea Islands, so attractive to Gaugin and Stevenson, were more lessons in disillusion. Always at the back of his mind, often at the front, had been America, the last frontier.

The culture of the American Indians was at first very alien to Lawrence, but he came to understand it and admire it deeply. It was right for them, their race, their spirit of place, but it was not in him to cluster to the drum. After his brush with death in Mexico, Lawrence's recovery at the ranch was a literal resurrection. He was happy there and as healthy as he was ever again likely to be. Why then did he choose to abandon it, on his fortieth birthday, to return to Europe? It was, in effect, an abandonment of the idea that travel might bring him to some promised land. As he was to say of Connie Chatterley, 'She had no faith in the newness of new countries. It was exile, always exile' (*LCL* 373). It was also a feeling that he could not justify his personal happiness if it were at the expense of turning his back on Europe and opting out of the fight he felt was his 'business' both as man and writer. He could justify the peace and happiness of the ranch only in terms of *reculer pour mieux sauter,* a brief withdrawal from the world to recoup his energies for another assault on it, the world, that is, of his own people, of Europe.

For health reasons, living in England was not an option. Lawrence's infallible instinct for beautiful places took him first to the Villa Bernarda at Spotorno, then to the Villa Mirenda. Perched in the Tuscan hills above Florence, the Mirenda was almost as far removed from the world of industry and politics and strife as the ranch had been. The Lawrence's neighbours, the Wilkinsons, had chosen to live there for that very reason, and marvelled that Lawrence seemed determined to import the world's problems. In fact Lawrence was at least as attracted to escaping from the world as they were. It is often assumed that after *The Plumed Serpent* Lawrence dropped Rananim. He dropped the name, certainly, and rejected Rolf Gardiner's invitation to join his relatively practical scheme… but he still oscillated between the claims of the 'societal instinct' and the needs of the individual. The 'extant social world', now he was back in Europe, filled him with rage and nausea. He felt an absolute need to cut himself off from it for his very survival. He began to feel that perhaps even Frieda was one too many 'other people'. The temptation was great to become a hermit, a temptation he had to exorcise in 'The Man Who Loved Islands' and 'The Man Who Was Through With the World'.

In stories such as these Lawrence could state very strongly the case against the isolated 'individual consciousness'. In essays such as 'The Individual Consciousness v. the Social Consciousness' and 'John Galsworthy' he could state equally strongly the case against the repressive 'social consciousness'. But in more ambitious works where he sought to heal that split, he floundered. The difficulty is evident in the fact that three of the works in which this may have been the intended theme were left unfinished – 'The Flying Fish', 'The Man Who Was Through with the World' and 'A Dream of Life'; not to mention *Lady Chatterley's Lover,* which, after three attempts, still leaves Mellors and Connie dangling at the end, and *The Escaped Cock,* which, as I shall argue, needed a part three, and might have had one if Lawrence's health had been up to another piece of sustained fiction.

***

In the time that remains to me I want to zoom in on two late texts, 'A Dream of Life', because it is such a revealing failure, and the story in which it seems to me Lawrence came nearest to achieving his quest, *The Escaped Cock.*

Two passages. First:

> A sunlit glade at the southern foot of a thickly wooded hill. On the west side of it, the steps and columned porch of a dainty little classic temple. … A dance of youths and maidens is in progress. The music is provided by a few flute-players seated carelessly on the steps of the temple. … Some of the youths have beards. Their dress, like the architecture of the theatre and the design of the altar and curved seats, resembles Grecian of the fourth century

> B.C., freely handled. They move with perfect balance and remarkable grace, racing through a figure like a farandole.

Second:

> It was a big gateway of yellow stone, and inside was a clear space, paved mostly with whitish stones, and around it stood buildings in the yellow stone, golden-looking, with pavement arcades supported on yellow pillars. … The crowd had gathered in order, a cluster of men on the left, in grey, grey-and-scarlet, and pure scarlet, and a cluster of women on the right, in tunics of all shades of blue and crocus lilac. In the vaulted porticos were more people. And the red sun shone on all, till the square glowed again. … The dance swept into swifter and swifter rhythm, with the most extraordinary incalculable unison.

Both these passages might be attempts to recreate some Etruscan ceremony. In fact both are set in England in the distant future. The first passage is George Bernard Shaw's vision of life in the year 31920, in the stage direction to part 5 of *Back to Methusalah*.[3] The second is Lawrence's vision of life in the year 2927, in his only futuristic fiction, which I have called 'A Dream of Life'.[4] Shaw published *Back to Methusalah* in 1921. Lawrence must have read it, or been somehow appraised of it, immediately, as he refers to it in *Fantasia of the Unconscious,* written in that same year:

> Our leaders have not loved men: they have loved ideas, and have been willing to sacrifice passionate men on the altars of the blood-drinking, ever-ash-thirsty ideal. Has President Wilson, or Karl Marx, or Bernard Shaw ever felt

[3] George Bernard Shaw, *Back to Methusalah* (Harmondsworth: Penguin, 1939), 259.

[4] It is printed in *Phoenix* and *LEA* as 'Autobiographical Fragment', a totally inappropriate title.

> one hot blood-pulse of love for the working man, the half-conscious, deluded, working man? Never. Each of these leaders has wanted to abstract him away from his own blood and being into some foul Methusalah or abstraction of a man. (*PU* 141)

The two passages I juxtaposed, despite their apparent similarity, are serving exactly opposite purposes. The main thrust of Lawrence's late works, particularly *Lady Chatterley's Lover, Etruscan Places, The Escaped Cock* and his paintings, can be seen as his attempt to refute *Back to Methusalah* and substantiate an exactly opposite vision of life.

Shaw believed in what he called Creative Evolution. He believed that evolution did not happen by chance, but by will; that men could will themselves to become almost anything. What had prevented man in the past from perfecting himself was the shortness of his life-span and fear of death, so the first stage in our future evolution must be to will ourselves to live much longer. Methusalah was supposed to have lived for nine hundred years. The final section of *Back to Methusalah* is called 'As Far as Thought Can Reach'. It envisages a time when man has evolved a body which dies only by accident. Early development and learning have been accelerated to the point where childhood and youth are compressed into about four years. After that men become Ancients, and are able to put away childish things and concentrate entirely on developing the one truly mature and fully human thing – thought. To this end they are willing themselves not to need bodies at all.

One would have thought that such projects had already been thoroughly discredited by Shaw's compatriot Jonathan Swift, with his Laputians, Struldbruggs and Houyhnmnmns, but Shaw seems to have lacked entirely Swift's common sense and humanity. As his Ancients have already divested themselves of all forms of love, all relationships, and are no longer subject to the needs, desires, instincts and pleasures of the body, there seems little need to dispense with that body;

but Shaw seems to have felt that mind is invariably tainted, degraded, by its close association with body, even with brain, and would be more free and powerful as a disembodied 'vortex'. Nowhere in the play or extensive preface does Shaw tell us what, having shed so much, there would be to think *about.*

In the passage with which we began, Shaw is evoking precisely that kind of art which Lawrence most admired, as closest to nature, expressing the very shapes and rhythms of life in song and dance, clothing, architecture; like the art of the Etruscans, which did not seek to defeat time, leaving 'burdens on the face of the earth' like the Romans, but celebrated the ephemeral, the passing seasons and cycles: an art not 'cooked in the artistic consciousness', like most of modern art: an art which was communal but not civic, not walled-off from the surrounding woods.

Shaw puts all this in his stage-direction, suggesting a Lawrencean Utopia, only to reject it all as merely childish. First one of the older maidens (aged four) announces to the youth who loves her that she is bored with all the songs and dances, with art and love, and finds the Ancients more interesting: 'They are fascinating, just fascinating. I want to get away from our eternal dancing and music, and just sit down by myself and think about numbers'.[5] Then two of the Ancients (of opposite sex, though this seems to make no difference: they are both bald and 'without sexual charm') attempt to explain to the 'children' how their own lives are superior. The explanation consists entirely of negatives – what is childish about everything other than thinking. What is so wonderful about thinking is apparently a secret the children are not yet old enough to be told.

The Ancients dismiss as worthless not only the body but the whole of nature: 'Your landscapes, your mountains, are only the world's cast skins and decaying teeth on which we live like microbes' (304). They have 'swept away the beasts of

[5] *Op. cit.,* 263.

the garden, and made an end of the crawling things and the flying things and of all them that refuse to live for ever' (313). The 'final reality', says the She-Ancient (with an uncomfortable pre-echo of the 'final solution') is 'myself', detached from body and become immortal. One of the youths describes the Ancients as 'unnatural, heartless, loveless, joyless monsters' (267), and nothing in the play detracts from the accuracy of this description.

The final speech of the play is delivered by our first parent, Lilith, who claims that the only worthy goal for her offspring is 'redemption from the flesh, to the vortex freed from matter, to the whirlpool in pure intelligence'. The cosmos, she says, is a desert, but 'my seed shall one day fill it and master its matter to its utmost confines' (314-15).

If Lawrence read this play, we can imagine his increasing horror. However, Shaw was only taking to its logical extreme an attitude to the body and the whole physical world which had been endemic in Western culture for two thousand years. This characteristic mind-set is evident even in a writer as sympathetic to Lawrence as Aldous Huxley, who wrote in his review of *Etruscan Places*:

> For the sake of the double flute and all it stands for, he [Lawrence] was prepared to sacrifice most of the activities upon which, for the last two thousand years or thereabouts, humanity, at any rate in the West, has set the highest value. The philosophy and practice of non-acceptance have made it possible for man to become, in some respects, more than human. But in the process he has had to sacrifice much of his former happiness; and while he has become spiritually and intellectually more, emotionally and physically he has, too often, degenerated and become less than human.[6]

[6] Coombes, *op. cit.*, 273.

Huxley's mindset prevented him from reading what Lawrence had actually written in *Etruscan Places*. He is clearly unable to think in other than dualistic terms. Lawrence is not arguing that one distinct set of values should be sacrificed for the sake of another distinct set of values. He is arguing that the refusal to accept the given terms of life, the interdependence of man, flora, fauna, landscape, climate, and the fact of death, together with the hubristic impulse to become 'more than human', had alienated man from his birthright, his atonement with the rest of life, including its creative energies. He does not want to go back to a childish or prelapsarian innocence (or ignorance), rather to develop a more selfless awareness, a holistic and biocentric consciousness, which would enable us to reaccept nature with that Blakean adult innocence which can only be attained on the far side of experience. He wants, above all, wholeness.

It is tempting to see *Etruscan Places* as the culmination of Lawrence's quest. After years of fruitless searching for the Holy Grail, Parzival is advised to cease his search, to relax and simply let the reins lie on his horse's neck. The horse takes him straight to the grail. So with Lawrence it seems that no sooner had he given up his savage pilgrimage and relaxed into Tuscan insouciance than chance took him on his Etruscan tour. And there in the vivid frescoes of Tarquinia was the very life he had been searching for:

> Behind all the dancing was a vision, and even a science of life, a conception of the universe and man's place in the universe which made men live to the depth of their capacity. To the Etruscan, all was alive: the whole universe lived: and the business of man was himself to live amid it all. He had to draw life into himself, out of the wandering huge vitalities of the world. (*SEP* 56-7)

Etruscan Places is perhaps the nearest Lawrence came to describing a utopia, but it does not really address the split because, unlike a work of fiction, it carries no obligation to describe individuals and their relationships. They are just 'the Etruscans', undifferentiated. Their art records only their communal life and religious rituals. And Shaw was surely right at least in his recognition that you cannot make a complete human life out of these elements alone. Lawrence would never have been content to spend his days in dancing, feasting, hunting, games and lovemaking, however close that might have brought him to the sources of life. He was too thoroughly an heir of the Romantic definition of life as

> Effort and expectation and desire,
> And something evermore about to be.[7]

A utopia is not a place to inhabit. That would be a Lotus Land. It is a state to strive for.

When, in 'A Dream of Life', Lawrence tried a fictional transportation of Etruscan civilization to the English midlands, he could not get beyond a description of the architecture, uniform costumes and communal dances:

> All the time the sun was slowly sinking, shadow was falling, and the dance was moving slower, the women wheeling blue around the obliterated sun. They were dancing the sun down, and dancing as birds wheel and dance, and fishes in shoals, controlled by some strange unanimous instinct. It was at once terrifying and magnificent. I wanted to die, so as not to see it, and I wanted to rush down, to be one of them. To be a drop in that wave of life. (*LEA* 64)

In 'The Flying Fish' Lawrence's image of 'swift, laughing togetherness' had been a school of dolphins. Here it is a flock of birds. Why did Lawrence never finish the story? The problem is that birds and dolphins cannot achieve and

[7] William Wordsworth, *The Prelude: a Parallel Text* (Harmondsworth: Penguin, 1971), 238.

maintain their marvellous togetherness, complete unison, and at the same time be unique individuals. Ted Hughes was surely right in claiming that the 'state of steady bliss' which he calls 'the heaven of the animals' is not achievable nor ultimately desirable for man. Much as he admired birds, dolphins, Etruscans or American Indians, Lawrence felt that modern Western man had come too far to submerge his individuality. He could not bring himself to abandon his belief in the sanctity of the unique individual. And how could fiction be written about individuals who had become indistinguishable from one another?

The difficulty is clearly stated by Lawrence in his review of Trigant Burrow's *The Social Basis of Consciousness*:

> Man is a prey to the division inside himself. Helplessly he must strive for more consciousness, which means, also, a more intensified aloneness, or individuality; and at the same time he has a horror of his own aloneness, and a blind, dim yearning for the old togetherness of the far past, what Dr. Burrow calls the preconscious state. What man really wants, according to Dr. Burrow, is a sense of togetherness with his fellow men, which shall balance the secret but overmastering sense of separateness and aloneness which now dominates him. (*IR* 333)

But if the delicate balance tips the other way, that can be suicidal:

> As a matter of fact, the mass is more neurotic than the individual patient. This is Dr. Burrow's finding. The mass, the normals, never live a life of their own. They cannot. (334)

The review ends with what is virtually the programme of *The Escaped Cock*:

> Men must get back into *touch*. And to do so they must

> forfeit the vanity and the *noli me tangere* of their own absoluteness: also they must utterly break the present great picture of a normal humanity: shatter that mirror in which we all live grimacing: and fall again into true relatedness (336).

The man who had died begins the process of re-establishing 'the living organic connections', but we are left in doubt as to how this will be achieved in relation to 'mankind and nation'.

There is no evidence to suggest that Lawrence knew much Blake, or was much influenced by him. But it seems to me that Lawrence ended up with a scheme which has much in common with Blake's idea of 'fourfold vision'. What Blake called 'single vision and Newton's sleep' was, for Lawrence, the materialism of Western culture, what in *Lady Chatterley* he called 'the din-din-dinning of books, schools, cinemas, clergymen, the whole national and human consciousness hammering on the fact of material prosperity above all things'. It was also that hubris, man's 'self-importance', which the Ancient Greeks had recognized as the original sin (or perhaps genetic flaw) in man's make-up. Two-fold vision is the recovery of the Energies, the charge of vitality which flows from a renewed connection with the larger life, the Greater Day, of the cosmos. One aspect of this charge is desire. The man who loved islands, once 'free from desire' is already virtually dead. In contrast the man who had died is painfully reborn into the world of clamorous desire embodied in the escaped cock.

His atonement with the phenomenal world frees the man to embark on his quest for a more complete human life than that of the self-sacrificing saviour. His marriage to the Priestess of Isis and subsequent fatherhood constitute his three-fold vision, his recovery of primal innocence. This is not the vulnerable innocence of childhood, but the innocence on the far side of experience, an innocence which is well aware of the need to fight to maintain itself in a hostile world; which sallies out into that world to confront its adversaries.

The man who had died rejects, first, the temptations of the hermit life, which is no better than the grave, then the temptation to settle for domestic contentment with the woman of his choice and their child. He sails out at the end into the dangerous world where Rome rules. He will support himself as a healer, and return in due season to his family. What else he will he do? The story cries out for a part 3 describing the complete life of a risen man, a man who has come through to fourfold vision. Though Lawrence never felt strong enough to undertake any more fiction, he did leave us in an essay called 'The Risen Lord' what amounts to a sketch for a third part of the story.

> If Jesus rose in the full flesh, He rose to know the tenderness of a woman, and the great pleasure of her, and to have children by her. He rose to know the responsibility and the peculiar delight of children, and also the exasperation and nuisance of them. If Jesus rose as a full man, in the flesh, He rose to have friends, to have a man-friend whom he would hold sometimes to His breast, in strong affection, and who would be dearer to Him then a brother, just out of the sheer mystery of sympathy. And how much more wonderful, this, than having disciples! If Jesus rose a full man in the flesh, He rose to do his share in the world's work, something he really liked doing. And if He remembered His first life, it would neither be teaching nor preaching, but probably carpentering again, with joy, among the shavings. If Jesus rose a full man in the flesh, He rose to continue His fight with the hard-boiled conventionalists like Roman judges and Jewish priests and money-makers of every sort. But this time, it would no longer be the fight of self-sacrifice that would end in crucifixion. This time it would be a freed man fighting to shelter the rose of life from being trampled on by the pigs. (*LEA* 271)

Etruscan Places, *The Escaped Cock* and 'The Risen Lord' are not about ancient history. Every age has its equivalent of the Romans, Philistines and money-changers. Lawrence identified them in his own day; they are not difficult to identify in ours. He knew that to drive the money-changers from the temple was simply to license them to operate everywhere else; that to render unto Caesar that which is Caesar's is to give Caesar a carte blanche. Lawrence loathed whiteness. Whiteness represented for him what remained when the multicoloured diversity and potentiality of the rainbow had been extinguished. Today Caesar lives in a White House, and his stooge across the pond operates from a White Hall.

If Lawrence were able to come back today, how might he need to modify his metaphysic? He would, of course, be appalled by the degradation and desecration of the earth, our only home, in the last three-quarters of a century, the triumph of Mammon, the fact that the multinational corporations now literally have the power (and, it seems, the will and the public support) to extinguish life; more specifically by such things as the rape of the rain-forests and the destruction of indigenous peoples. In his darker moments he would feel that our world simply confirmed what he said in his last work, *Apocalypse,* that man was doomed ultimately to destroy himself 'in conflict with the cosmos' (*A* 200). But he might salvage some hope from the convergence of so many creeds and disciplines towards deep ecology (and the knowledge of how much he had himself has contributed to that), and from the emergence of a world-wide network of individuals, groups and organizations, of activists, conservationists, writers, educators, dedicated to preventing, or at least deferring a little longer, the extinction of the rose of life.

Three Risen Christs:
the Genesis of *The Escaped Cock*

Early in 2006 I sent a copy of Literature and the Crime Against Nature *to Sangharakshita, a Londoner who had founded the Order of Western Buddhists in 1968, and who had reviewed my biography of Lawrence enthusiastically in 1980. In return he sent me his latest book,* From Genesis to the Diamond Sutra: A Western Buddhist's Encounters with Christianity *(Birmingham: Windhorse Publications, 2005). His chapter on Jesus ends with a three-page summary of George Moore's* The Brook Kerith, *of which I had never heard. The parallel with* The Escaped Cock *was glaring., and provided a perfect topic for the Lawrence conference in Eastwood in 2007. I am extremely grateful to Howard Booth for alerting me at the conference to the connection between* Pilate's Wife *and* The Escaped Cock.

The text for this conference was a quotation from a letter Lawrence sent on his last visit to England in 1926:

> Curiously, I like England again, now I am up in my own regions. It braces me up: and there seems a queer, odd sort of potentiality in the people, especially the common people. One feels in them some odd, unaccustomed sort of plasm twinkling and nascent. They are not finished. And they have a funny sort of purity and gentleness, and at the same time, unbreakableness, that attracts one. (*5L* 519-20)

Surely this reminds us of Ursula's rainbow vision at the end of *The Rainbow*:

> She knew that the sordid people who crept hard-scaled and separate on the face of the world's corruption were living still, that the rainbow was arched in their blood and would quiver to life in their spirit, that they would cast off their horny covering of disintegration, that new, clean,

> naked bodies would issue to a new germination, to a new growth, rising to the light and the wind and the clean rain of heaven. (*R* 258-9)

Lawrence's continuing interest in resurrection was no mere abstract theory. It was grounded in personal experience. Ursula's virtual rebirth after her encounter with the horses was based on his own sense of having emerged into a new and bigger life after having almost followed his mother to the grave in 1911. In 1925 he had once again almost died, in Mexico City, and had experienced another resurrection back at the ranch. His belief in resurrection was to find its final and most fully embodied expression in *The Escaped Cock*.

All this has been well documented. Those of us who have described the genesis of *The Escaped Cock* have assumed that having discussed Lawrence's early reading of such rationalist texts as Ernest Renan's *Life of Jesus,* the resurrection theme, and Lawrence's revelatory Etruscan experience, culminating in the escaped cock itself in a Volterra shop window, with, perhaps, a footnote on his reading of Rozanov on his return from the Etruscan adventure, we have said all that needed to be said.[1] We were wrong. Two major sources have, as far as I am aware, been completely overlooked.

George Moore long ago dropped out of the canon of early twentieth century novelists. Nobody reads him now. But in Lawrence's day he was a very important figure, at least the equal of Wells, Bennett and Galsworthy. On 1 November 1909, Lawrence asked Blanche Jennings to send him a novel by Moore, preferably *Esther Waters* (1894). He repeated the request in January 1910, but there is no evidence as to whether he received it. He read Moore's autobiography *Salve* shortly after its publication in October 1912, and thought it 'not up to much' (*1L* 524). There is no other mention of Moore in Lawrence's correspondence until the end of 1916.

[1] See '"The Secret of the Etruscans": The Genesis of *The Escaped Cock*' in Sagar, *D. H. Lawrence: Life into Art*, Penguin, 1985.

Lawrence finished the first version of *Women in Love* in November 1916, and sent one copy to his agent Pinker and the other to Catherine Carswell. He was not sanguine about the chances of publication, and wrote to Catherine:

> I wonder if it would be wise to get some well-known and important person to take the novel under his protection. (*3L* 58)

Marooned in Cornwall, Lawrence was desperate for reading matter, and asked Catherine to send him a few books. The parcel she sent included a novel by Moore, which Lawrence described as 'clever', but not 'very simpatico to me' (75). It is not named, but could well have been *The Brook Kerith,* published earlier that year, and already embroiled in controversy.

In December 1917, with *Women in Love* no nearer publication, Lawrence heard that Moore had read the manuscript (sent to him without Lawrence's knowledge) and praised it highly. He decided that Moore would make an excellent protector: 'I should like him to back me up in the novel' (195). Lawrence wrote to Moore, whose reply was not encouraging. Though Moore thanked him 'for the pleasure your novels have given me', his detailed criticism made it clear that he would be no champion of *Women in Love,* as he felt Lawrence should return to the style of *The White Peacock* and *Sons and Lovers,* concentrating on description and characterization and keeping ideas out of his novels (196). This was odd coming from Moore, as he had himself progressed from the naturalism of his early novels such as *Esther Waters* to the novel of ideas in *The Brook Kerith,* most of them the very same ideas Lawrence himself was to use as the basis of his last novel, *The Escaped Cock.*

On the 3 May 1927, shortly after his return from their Etruscan tour, Lawrence wrote to Earl Brewster:

> I wrote a story of the Resurrection, where Jesus gets up and feels very sick about everything, and can't stand the old crowd any more – so cuts out – and as he heals up, he begins to find what an astonishing place the phenomenal world is, far more marvellous than any salvation or heaven – and thanks his stars he needn't have a 'mission' any more. It's called *The Escaped Cock,* from that toy in Volterra. (*6L* 50)

This could serve equally as a summary of *The Brook Kerith.* In both stories, Jesus is taken down from the cross too soon, and regains consciousness in the tomb. He is rescued and nursed back to health by a man and a woman. His recovery is slowed by his loss of interest in life, especially in his former mission. He is out of touch with his fellow men, the sight and sound of whom is a torture to him. The first things to awaken his interest in life are the animals of the household, including the hens. It is unsafe to remain in Judea, and he plans to go south, perhaps to Egypt, as soon as he is strong enough. At last Jesus departs, his favourite animal under his arm.

Surely such a close resemblance could hardly be mere coincidence. There are several reasons, beyond the plot similarity, why I believe we can detect a direct influence of *The Brook Kerith* on *The Escaped Cock.* There are many incidents and details which may have lodged in Lawrence's memory. For example, in his revision of the ending of Part I Lawrence added a cock-fight, which might have surfaced from the vivid cock-fight described in *The Brook Kerith.*

But the main parallels between the two novels are thematic. As in *The Escaped Cock,* Moore's basic dichotomy is between Word and world. 'Quires and scrolls', his Jesus comes to believe, 'lead men from God'. His praise of the sensory incarnate world becomes Whitmanesque:

> Rites and observances, all that comes under the name of religion, estranges us from God. … God is not here, nor

> there, but everywhere: in the flower, and in the star, and in the earth underfoot.[2]

Moore's lengthy descriptions of Scripture and preaching are subtly undermined by a play of irony, whereas his evocations of what Lawrence calls 'the phenomenal world' are almost as fervent as Lawrence's own:

> But suddenly from among the myrtle bushes a song arose. It began with a little phrase of three notes, which the bird repeated, as if to impress the listener and prepare him for the runs and trills and joyous little cadenzas that were to follow. A sudden shower of jewels it seemed like, and when the last drops had fallen, the bird began another song, a continuation of the first, but more voluptuous and intense; and then, as if he felt that he had set the theme sufficiently, he started away into new trills and shakes and runs, piling cadenza upon cadenza till the theme seemed lost, but the bird held it in memory while all his musical extravagances were flowing, and when the inevitable moment came he repeated the first three notes. ... It was one of those moments when the soul of man seems to break, to yearn for that original unity out of which some sad fate has cast it — a moment when the world seems to be one thing and not several things: the stars and the stream, the odours afloat upon the stream, the bird's song and the words of Jesus: Whosoever admires the stars and flowers finds God in his heart, seemed to become all blended into one extraordinary harmony. (105)

This is very close to the sense of atonement to which Lawrence's Jesus comes through:

[2] George Moore, *The Brook Kerith* (Harmondsworth: Penguin, 1952), 289.

> But the man looked at the vivid stars before dawn, as they rained down to the sea, and the dog-star green towards the sea's rim. And he thought: How plastic it is, how full of curves and folds like an invisible rose of dark-petalled openness, that shows where dew touches its darkness! How full it is, and great beyond all gods. How it leans around me, and I am part of it, the great rose of space. I am like a grain of its perfume, and the woman is a grain of its beauty. Not the world is one flower of many-petalled darknesses, and I am in its perfume as in a touch –
> … And he said: 'This is the great atonement, the being in touch. The grey sea and the rain, the wet narcissus and the woman I wait for, the invisible Isis and the unseen sun, we are all in touch, and at one. (*VG* 160-1)

Nothing in *The Brook Kerith* corresponds to the man who had died's marriage to the priestess of Isis in Part 2 of *The Escaped Cock*. Moore's Jesus has no relationship with a woman. But he does make clear his new attitude to sexual love:

> But my passion was so great in those days that I did not see that my teaching was not less than blasphemy against God, for God has created the world for us to live in it, … and if he has put into the heart of man love of woman, and into the heart of woman love of man, it is because he wishes both to enjoy that love.[3]

The Essenes figure largely in Moore's story. Though they are in many ways preferable to the other sects described, their most striking characteristic is their belief that the life of the spirit can be fostered only by excluding all pleasure from life, especially the life of the body and senses. Indeed, their exclusion of women is threatening their continued existence. Typical of Moore's humour is the debate among the Essenes in which it is suggested that they might achieve reproduction

[3] *Ibid.*, 351.

without pleasure if they selected only elderly women – 'But a moment after, a brother reminded us that elderly women were not fruitful' (244). Jesus before his crucifixion had preached that man should 'mutilate his body till it conform perforce to his piety' (144). By the end of the novel he has swung to the opposite, the Lawrencean position, that 'God is but desire' (289).

We know, of course, that *The Escaped Cock* grew out of Lawrence's Etruscan experience. The Etruscans provided him with a standard of sanity. *The Escaped Cock* is almost the story of how Jesus became an Etruscan. The opposite of the Essenes and the equivalent of the Etruscans in *The Brook Kerith* are the Athenians, whom the fanatical Paul of Tarsus condemns: 'a race much given to enjoyment, like women, … given to milking goats and dancing in the shade to the sounds of a pipe' (327-8). What Paul condemns as frivolity Moore's risen lord, like Lawrence's, recognizes as a sane naturalness and insouciance. Paul's doctrine of 'salvation' was to lead, Moore affirms, directly to the Spanish Inquisition. Such bullying, Jesus claims, 'is the end of all worship. There is but one thing, Paul: to learn to live for ourselves, and to suffer our fellows to do likewise' (374-5). Repudiating the teaching of John the Baptist he claims 'it turned me from my natural self' (350).

Both Moore and Lawrence imagine the risen lord realizing that truth is not to be found in scriptures or law books or the words of charismatic or fanatical prophets, but only within, by an open and humane relationship to the world in all its unknowable multiplicity. In *The Brook Kerith* Moore's Jesus moves far from his earlier mission to save the world:

> I know myself, he said one day, but I do not know the God which is above, for he seems to be infinite; nor do I know nature, which is beyond me, for that, too, seems to run into an infinite, but an infinite that is not that of God. (280)

It is the same question Lawrence's Jesus is left asking himself at the end of Part I: 'From what, and to what, could this infinite whirl be saved?' (*VG* 140). Mara Kalnins writes that Lawrence at the end of his life:

> believed that the movement in 'the great *down* direction' would end the domination of the Logos, the Word, and would restore the balance between the spiritual and sensual planes of existence that Greece, Rome and Christianity, with their emphasis on the spirit and the mind, had destroyed. Man need not wait for a postponed spiritual salvation – he held the key to fulfilment within himself, bound in the 'physical psyche'. (*A* 7)

At the end of each story the risen lord is setting out alone on a journey. We do not know where he is heading, and neither does he. It is simply the next stage in the endless existential quest for what Jung calls 'self-effectuation', and Lawrence calls discovering how the life that is in you wants to be lived. In both cases the suggestion is that he might find in Buddhism or Hinduism a more humane balance between body and spirit than is to be found in Western thought. In Moore there are monks from India in the area, and it is possible that Jesus will accompany them back to India. Though Lawrence's Christ makes no literal move in that direction, his psychic state at the close is described in imagery drawn from Kundalini yoga: 'But the gold and flowing serpent is coiling up again to sleep at the root of my tree' (*VG* 163).

It is not surprising that nobody reads George Moore today. His style, especially in contrast with Lawrence's late style, is turgid. But Moore's brave humanization of Christ (especially brave for an Irishman) not only inspired Lawrence to write *The Escaped Cock*, but must also to some extent account for the relative lack of hostility towards it from the Christian establishment. They had spent most of their ammunition on George Moore.

***

As I have said, the influence of *The Brook Kerith* was almost entirely on Part 1 of *The Escaped Cock*. So when did Lawrence think of marrying his Christ-figure to a Priestess of Isis, and where did that idea come from? There does in fact exist an earlier novel in which the main character, who comes to think of herself as a Priestess of Isis, is responsible for saving Christ from death on the cross.

Hilda Doolittle, who wrote under the name of H. D., was exactly a year older than Lawrence. In 1913, on the rebound from Ezra Pound, she married Richard Aldington. By 1915 Aldington, accusing her of frigidity, had turned his attention to Brigit Patmore. Hilda's frigidity towards Aldington may have been caused in part by the fact that she had met and fallen deeply in love with Lawrence. She felt that he was the only man she had ever met who could understand her. Lawrence admired her both as woman and as poet. A decade later he was to use many of the facts of her life in the creation of Connie Chatterley (whose sister he named Hilda).

In 1917 H. D. was living at 44 Mecklenburgh Square. When the Lawrences had to leave Hampstead in October, she offered them a room there for several weeks. Cecil Gray was a frequent visitor. He called his book describing the goings-on there *Musical Chairs*. It could more aptly have been called *Musical Beds*. Dorothy 'Arabella' Yorke also had a room there, and when Aldington was home on leave he openly slept with her. Gray himself had affairs with both Hilda and Frieda. Meanwhile both Hilda and Arabella were throwing themselves at Lawrence's feet in a manner Gray found disgusting:

> I accused him, in point of fact, of allowing himself to become the object of a kind of esoteric female cult, an Adonis, Atthis, Dionysos religion of which he was the central figure, a Jesus Christ to a regiment of Mary Magdalens. (*3L* 179)

He could well have added Osiris to this list of resurrected

gods. Defending himself against Gray, Lawrence wrote to him:

> If Jesus had paid more attention to Magdalen, and less to his disciples, it would have been better. … And my 'women', Esther Andrews, Hilda Aldington etc, represent, in an impure and unproud, subservient, cringing, bad fashion, I admit, – but represent none the less the threshold of a new world, or underworld, of knowledge and being. (179-80)

It was this worship and Hilda's idea of an 'underworld' which led Lawrence to create the figure of Count Dionys in 'The Ladybird', perhaps the lowest point in all his fiction. Hilda was still speaking of herself and Lawrence in these terms in her sessions with Freud after Lawrence's death.

In March 1919 Hilda gave birth to a daughter whom she named Perdita. Shakespeare's Perdita spends most of *The Winter's Tale* not knowing her real father. There was much speculation as to who Perdita Aldington's father might be. One of the candidates was Lawrence. However, H. D.'s autobiographical novel *Bid Me to Live* suggests that Lawrence kept the relationship on the 'ecstatic subtly-intellectual' plane, in the mistaken belief that that was what she wanted. Frieda would have preferred them to be simple lovers rather than 'mushy' soul-mates. Not until 1983 did Perdita reveal that she had come to believe that her father was Cecil Gray.

In 1924 H. D. began a novel called *Pilate's Wife*. The novel is not primarily about the Christ figure, but about Pilate's wife, whom she names, unhistorically, Veronica, and who is given Etruscan forbears. In her introduction to the novel, Joan A. Burke describes it as 'a woman's self-directed quest for a life-affirming "feminine counterpart of deity", supplanting the messianic focus of the New Testament'.[4]

[4] Hilda Doolittle, *Pilate's Wife* (New York: New Directions, 2000), vi.

Veronica embarks on a journey towards resurrection, culminating in 'a complete change, spiritual, emotional, physical' (35).

The style of the novel's opening chapters is almost insufferably precious and contrived. Of one of her characters H. D. says: 'His least word fell like chipped stone on marble', and this is true of her own lapidary style, which entirely lacks the natural rhythms of prose, substituting a static 'metallic glitter' for the movement and colour of life. Gradually the reader comes to realize that she is using a device Lawrence had perfected in *St Mawr* (published in 1925). There the flippant, throwaway style of the opening exactly corresponds to the frivolous 'cardboard' lifestyle in which Lou is trapped. This style is transformed the moment the stallion St Mawr enters the story. He testifies to a deeper reality than any she has known, and challenges her to abandon Vanity Fair and embark on a quest for self-effectuation.

Veronica lives in a world of wealth and privilege, tinsel and vanity. She is insulated from life by her splendid clothes, jewellery, costly fabrics and furnishings, grandiose architecture. Her life and perceptions are confined to 'the surface of things' (7). Her first inkling of a world beyond all this comes, again, from an animal, her exotic pet, cat or marmot or monkey,[5] whose 'vivid presence' brings a 'living pulse' into her dead room (5). She has tried to fill the vacuum of her marriage with many lovers, but 'she preferred the animal to these men' (7).

Other hints of a more meaningful life come from a friend, Memnonius, who brings her the wisdom of lower Egypt and introduces her to the cult of Isis, which flames her imagination. He likens her to 'a Nile flower, infolded' (23), waiting to blossom into the Goddess, Isis. He introduces her

[5] As the creature is extremely agile, climbing the curtains and performing prodigious leaps, it is hardly likely to have been a cat, still less a marmot, whose American name is groundhog. Perhaps H. D. was thinking of a marmoset, which would fit her description quite well.

to a prophetess, Mnevis, who (exactly like St Mawr) convinces her of 'the banality of the particular brand of unreality , that her world offered' (54), and who, at the mid-point of the novel, tells her of Christ, his teachings and his imminent crucifixion.

The Christ H. D. introduces here suggests Lawrence, 'too slight' and 'a sort of poet'. The religion he is preaching is a sacramental pantheism:

> By minute contemplation of the unfolding of a wild-flower, you gain, he claims, hieratic knowledge of the inner mystery. [...] He claims that no bird shall fall, no grass-blade pierce the earth, no grain rise and uncurl stem and leaf and fruit, no serpent lift a head and no dove spread fan-tail or unfold wing-feather, without the conscious and intimate knowledge of the supreme Diviner, who is the father of wind and bird and man equally. (65)

Later Veronica identifies the man specifically with Osiris:

> This man was as great as Osiris, greater than the Hellenic sun-god. Yet for all that, he *was* Osiris, *was* the Hellenic sun-god, demonstrably in beauty and in wisdom. ... His *consider the lilies* linked his cult of nature with the old shrines – where lilies always floated before the feet of the blue-robed Isis. (The lilies were the flower, notoriously, of Isis.) (106)

The scales fall from her eyes. Prophetically she sees the 'accustomed grandeur' of Rome for what it will be:

> She saw the palace in ruins: it lay heavy, lizards ran in and out of broken crevices. The old palace had no rose-trees, no flap even of a torn bit of cloth, no tapestries, no candles set stark and glowing, nor any live torch. The palace was in ruins – half of it worn off, gnawed by

> countless weathers; in and out of crevices, snails crawled, one snail had eaten away a half of a dock-leaf – no lilies anywhere. The palace was dead, lost in stubble, sheep-pens, tents, a row of crumbling houses. The palace would house the ass and the wild-sheep, the goat would sniff at the fallen water-basin. (107-8)

Earl Brewster's recollection of the origin of *The Escaped Cock* was slightly different from Lawrence's:

> My memory is that Easter morning found us at Grosseto: there we passed a little shop, in the window of which was a toy white rooster escaping from an egg. I remarked that it suggested a title – *The Escaped Cock – A Story of the Resurrection.*[6]

In *Etruscan Places* Lawrence describes a man 'holding up the egg of resurrection, within which the germ sleeps and the soul sleeps in the tomb, before it breaks the shell and emerges again' (*SEP* 53). Veronica's resurrection is expressed in terms astonishingly close to these:

> Jehovah was a policeman. … This Jesus dared put forward a new axiom: God has imagination. He insisted that God, though he had the eye of the eagle (that bird of Jupiter), yet had the tenderness of the dove, or even the common domestic fowl who fluffs out her feathers, to collect her chicks. He stripped off the outer shell of the soul. Veronica herself was now as defenseless as a new-hatched chick; why, all this, she thought, was my egg-shell![7]

She accepts her vocation as Isis in Search, as destined bride of Christ, and organizes, through a commander who is a

[6] Brewster, *op. cit.,* 123.
[7] Doolittle, *op. cit.,* 126.

convert to Christ, that Jesus should be taken down too soon, and smuggled away to safety in Cyprus: 'Would he visit, in Cyprus, the famous temple of Aphrodite?' (125). The novel was originally intended to have a sequel called *Christ in Cyprus.* Presumably Veronica was to have joined him there: 'Surely the Prophet was human, he would have time now (as would she) for all the things that had escaped him' (133).

***

It may seem from this account that the case for *Pilate's Wife* as a direct source for Part 2 of *The Escaped Cock* is at least as strong as the case for *The Brook Kerith* as a source for Part 1. But this cannot be the case. Lawrence finished Part 2 in July 1928. H.D. did not finish *Pilate's Wife* until several months later. She certainly did not show him her work in progress. It was not to be published until 2000. However, this does not necessarily mean that the parallels were entirely coincidental. In 1933 H. D. wrote:

> Stephen Guest brought me a copy of *The Man Who Died.*[8] He said, 'Did you know that you are the priestess of Isis in this book?' Perhaps I would never have read the book if Stephen had not brought it me. Actually, I might have had

[8] *The Escaped Cock* was first published by the Black Sun Press in September 1929. In February 1930 Lawrence was negotiating with Charles Lahr for a public edition. Lahr wanted a different title, and, on the strength of Lawrence's earlier stories 'The Woman Who Rode Away', 'The Man Who Loved Islands' and 'The Man Who Was Through with the World', suggested *The Man Who Had Died.* Lawrence approved this title, with the proviso that it should have *The Escaped Cock* as a subtitle. In the event, Lahr did not publish the novel. Martin Secker published the English trade edition in 1931 under the meaningless title *The Man Who Died.* The novel continued to be published under that title until the Black Sparrow Press edition of 1973. The Cambridge U. P. edition has permanently restored the original title.

> at first a slight feeling of annoyance. I had told friends of a book that I wanted to write, actually did write. I called it *Pilate's Wife*. It is the story of the wounded but living Christ waking up in the rock-tomb. I was certain that my friends had told Lawrence that I was at work on this theme. My first reaction was, 'Now he has taken my story'. It was not my story. George Moore, among others, had already written it. There is the old myth or tradition that Christ did not die on the Cross.[9]

H.D. seems surprisingly unsurprised by the many similarities between her novel and Lawrence's. *The Escaped Cock is*, in a sense, her story, told from the point of view of the risen Christ rather than that of the Priestess of Isis. In this note H. D. implies that there were common friends to whom she had told enough of the story to enable them to give Lawrence a fairly detailed account of it. The most obvious candidate is Richard Aldington. Though he had been living for several years with Arabella Yorke, Aldington was still married to H. D., and in frequent contact with her. The Lawrences visited Richard and Arabella in London in August 1926, and the Aldingtons visited the Lawrences at the Villa Mirenda in October. What more likely than that Aldington would bring Lawrence up to date with what he knew of Hilda's most recent, most ambitious and most daring project? Such a conversation could have planted in Lawrence the seed of a 'story of the Resurrection',[10] in which, in a 'phallic second half' (*6L* 326), the man who had died meets, marries and is healed by a Priestess of Isis in Search, a woman who, far from being 'impure and unproud, subservient, cringing', is sufficiently pure, proud and brave to embody a 'feminine counterpart of deity', to complement and complete his own manhood and godhead.

[9] Hilda Doolittle, *Tribute to Freud* (New York: New Directions, 1974), 141-2.
[10] Brewster, *op. cit.,* 123-4.

The 'Shame' Chapter of *The Rainbow*

This piece was first published in the Journal of D. H. Lawrence Studies, *vol. I, no. 3. 2008.* The Rainbow *has always been the first of Lawrence's full-length novels in my estimation and affection, combining as it does the virtues of the nineteenth-century social-realist novel with those of such modernist psychological-poetic novels as* Wuthering Heights, Heart of Darkness *and* Portrait of the Artist as a Young Man *(though Lawrence had read only the first of these).* The Rainbow *was the first Lawrence first-edition I ever acquired – a fine copy for fifteen pounds, with a Lawrence postcard inserted as a gift from the bookseller! Our first child was born in Lawrence's centenary year, and we called her Ursula (whom I had described in my first book as 'the first free soul in the English novel').*

But no great writer, not even Shakespeare, writes well all the time. 'The bad man calls the misses, the good man calls the hits' is a proverb Ted Hughes was fond of quoting. But to describe the misses often helps us to appreciate what is so good about the hits.

It is ironic that 'Shame', the chapter most frequently quoted in the court proceedings against *The Rainbow*, should be also the weakest and most dispensable artistically. Few of what we now recognize as Lawrence's characteristic strengths are evident there. The structure of the third generation story is very similar to that of Joyce's *Portrait of the Artist as a Young Man* (though there is no evidence that Lawrence had read it). There each chapter ends with an epiphany, a moment when all Stephen's problems seem to dissolve, and a radiant future opens up before him. But each is a false epiphany, betrayed by the inflated language of his vision, and totally exposed by the deflating, often sordid, opening to the next chapter, at the end of which Stephen bounces back with a new vision. Similarly Ursula is seduced by a series of false rainbows, shining doorways to a radiant future. Clearly Lawrence wanted Ursula to run the whole gamut of possible errors in her 'trial and error' progress. In the 'Shame' chapter she was to meet, to embrace, but finally to reject materialistic science, rational humanism, lesbianism and industrialism. He believed that there are links between these, and attempts to dispose of them simultaneously in one short chapter, as exemplified by two characters, Winifred Inger and Uncle Tom Brangwen; but he jumps into authorial condemnation of them before he has presented us with adequate 'objective correlatives' for their alleged perversity and corruption.

There is some telling description of Wiggiston, where 'living human beings must be taken and adapted to all kinds of horrors' (*R* 322), where life is reduced to a 'squalid heap of side-shows. The pit was the main show, the *raison d'être* of all' (324), but there is far too much reliance on jargon. We are told again and again that everything is rigid, sterile, sordid, barren, ugly, dead, inchoate, and, four times, amorphous. Lawrence is concerned to present the Wiggiston experience as nightmarish and unreal for Ursula, but the price he has to pay for this is to make it insubstantial for the reader also. The dehumanization of the miners is (in comparison with, say, the opening of 'Odour of Chrysanthemums') merely gestured at:

> Like creatures with no more hope, but which still live and have passionate being, within some utterly unliving shell, they passed meaninglessly along, with strange, isolated dignity (321).

Winifred Inger is presented to us as sharing some of the characteristics of Ibsen's Lady Inger,[1] a proud, spirited, intelligent and independent noblewoman, who pits herself against the leading men of her time. But her independence

[1] Lawrence had sent a volume of Ibsen plays, including *Lady Inger*, to Louie Burrows in February 1909. He told her that *Lady Inger* was the least good of the three plays. However, he was sufficiently impressed by the Don Juan-like character Nils Lykke to write a poem in 1910, 'Nils Lykke Dead' (revised as 'The Bitterness of Death') which is spoken by one of his female victims grieving over his corpse. (He does not die in the Ibsen play.) The poem is in the Nottingham University College notebook, Roberts E320.1.

leads her to murder and tragedy. Winifred Inger is introduced to us as 'a fearless-seeming, clean type of modern girl whose very independence betrays her to sorrow'. She has 'a look of nobility' and 'a fine, clear spirit ... Her eyes were blue, clear, proud, she gave one altogether the sense of a fine-mettled, scrupulously groomed person, and of an unyielding mind' (311-12). Yet, behind all this, there is 'a great pathos'. We wait in vain for a sympathetic account of what is wrong with her life and what is damaging to Ursula in their relationship. We are told that in religious matters she is a humanist, that she is disillusioned with men, and, in one sentence, that she is 'interested in the Women's Movement' (318). Within a page this has become 'the perverted life of the elder woman'! She is even physically transformed to account for Ursula's sudden nausea: 'And sometimes she thought Winifred was ugly, clayey. Her female hips seemed big and earthy, her ankles and her arms were too thick' (319).

Uncle Tom is similarly sketchy. It is not clear why he should have chosen to become an industrial magnate, nor how he detects in Winifred 'a kinship with his own dark corruption' (322). Again Lawrence tries to use physique as a substitute for fuller presentation:

> The fine beauty of his skin and his complexion, some almost waxen quality, hid the strange, repellent grossness of him, the slight sense of putrescence, the commonness which revealed itself in his rather fat thighs and loins. (322)

This is a far cry from the inwardness and inevitability with which Lawrence conveys the rather similar attraction of Gerald and Gudrun to each other in *Women in Love.*

What unifies Tom and Winifred is, we are told, their worship of the machine:

> She too, Winifred, worshipped the impure abstraction, the mechanisms of matter. There, there, in the machine, in

> service of the machine, was she free from the clog and degradation of human feeling. There, in the monstrous mechanism that held all matter, living or dead, in its service, did she achieve her consummation and her perfect unison, her immortality. (325)

What did Lawrence expect his readers to make of this? It is prose devoid of human feeling or common human experience. Nothing here is 'realized'. The single short paragraph in which this is stated is not enough to convince us that what we know of these characters would necessarily lead to machine-worship. Indeed, such phrases as 'the mechanisms of matter' seem to be taking for granted in the reader a close familiarity with the theories of Bergson. Whether or not Lawrence had read *Creative Evolution*[2] by this time, he had certainly read, in 1911, an article on it in which A. J. Balfour had written:

> Reason is at home, not with life and freedom, but with matter, mechanism, and space – the waste products of the creative impulse. We need not wonder, then, that reason should feel at home in the realm of matter; that it should successfully cut up the undivided flow of material change into particular sequences which are repeated, or are capable of repetition, and which exemplify 'natural laws'.[3]

This piece had so impressed Lawrence that he had lent it to several friends.

To measure the failure to incorporate Bergsonian ideas in this chapter as anything more than obscure jargon, we need only compare Ursula's subsequent experience with the microscope, where similar ideas from Bergson are completely, wonderfully, incorporated.

[2] The English translation had been published in 1911, and may have been the book by Bergson sent to Lawrence by Arthur McLeod in April 1913 [*1L* 544].

[3] *Hibbert Journal*, October 1911, 12.

Lawrence's God

An extended version of the 'D. H. Lawrence Birthday Lecture' given, at the invitation of the D. H. Lawrence Society, in Cossall Church on 11 September 2008 as part of the Eastwood Lawrence Festival. This was the first time I had given a lecture in a 'house of God'. It seemed appropriate to ask what the word 'god' meant to Lawrence.

Lawrence knew Cossall well. The Burrows family lived at Church Cottage, next door to this church. Lawrence had known Louie Burrows, who was three years younger than himself, from childhood. From 1902 to 1905 they both attended the part-time Pupil-Teacher centre at Ilkeston, and from 1906 to 1908 they were both students at Nottingham University College. He was a frequent visitor to the Burrows home until the family left Cossall in 1908. He kept in touch with Louie, and became engaged to her in December 1910. The engagement lasted until February 1912, the month before Lawrence met his future wife Frieda Weekley.

When he came to write the second-generation story in *The Rainbow* in 1914, Lawrence drew very heavily on Louie's parents as models for Will and Anna Brangwen. Cossall becomes Cossethay, where Will and Anna live in Church Cottage after their marriage in this church, which Lawrence calls 'the old, little church, with its small spire on a square tower'. Later Will, like Alfred Burrows, starts a woodwork class for the village boys. Alfred and his class made the ornamental screen behind the altar here, in 1891.

***

It therefore seemed to me appropriate today, on Lawrence's birthday, to ask what the word 'god' meant to Lawrence. The Lawrence family attended Eastwood congregational church. It is easy to condemn the chapel for the predicament of many young people of whom Lawrence and Jessie Chambers and Louie Burrows were representative. But the chapel influence was by no means wholly negative. Lawrence's formal education had behind it that strong tradition of self-education, open serious discussion, wide reading (thanks to the Mechanics' Institute library) and free-thinking that is associated – in a strange, uneasy alliance – both with Congregational/Unitarian nonconformity and with a largely atheistic radicalism of which Willie Hopkin was the shining local example – councillor and magistrate, host to many of the great left-wing figures of the day and to weekly meetings of Eastwood 'progressives', shaper of local opinion for many years in his weekly column in the *Eastwood and Kimberley Advertiser,* and vocal participant in the meetings of the Literary Society. He became a mentor to the young Lawrence, and introduced him to many rationalist writers.

In 1907, in the middle of his course at Nottingham University College, Lawrence experienced a crisis of faith and confided in the Congregational minister Robert Reid that his reading of Darwin, Herbert Spencer, Renan, J. M. Robertson, Blatchford, and Vivian in his *Churches and Modern Thought*, had 'seriously modified' his religious beliefs. He asked Reid to tell him the 'precise position of the Church of today' on such matters as evolution, the origin of sin, heaven and hell. He was worried also by the problem of suffering, and could no longer believe in 'a personal human God'. He revealed to Reid his belief that men are born twice, the second time on entering manhood:

> Then they are born to humanity, to a consciousness of all the laughing, and the never-ceasing murmur of pain and sorrow that comes from the terrible multitudes of brothers. Then, it appears to me, a man gradually formulates his religion, be it what it may. A man has no religion who has not slowly and painfully gathered one together, adding to it, shaping it; and one's religion is never complete and final, it seems, but must always be undergoing modification. So I contend that true Socialism is religion; that honest, fervent politics are religion; that

> whatever a man will labour for earnestly and in some measure unselfishly is religion. (*1L* 40)

Lawrence's rejection of Christian orthodoxy as it was commonly taught at that time does not imply a rejection of religion. Lawrence later described himself as a 'passionately religious man', and no-one familiar with his work can doubt the truth of this. But the word 'religious' has a wide range of meanings. There are religions with many gods, with strange gods, and with no gods at all. Those which do have a god or gods have very different concepts of the nature of deity. Even within Christianity there are many versions of God.

***

The word 'god' occurs infrequently in Lawrence's early fiction. Some foreign novelists, for example Melville in *Moby Dick,* Dostoevsky in *The Brothers Karamazov*, and Camus in *The Plague,* have used the novel to explore the nature of god. But Lawrence began his career as a novelist firmly within the English social-realist tradition, which means that the subject matter is human psychology and relationships within the family, the community, the nation and the prevailing inherited culture. It was not, in the English tradition, a medium suitable for expressing one's sense of god.

One could read the complete fiction of the leading English novelists of Lawrence's youth, Meredith, Wells, Bennett, Galsworthy, without getting a hint that God played any part in English life and consciousness. Even Thomas Hardy, whom Lawrence admired for his 'setting behind the small action of the protagonists the terrific action of unfathomed nature', introduces god rarely, and only as a pseudo-classical personification of malign Fate.

Rupert Birkin, the Lawrence figure in *Women in Love*, begins a sentence to his friend Gerald Crich: 'Since there's no god'. Yet one might say that the very absence of God from modern human life, creating a spiritual vacuum, is the theme of Lawrence's modernist middle novels, *Women in Love, The Lost Girl, Aaron's Rod* and *Kangaroo.* Lawrence believed that England was unique in its complete separation of daily life from religious or spiritual experience. He transplanted himself and then his characters to Italy, Australia, New and Old Mexico in a search for a culture in which human relationships included their relationship with nature and the sacred. Lawrence's so-called savage pilgrimage could be described as a search for god in other cultures, distant from us in either space or time or both, a god more consistent with his own experience of the sacred than the God mediated to him by English Christianity. In *Birds, Beasts and Flowers* the presiding gods are Dionysos and Persephone. In *The Plumed Serpent* he evokes Quetzalcoatl, the primary god of pre-Columbian Mexico. In New Mexico, in *St Mawr,* he finds 'the Great God Pan'. In *The Escaped Cock* he names his gods Isis, Mother of the Gods, and her consort Osiris. In the last poems, the poems about death, the name of god is Pluto, god of the underworld. These are not different gods, rather the names which have been used at different times and in different places for the same experience of something which seems to require the name 'god'.

Like Blake and Coleridge before him, Lawrence believed that the awareness which can be achieved from the full flow of imagination is necessarily religious. 'At the maximum of our imagination', he wrote, 'we are religious. And if we deny our imagination, and have no imaginative life, we are poor worms who have never lived' (*LEA* 193). In his last few years, Lawrence did find ways to bring god into his fiction, but as a concept rather than a personal experience. It is in poetry that he found a perfect medium for conveying what was deepest and most constant in his sense of god. God is present in his poems from the beginning, and omnipresent by the end. What I want to do now is trace Lawrence's developing thought about god through a selection of his poems.

***

Another rationalist writer whose influence on Lawrence was perhaps deeper and more lasting than any of those he mentioned in his letter to Robert Reid was Haeckel. As early as 1905 he had written a poem called 'The Wild Common' in which this influence is evident.

The theme is, by the standards of the young man brought up with a dualistic consciousness and transcendental religion, heretical. His spirit, he imagines, would prefer to 'bereave' him and wander free as the wind. But, could it do so, his 'insolent soul' would be lost, and would quickly wither, since the soul is to the body only as the blossom to the plant, as the gold to the gorse; it needs flesh and blood as a flower needs humus and 'pulsing waters'. The poem works through strong images, beginning with that of the poet standing naked looking at his own reflection in a deep pond. His reflection quivers as if it would leave him, but must cleave to his flesh. It is as though this going naked in imagination frees the young man from some of his usual constraints, both of thought and expression. The penultimate stanza rises to an ecstatic atonement with the natural world:

> Over my sunlit skin the warm clinging air
> Rich with the songs of seven larks singing at once,
> goes kissing me glad.

And the final stanza translates this intercourse into frankly sexual terms:

> Oh but the water loves me and folds me,
> Plays with me, sways me, lifts me and sinks me as
>   though it were living blood
> Blood of a heaving woman who holds me,
> Owning my supple body a rare glad thing,
>   supremely good.

The monism of this poem comes close to that of Haeckel, who writes in *The Riddle of the Universe*:

> Monism recognizes one sole substance in the universe, which is at once 'God and Nature'; body and spirit it holds to be inseparable. [...] Our scientific experience has never yet taught us the existence of forces that can dispense with a material substratum, or of a spiritual world over and above the realm of nature. Like all other natural phenomena, the psychic processes are subject to the supreme, all-ruling law of substance. [...] The idea of God is identical with that of nature or substance.[1]

'Substance' is the key word in Haeckel's philosophy. When Lawrence rewrote 'The Wild Common' in 1928, he introduced the word five times, culminating in the purely Haeckelian:

> All that is right, all that is good, all that is God takes substance!

This insistence that spirit exists only insofar as it is incarnate in the physical, temporal creation, remains a constant throughout Lawrence's poetry. It is a form of Pantheism, the belief that all creation is divine, but that divinity does not exist outside creation.

***

Lawrence was to describe himself as a 'priest of love'. The early months of his relationship with Frieda Weekley confirmed for him that sex is, or can be, not just a metaphor for religious experience, but a crucial example of it, a means of releasing the individual from the hard shell of the ego, and making possible a fertilizing intercourse not only with the sexual partner, but with the not-self in all its manifestations, with Nature, with what he called 'the circumambient universe'. Many of the poems in '*Look! We Have Come*

[1] *Hibbert Journal*, October 1911, 12.

Through!' testify to this.

The opening of the self to the other in sexual love is close to the suspension of self required by the poetic inspiration. Settled on Lake Garda with Frieda in 1913 Lawrence wrote:

> Isn't it hard, hard work to come to real grips with one's imagination – throw everything overboard. I always feel as if I stood naked for the fire of Almighty God to go through me – and it's rather an awful feeling. One has to be so terribly religious, to be an artist. (*1L* 519)

The following year, probably close to his wedding day, he wrote 'Song of a Man Who has Come Through'. It is a poem simultaneously about life and art and religion, about Lawrence the married man and the poet and the priest.

> Not I, not I, but the wind that blows through me!
> A fine wind is blowing the new direction of Time.
> If only I let it bear me, carry me, if only it carry me!
> If only I am sensitive, subtle, oh, delicate, a winged gift!

The poem consists almost entirely of images – wind, chisel, fountain, angels. Whatever the wind is, it is the opposite of the 'I'. The 'I', the self-conscious, self-centred, self-protective, habituated, mechanical ego must be yielded to it. The self must be opened to the not-self, the other, the invisible wandering energies of the world. In a poem so full of echoes of the bible and the non-conformist hymns, wind also suggests the Holy Spirit, the breath of God, which is also, of course, poetic inspiration.

> If only, most lovely of all, I yield myself and am borrowed
> By the fine, fine wind that takes its course through the
> chaos of the world
> Like a fine, an exquisite chisel, a wedge-blade inserted;
> If only I am keen and hard like the sheer tip of a wedge
> Driven by invisible blows,

> The rock will split, we shall come at the wonder, we shall
> find the Hesperides.

Lawrence wants to be borrowed by the wind so that it might use him as a chisel to split a rock. This rock is surely the closed ego once more, hardened into a thick shell of callousness, of insulation against the unknown and potentially dangerous. This shell seals people off from each other, from nature and spirit, reducing them to insentient monads incapable of love, wonder or worship. The splitting of this shell can be a painful, even tragic experience (as it is for Ursula at the end of *The Rainbow*), but it is a necessary prelude to rebirth.

> Oh, for the wonder that bubbles into my soul,
> I would be a good fountain, a good well-head,
> Would blur no whisper, spoil no expression.

The split rock releases a fountain, which is the free flowing of life's energies, creativity. Again it is impossible to tell whether Lawrence is thinking of his art or his life. The distinction disappears. Lovers who have in this sense come through have regained Paradise, but a Pagan paradise (the garden of the Hesperides) whose apples are not the bitter apples of sin but the golden apples of Aphrodite.

> What is the knocking?
> What is the knocking at the door in the night?
> It is somebody wants to do us harm.
>
> No, no, it is the three strange angels.
> Admit them, admit them.

The three strange angels are those who came to Abraham and Sarah to announce that they had been chosen to bear the seed of the future – 'the new direction of Time'– while all in nearby Sodom perished. Lawrence felt that his marriage was an ark in which he and Frieda might be saved, while Europe rushed towards the ruin of the war. When the angels knock on the door, the defensive ego fears to open. They are dangerous, they make all-or-nothing demands. But it is only by total exposure to them and acceptance of those demands that blessedness can be achieved.

***

Lawrence spoke of the cyclamens of Lake Garda as 'little living myths that I cannot understand'. All the creatures of *Birds, Beasts and Flowers* are such living myths, embodiments of godhead. The not understanding is the whole point. How arrogant to presume to understand non-human creatures. It can only be done by anthropomorphizing them. In 'Fish' Lawrence tries to bully the creature, by anthropomorphic metaphor, into yielding its being to the understanding, but the effort fails:

> A slim young pike, with smart fins
> And grey-striped suit, a young cub of a pike
> Slouching along away below, half out of sight,
> Like a lout on an obscure pavement [...]
> Aha, there's somebody in the know!

As the most supposedly objective description is necessarily filtered through and coloured by 'human feelings and consciousness', and obliged to use language, which is essentially anthropomorphic, the challenge seems impossible – the challenge to discover or create a language and a perspective capable of testifying to the otherness not only of non-human creatures, but even of their barely-conceivable gods.

> But watching closer
> That motionless deadly motion,
> That unnatural barrel body, that long ghoul nose, [...]

I left off hailing him.
I had made a mistake, I didn't know him,
This grey, monotonous soul in the water,
This intense individual in shadow,
Fish-alive.
I didn't know his God.
I didn't know his God.

In 'St Matthew' Lawrence asks 'What, then, is a man?' For man to desire to live entirely the life of the spirit, either before or after death, is another form of human arrogance, man denying his utter dependence on the given material world, the world of flora and fauna, of climate, of air and water and earth, which, because he cannot live for ever in perpetual bliss, is not good enough for him. Matthew, as spokesman for man, argues that Christ, in seeking to draw all men unto him, is thereby denying their nature. Matthew, like Will Brangwen in *The Rainbow*, responds passionately, with wildly beating heart, to the promise of being lifted up; but like Anna, he insists also on the life of the body and the horizontal land:

So I will be lifted up, Saviour,
But put me down again in time. Master,
Before my heart stops beating, and I become what I am not.
Put me down again on the earth, Jesus, on the brown soil
Where flowers sprout in the acrid humus, and fade into humus again.
Where beasts drop their unlicked young, and pasture, and drop their droppings among the turf.
Where the adder darts horizontal.
Down on the damp, unceasing ground, where my feet belong
And even my heart, Lord, forever, after all uplifting;
The crumbling, damp, fresh land, life horizontal and ceaseless.

Man's being contains many beasts, and there is a time for each to receive expression; a time for lark-like exaltation on the wings of the spirit, but also for moving among the ordinary creatures of earth, and the mysterious creatures of under-earth and under-water, creatures of the darkness:

> Matthew I am, the man.
> And I take the wings of the morning, to Thee, Crucified,
> Glorified.
> But while flowers club their petals at evening
> And rabbits make pills among the short grass
> And long snakes quickly glide into the dark hole in the
> wall, hearing man approach,
> I must be put down, Lord, in the afternoon,
> And at evening I must leave off my wings of the spirit
> As I leave off my braces,
> And I must resume my nakedness like a fish, sinking
> down the dark reversion of night.
> But remember. Saviour,
> That my heart [...]
> Throws still the dark blood back and forth
> In the avenues where the bat hangs sleeping, upside-down
> And to me undeniable, Jesus.

***

In *More Pansies* and *Last Poems* God becomes Lawrence's most frequent theme. The group of swan poems is contemporary with his painting *Leda.* In 'Give Us Gods' he recapitulates, backwards, the images in which man has conceived his gods. He rejects the patriarchal gods, and Jesus, 'shelving substance onto the woman', and the Greek gods with their all-too-human foibles. He rejects the bull, the eagle, the phoenix, the ram, the swart beetle, even the 'sly gold serpent', seeking 'gods before these', 'the father of all things'. And the ultimate image he finds is the swan or goose 'honking in the gloom the honk of procreation from such throats'.

Lawrence's God

Scientific man's search for the origins has brought him to conceive no gods at all, just mists of random atomic energy:

> Mists
> where the electron behaves and misbehaves as it will,
> where the forces tie themselves up into knots of atoms
> and come untied;
> mists
> of mistiness complicated into knots and clots that barge
> about
> and bump on one another and explode into more mist, or
> don't,
> mist of energy most scientific –

This prophetic vision of the attempt at CERN to discover 'the god particle' 'in a mist of atoms / electrons and energies, quantums and relativities' provokes Lawrence to look for god 'in the dark unscientific' where he feels 'the drum-winds of his wings' as he comes to tread our women.

> Gods, do you ask for gods?
> Where there is woman there is swan.

The 'marshy flesh' of woman is for ever the birth place, the homing place of the swan:

> The vivifier exists, but for me is neither man-like nor
> woman-like
> nor even like an animal, bull, ram, or lion, or lamb.
> Yet when I think of the wild swan, or the ripple-marked
> black-headed goose
> far off upon the misty waters of the depths of space
> silently swimming and sleeping, and pressing the flood
> with webbed fecundity, plunging the seed of life in the
> wet wilderness
> and honking with a horn-like annunciation of life from
> the marshes of chaos

something thrills in me, and I know
the next day is the day of the goose, the wild swan's day.
'Gods'

Procreation is the ultimate secret, the miracle. The mist is a crucible of all the potentialities of unformed life awaiting the fusion of opposites, the chemical wedding, which will generate life. The opposites are fire and water, male and female. The mind of man cannot conceive new life, nor his body create it except as a transmitter of the divine, the superhuman. Every conception is a visitation from god:

Yet, O my young men, there is a vivifier.
There is a swan-like flame that curls round the centre of
space
and flutters at the core of the atom,
there is a spiral flame-tip that can lick our little atoms
into fusion
so we roar up like bonfires of vitality. …
O ruddy god in our veins, O fiery god in our genitals!
'Spiral Flame'

We can, of course, be transmitters of life in many other ways. Whenever life flows through us, however casual or commonplace the occasion, we partake of the divine, are, for the moment, in a state of grace. The young tram-conductor, as he unselfconsciously lifts his face to the electric rod in the yellow evening light is, for a moment, Hyacynthus. The young woman swiftly taking in her washing and running before the rain, is, for a moment, Io, or the Danaë. The woman coming towards him on the hotel terrace is, at that moment, 'Isis, gleaming, having found her Osiris' ('For a Moment'). The Gods, in other words, are 'only ourselves, as we are in our moments of pure manifestation' ('The Gods'). This is not anthropocentric, as 'pure manifestation' includes awareness of the larger life of the cosmos flowing through us, as through all creation, on which we are totally dependent if we are not to be reduced to 'men minding machines'.

Lawrence himself when alone often experiences a sense of oneness with the divine, the source:

> whose is the presence
> that makes the air so still and lovely to me?
>
> Who is it that clasps and kneads my naked feet, till
> they unfold,
> till all is well, till all is utterly well? the lotus-lilies of
> the feet!
>
> And I fall asleep with the gods, the gods
> that are not, or that are
> according to the soul's desire,
> like a pool into which we plunge, or do not plunge.
> 'There are No Gods'

In 'Name the Gods' Lawrence refuses to name or describe them 'because they have no form nor shape nor substance'. Yet at the end of the poem he names Priapus, in 'The Man of Tyre' he names Aphrodite, in 'Bavarian Gentians' he names Pluto and Persephone, and in 'For a Moment' he names several gods. How can he claim to refuse to name them?

As Bethan Jones has pointed out,[2] Lawrence had been familiar with Gilbert Murray's *The Four Stages of Greek Religion* since 1916. There Murray claims that originally all gods were nameless, or were referred to by the names of aspects of the cosmos, of nature, or of common human experience. But as Lawrence says 'the simple ask for images', and the artists gave them images, which were inevitably personifications, leading to names, specific features, and Homeric stories.

In these poems Lawrence is reversing this process, stripping the names of their specific association with what

[2] Bethan Jones, *The Last Poems of D. H. Lawrence* (Farnham: Ashgate, 2010).

Murray called 'the sharp-cut statue kind of god', restoring the multiplicity and immediacy of the phenomena and experiences from which these gods had originated.[3] Lawrence was not very interested in the Olympian gods, rather in those gods who had resisted becoming their own statues, Pan and Dionysos, gods whose myths remained grounded in the sexual and seasonal realities, Pluto and Persephone, Isis and Osiris.

***

In 'God is Born' Lawrence gives us his 'unscientific' account of evolution, every stage of which is a new birth of god. God is light and dark, water and vapour, sapphire and gold, the 'little eggy amoeba', the narcissus. Lizard, peacock, leopard are all god.

> And when at last man stood on two legs and wondered,
> then there was a hush of suspense at the core of every
> electron:
> Behold, now very God is born!
> God Himself is born!
>
> And so we see, God is not
> until he is born.
> And also we see
> there is no end to the birth of God.

Lawrence is here closer to Darwin than were T. H. Huxley

[3] Lawrence's resistance to the process of naming and describing the gods hardened at the end of his life to the point when he wrote, in 'Tabernacle':

> But anyone who shall ascribe attributes to God or oblivion
> let him be cast out, for blasphemy.
> For God is a deeper forgetting far than sleep
> and all description is a blasphemy.

and his rationalist successors. Darwin ended *The Origin of Species* with an expression of his awe that 'from so simple a beginning endless forms most beautiful and most wonderful have been, and are being evolved'.

What this poem and others embody is the conviction that propelling evolution is a motive force which favours multiplicity, diversity, distinctiveness. Lawrence calls this force the demiurge:

> God is the great urge that has not yet found a body
> but urges towards incarnation with the great creative urge.
> And becomes at last a clove carnation: lo! that is god!
> . . .
> There is no god
> apart from poppies and the flying fish,
> men singing songs, and women brushing their hair in the
> sun.
> The lovely things are god that has come to pass, like
> Jesus came.
> The rest, the undiscoverable, is the demi-urge.

'The Body of God'

But he mocks the idea of a humanoid super-intelligent god making advance designs of all his creatures:

> as if any mind could have imagined a lobster
> dozing in the under-deeps, then reaching out a
> savage and iron claw!
> Even the mind of God can only imagine those things that
> have become themselves:
> bodies and presences, here and now, creatures with a
> foothold in creation
> even if it is only a lobster on tip-toe.

'Demiurge'

Lawrence finds the idea of a designer god ludicrous. Shapes

and colours and smells are sensual experiences, which can never be imagined without senses:

> You can't imagine …
> the Most High, during the coal age, cudgelling his
>   mighty brains
> even if he had any brains: straining his mighty mind
> to think, among the moss and mud of lizards and
>   mastodons
> to think out, in the abstract, when all was twilight
>   green and muddy:
> 'Now there shall be tum-tiddly-um, and tum-tiddly-um,
> hey-presto! Scarlet geranium!'
> We know it couldn't be done.
>
> But imagine, among the mud and mastodons
> God sighing and yearning with tremendous creative
>   yearning, in that dark green mess
> oh, for some other beauty, some other beauty
> that blossomed at last, red geranium, and
>   mignonette.
>
> 'Red Geranium and Godly Mignonette'

Darkness had always been a positive for Lawrence, associated with origins, powers, and the resources of the unconscious. As his death approached, it acquired more urgent and specific meaning. In what he knew would be the last autumn of his life he imagined death as a privileged invitation to attend the annual reunion of Pluto and Persephone in the underworld, the 'marriage of the living dark' which guarantees the renewal of life. His last poems were the building of his ship of death to carry him on his 'longest journey, over the last of seas' (*Poems* 965). The journey is not to any heaven or spiritual afterlife; it is to 'the last wonder of oblivion'. Oblivion is the complete darkness of disintegration which must precede reintegration to a new form and life. It was the eating of pomegranate seeds, the food of the dead, which committed

Persephone to return to Hades. Any ripening and rotting fruit enacts this dual process, of breaking down and losing its identity, returning to the source, and, at the same time, nurturing the seed in darkness –

> then I shall know that my life is moving still
> with the dark earth, and drenched
> with the deep oblivion of earth's lapse and renewal.
>
> 'Shadows'

Lawrence was dying at forty-four after a life with more than his share of sickness. There is no underplaying of the suffering of death to shore up this trust:

> And if, in the changing phases of man's life
> I fall in sickness and in misery
> my wrists seem broken and my heart seems dead
> and strength is gone, and my life
> is only the leavings of a life
> …
>
> then I must know that still
> I am in the hands of the unknown God,
> he is breaking me down to his own oblivion
> to send me forth on a new morning, a new man.

Keith Sagar: Publications on D. H. Lawrence

1960

'What Mr Williams has made of D. H. Lawrence', *Twentieth Century,* August.

1962

'Lawrence and the Wilkinsons', *Review of English Literature* 3, October.

1965

'Three separate ways: unpublished D. H. Lawrence letters to Francis Brett Young', *Review of English Literature* 6, July.

1966

The art of D. H. Lawrence, Cambridge University Press. (Reprinted 2010)

1967

'The best I have known: D. H. Lawrence's 'A modern lover' and 'The shades of spring'', *Studies in Short Fiction* 4, Winter.

1968

'The genesis of *The rainbow* and *Women in love*', *DHL Review* 1, Fall.

1970

'Little living myths: a note on Lawrence's *Tortoises*, *DHL Review* 3, Summer.

1971

Ed. *The mortal coil and other stories.* Penguin.

Ed. *The princess and other stories.* Penguin.

'D. H. Lawrence: dramatist', *DHL Review* 4, summer.

'The Red Wolf', *Times Literary Supplement,* 10 September.

Keith Sagar: Publications on D. H. Lawrence

1972

Ed. *D. H. Lawrence: selected poems*. Penguin.

1973

'*Goats and compasses* and *Women in love* again', *DHL Review* 6, Fall.

1975

'The genesis of "Bavarian gentians"', *DHL Review* 8, Spring.

1976

'Lawrence and Frieda: the alternative story', *DHL Review* 9, Spring.

1978

'The strange history of *The daughter-in-law*', *DHL Review* 11, Summer.

1979

D. H. Lawrence: a calendar of his works. Manchester University Press.

1980

The Life of D. H. Lawrence. Methuen/Pantheon.

'How Edward Garnett made Lawrence's novels fit for public consumption'. *Times Higher Education Supplement*, 11 January.

'A Lawrence for today: art for life's sake', *Times Higher Education Supplement,* 29 February.

'Beyond D. H. Lawrence' in *D. H. Lawrence: The man who lived.* Eds. Partlow and Moore. Carbondale and Edwardsville: Southern Illinois University Press.

1981

Ed. *D. H. Lawrence: Sons and lovers*, Penguin English Library

1982

Ed. *A D. H. Lawrence handbook*, Manchester University Press.

'A Lawrence travel calendar'. In *A DHL Handbook*.
(with S. Sklar) 'Major productions of Lawrence's plays'. In *A DHL Handbook*.
Ed. *D. H. Lawrence and New Mexico*. Salt Lake City: Peregrine Smith.
Ed. *D. H. Lawrence: The complete short novels*. Penguin English Library.

1985
D. H. Lawrence: Life into Art. Penguin/Viking.

1986
'Which "Bavarian gentians"?'. *Words* 8, January.

1987
'Which "Ship of death"?'. *DHL Review* 19, Summer.
'Six paintings by D. H. Lawrence', *Words International* 1, November.
'D. H. Lawrence: the man and the artist' in *The modernists: essays in honor of Harry T. Moore*. Eds. L. Gamache and I. MacNiven.

1988
Introduction to *D. H. Lawrence: Foreword to Pansies*. Libanus Press.

1991
'Studies on D. H. Lawrence'. *Newsletter of the D. H. Lawrence Society of China* 3.
With Keith Cushman. 'An Achsah Brewster painting misattributed to Lawrence', *DHL Review* 23, Summer/Fall.

1992
'Open self and open poem: the stages of D. H. Lawrence's poetic quest', *DHL Review* 24, Spring.
'Lawrence and the resurrection of Pan' in *The centre and the circles*, D. H. Lawrence Centre, University of Nottingham.

'D. H. L and R. L. S.', *DHL Review* 24, Summer.

1993

Ed. (with J. T. Boulton). *The letters of D. H. Lawrence*, vol.VII. Cambridge University Press.

1999

'The genesis of "Snake"'. *Études Lawrenciennes* 20.

2001

'The resurrection of Pan: teaching biocentric consciousness and deep ecology in Lawrence's poetry and late nonfiction'. In *Approaches to teaching the works of D. H. Lawrence.* Eds E. Sergent and G. Watson. MLA.

2003

'Lawrence's debt to Whitman'. *Symbiosis* 7 i, April.

Ed. *D. H. Lawrence's paintings.* Chaucer Press.

2004

The Life of D. H. Lawrence. (Revised edition.) Chaucer Press.

Preface to *The collected art works of D. H. Lawrence.* Tetsuji Kohno. Japan.

2005

'Lawrence and the resurrection of Pan' in *Literature and the crime against Nature.* Chaucer Press. [This is much longer than the 1992 version.]

2006

'D. H. Lawrence: visionary'. In *Visionaries of the twentieth century.* Eds. S. Kumar and F. Whitefield. Green Books.

'The Wilkinsons revisited'. *Journal of D. H. Lawrence Studies.* 1. i.

2007

D. H. Lawrence: Poet. Humanities EBooks.

2008

'The "Shame" chapter of *The Rainbow*'. *Journal of D. H. Lawrence studies.* 1. iii.

2009

'How to live: the end of Lawrence's quest'. In *Windows to the sun: D. H. Lawrence's thought adventures.* Eds. V. Hyde and E. Ingersoll. Fairleigh Dickinson University Press.

'"Straight oxygen": Ted Hughes' debt to D. H. Lawrence'. *Journal of D. H. Lawrence Studies.* 2. i.

Index of Works by D. H Lawrence

General Index

General Index

Also in this series

Talking Lawrence: Patterns of Eastwood dialect in the work of D. H. Lawrence
by Hilary Hillier

Hilary Hillier is, quite simply, the most acute student of the dialect to have issued from Eastwood since Lawrence himself.
John Worthen

The book will be of particular interest to speakers of other languages interested in Lawrence studies but it also provides an authoritative platform for anyone concerned to explore more fully and systematically the key meanings which always emerge when language and its use for literary purposes is at stake. **Ronald Carter**

ISBN 978-1-905510-18-4 (64 pp.)

PRICE £5.00

The dialect of Eastwood lies at the heart of many of Lawrence's best-loved works. It is unique to the local community in which he grew up and in which many of his works were set. In this indispensable study Hilary Hillier presents a framework for understanding the dialect, tracing the key elements of its grammar and its accent, and detailing ways in which these differ from so-called 'correct' English. Each feature is illustrated by examples from both Lawrence's works and contemporary speech to demonstrate how this dialect continues to live in the Eastwood area today. *Talking Lawrence* reveals the precision with which Lawrence's use of language exposes significant social distinctions between his characters. Some of his most remarkable characters, truculent colliers such as Morel or formidable women such as Mrs Gascoyne, are brought to sparkling life by the language they speak. Lawrence knew these people, and he knew their language. He was able to use that language with skill, insight, subtlety and, perhaps most surprising of all, humour. Hilary Hillier's study is a resource for all readers of Lawrence, and an unparalleled introduction to this fascinating subject.

Two Lawrence Plays: Empty Bed Blues and The Fox ... and the Little Vixen
by Stephen Lowe

ISBN 978-1-905510-28-3 (156 pp.)

PRICE £6.99

"Art for Life's Sake": essays on D. H. Lawrence

by Keith Sagar

Keith Sagar has produced over fifty years a stream of essays, introductions and lectures on Lawrence, fourteen of which are collected here. Four have not been previously published, and this collection brings most of others back into print. Of Keith Sagar's first book, *The Art of D. H. Lawrence* (1966), Vivian de Sola Pinto wrote that it marked the start of serious Lawrence scholarship in England. Alastair Niven described Sagar's *Calendar* of Lawrence's works (1979) as 'indispensable, fascinating and almost certainly as authoritative a literary calendar as we could expect for any writer'. John Worthen described *The Life of D. H. Lawrence* (1980) as 'the best single-volume biography of Lawrence'. Keith Brown, reviewing *D. H. Lawrence: Life into Art* in the *Times Literary Supplement* in 1985 wrote: 'Criticism of Dr Sagar's book is well-nigh impossible. It is clearly going to be there as long as formal Lawrence studies survive'. Of his latest book, *D. H. Lawrence: Poet* (2008), Christopher Pollnitz wrote: 'Keith Sagar has done more than any other critic to reshape understanding of Lawrence as poet.'

ISBN 978-1-905510-31-3 (248 pp.)

PRICE £7.99

Working with Lawrence: Texts, Places, Contexts

by Peter Preston

Working with Lawrence: Texts, Places, Contexts draws together a representative selection of essays by the late Peter Preston, who retired in 2005 as Director of the Centre for Continuing Education at the University of Nottingham, where he was Special Lecturer in English Studies and Academic Consultant to the D. H. Lawrence Research Centre, which he founded in 1991. The essays adopt a range of approaches, drawing closely on textual, biographical and bibliographical sources whilst engaging with genetic and comparative criticism, and reception studies. They are distinguished by their author's wide-ranging and comprehensive understanding of Lawrence's aesthetic, political and cultural positioning, and by his characteristically meticulous attention to textual detail and sensitivity to the ambition and effects of Lawrence's writings.

ISBN 978-1-905510-31-3 (300 pp.)

PRICE £9.99

www.ingramcontent.com/pod-product-compliance
Lightning Source LLC
Chambersburg PA
CBHW032003050726
47590CB00006B/2032

* 9 7 8 1 9 0 5 5 1 0 3 4 4 *